Toward a Freudian Theory of Literature

FRANCESCO ORLANDO

Toward a Freudian Theory
of Literature WITH AN ANALYSIS

OF RACINE'S *PHÈDRE*

Translated by Charmaine Lee

The Johns Hopkins University Press
Baltimore and London

The Johns Hopkins University Press, Baltimore, Maryland 21218
The Johns Hopkins Press Ltd., London

Library of Congress Catalog Card Number 78-7577

Library of Congress Cataloging in Publication Data

Orlando, Francesco, 1934-
    Toward a Freudian theory of literature

    Translation of 2 works, Lettura freudiana della Phèdre and Per una teoria freudiana della letteratura, published in 1971 and 1973 respectively; with new appendices.
    1. Freud, Sigmund, 1856-1939. 2. Psychoanalysis and literature. 3. Racine, Jean Baptiste, 1639-1699. Phèdre. I. Orlando, Francesco, 1934-   Per una teoria freudiana della letteratura. English. 1978. II. Title.

BF173.F8506813   809'.933'1   78-7577
ISBN 0-8018-2102-9

Contents

Preface TO THE ENGLISH EDITION

The two parts of the present volume originally appeared in Italy as two separate books, in 1971 and 1973 respectively. The first was conceived as a course at the University of Pisa (1969-71), and in publishing it I left intact the simplicity of the exposition, which had been required for didactic purposes, but which also seemed continually to put the preciseness of my thought to the test. The second arose out of a reconsideration and a more detailed examination of the theoretical questions raised by the earlier book, and is thus in some ways a sequel to it. In presenting them together in a single volume to an English-speaking audience, I am merely fusing an analytical half with a theoretical half, each of which, I believe, called for the other.

As for the results of continuing theoretical reflection from 1973 onward, only in a few instances has it been possible to incorporate these into the text of the second part, by adding or modifying a few sentences or paragraphs. I have, therefore, decided to include a series of appendixes dealing with the most important of these issues. I have had cause to refer to more than one of them from various points in the text, just as more than one, in turn, refer back to various points in the text or to the text as a whole. Consequently, it would be advisable for the reader (unless he merely notes their presence and then uses them as he pleases) to go through the whole series.

I should like to thank the editors of the *Yearbook of Italian Studies* and *Strumenti critici* for having allowed me to reuse in these appendixes passages from an interview appearing in the former in 1975 and from my reply to a review published in the latter in 1976. My thanks also go to the translator, Charmaine Lee, for offering me her full collaboration in our revision of the entire translation.

I
Analytical Part

Mon unique espérance est dans mon désespoir.
    RACINE, *Bajazet*

The task to be accomplished is not the conservation of the past,
but the redemption of the hopes of the past.
    HORKHEIMER AND ADORNO, *Dialectic of Enlightenment*

1
Reasons for the Choice of Method

Voilà le hic, mon cher collègue. Allons, quittez cet air empesé.
Quand donc vous sentirez-vous à l'aise, là où vous êtes chez
vous?

      LACAN, *D'une question préliminaire à tout traitement pos-*
      sible de la psychose

What does "Freudian interpretation" mean? This announcement of a
method requiring some preliminary explanation is rather unusual in the
context of Italian culture, still impregnated with a long tradition of
idealism originating with Benedetto Croce. The reader who is not a
specialist in literary studies, and even many who are adept and well
informed, will not at first understand what the name of Freud, and
therefore psychoanalysis, might have to do with the interpretation of a
literary masterpiece. Psychoanalysis is commonly regarded as a method
for treating certain nervous disorders and a form of psychology aiming
at a particular subtlety and depth, which harks back to an individual's
childhood in order to explain his personality as an adult and refers
constantly to sex. Is the same technique adopted here in order to shed
light on Racine's life, on the relationship between his personality and his
early childhood, on any possible pathological aspects of this personality,
or on the relationship between his life and his work? Or does "Freudian
interpretation" mean adopting this technique in order to consider the
characters in *Phèdre* as though they were people who actually lived? The
most common Anglo-American and French applications of Freudian
psychoanalysis to art are always aimed in one of these directions.[1]

In fact, we are dealing with something quite different. Certainly the
extraordinary revolution in psychology brought about by Freud's discoveries has modified our view of Racine's life (as it would do for the life
of any individual), and the problem of artistic creativity and the conception of the characters. Yet neither the author's biography nor the
psychology of his creativity can be a decisive factor in understanding his

---

1. The remarkable works of Charles Mauron, and his concept of "psychocriticism," which
I shall discuss in Chapter 10, are no exception, though in some places they come very close
to the methodological objective that I am about to indicate.

work, for the simple reason that he addresses a literary work not to himself but *to others*. As soon as it is a finished product, a work begins to function in a way that presupposes an indeterminable number, and a more or less exactly definable type, of readers, spectators, interpreters, critics, and so on. If I were to speak of artistic success in terms borrowed from the field of economics, I could say that the *consumers* of the object, the work of art, are at least as important as the *producer* in explaining it. Were it to be generated only according to personal needs of the producer not shared by the consumers, the object could not be successful. In this case, the object consists of words, so that, substituting terms borrowed from linguistics for those borrowed from economics, I may say, for example, that *Phèdre* is a *message,* which goes from an *addresser* (Racine) to a number of *addressees,* who, since all works of art arise in the context of a particular social class, were originally a fairly well-defined group. It should be said, however, that their quality and number have become increasingly less definable because with *Phèdre* we are dealing with a success continuous over almost three centuries. We must consider as addressees not only the members of the audience of Racine's age but also those distributed in time over many generations up to our own.

Thus, in that message which is the text, an addresser dead for hundreds of years continues to encounter an infinite succession of addressees. This is a phenomenon that is both social and historical in nature, one that literally transcends both the person of the addresser, who remains trapped in the age in which he lived and died, and that of the addressee, who remains elusive because he is forever changing. The only enduring, unchanging constant in all of this is the message, at least insofar as the editions correctly reproduce the original text. It therefore seems clear that to understand *Phedre* no psychological approach, however deepened by the psychoanalytical contribution, can be adequate. This is true regardless of whether it deals with the psychology of artistic creativity, which concerns the addresser of the work of art, or the psychology that could concern the addressee, that of artistic enjoyment (and the inadequacy is greater still with the psychology that considers the characters as living beings). In order to overcome the risk of onesidedness and to include, in any case, both the entities that meet within the message, whichever of the two is taken as a point of departure, the psychological problems must become *historical problems*. What I mean is that one ought not so much to ask how that individual could produce that particular work, but rather how it could have occurred to that individual to express certain values of his age, to impose them on that age and beyond, by producing that particular work. At the same time, any question as to how, why, which, and how many readers or spectators have enjoyed *Phèdre* from the seventeenth to the twentieth centuries must lead to the question: which and how many values of signification are contained in the text of *Phèdre* that it should have attracted attention for three centuries and does so still? History selects the individuals who are capable of the greatest artistic services. It is through history that their success, made up of innumerable encounters between addresser and addressee, is confirmed and prolonged. Nevertheless the variety in the *time* of this encounter inevitably refers back to what we might call the imaginary *place* of the encounter, which is the message, an object, as stated already, made up of words. Thus the historical problem must in turn become a *semiotic problem*, a problem of the values of meaning contained in the text.

Recourse to psychoanalysis, at this point, may still seem useful only if the knowledge we derive from it enables us to understand something other than a psychology, whether that of the creator, the reader, or the character; only if it enables us better to understand an object consisting of words, which is precisely the case at hand. It is quite legitimate to expect a benefit of this type—semiotic rather than strictly psychological —from a knowledge of psychoanalysis. Clearly, in saying this, I refer to the concept of language in the broad sense, the sense in which language is not only words but any other sign system (for example, gestures, signals, visible symbols, images, music, etc.). Freud's discovery of the human unconscious was not only the discovery of something *that has a language,* but also a discovery made possible, and susceptible to further control and probing, only through manifestations of this language. Let us turn to the *Introductory Lectures on Psycho-Analysis,* where Freud masterfully assumes the task of popularizing and synthesizing his doctrine. Fifteen of the twenty-eight lectures in the 1915-17 series, more than half and, moreover, the first ones, deal with parapraxis and dreams, two phenomena which had not found their real meaning before Freud, which had not been delivered from the realm of chance. By abolishing the element of chance and revealing their meaning, Freud accomplished the discovery of the unconscious. In effect, he discovered a language (parapraxis) where none had been suspected and deciphered one (dreams) which until then had been indecipherable. Something similar may be observed for the other category of phenomena, neurotic symptoms, through which Freud demonstrated that the unconscious speaks, although the subject does not know it and others do not understand it. All the information that Freud and, subsequently, Freudian psychoanalysis have been able to give us about the human unconscious passes through an interpretation of these unsuspected phenomena of involuntary and generally misunderstood language; or it passes through an equally involuntary and equally misunderstood use of the most common of these languages—speech.

Inevitably must now be asked the question of the relationship between the language—since this is indeed a matter of language—of parapraxes, dreams, and symptoms and the normal one of speech. On the one hand the differences are evident and may be synthesized into one. Even when it provides some insight into the unconscious, speech by nature involves voluntary and conscious communication between an individual and others, between addresser and addressee, as we observed while discussing the literary work comprised of words. On the contrary, parapraxes, dreams, and symptoms are always an involuntary language, generally incomprehensible not only to others but to the very individual who commits the slip, dreams the dream, betrays the symptom. This incommunicable language, on the other hand, has a coherence, a logic, and laws of its own, which, though secret and different from those of rational thought, are no less rigid. Is it not possible for the language of human communication, speech, to participate in this kind of coherence, logic, and laws, which Freud's genius has described for us and whose description is synonymous with a knowledge of the unconscious? I am obliged to answer yes, above all because of the fact, already mentioned, that an understanding of the unconscious may also be reached through speech. It is exclusively on this assumption that the therapeutic use of psychoanalysis is founded (defined by one of its first patients as a *talking cure*, a cure that knows nothing but words). What is even more interesting for the literary scholar is the fact that, after having exhaustively examined the phenomena of dreams (*The Interpretation of Dreams*, 1900), and of parapraxes (*The Psychopathology of Everyday Life*, 1901), Freud turned his attention to a phenomenon which fits perfectly into the realm of speech used for voluntary and conscious communication with others, or even into the realm of speech used for artistic aims—the joke (*Jokes and Their Relation to the Unconscious*, 1905). Freud could not have known of modern linguistics, whose actual founder, Ferdinand de Saussure, was born a year later than he and was to die in 1913 without having published the results of his research. Perhaps because of this, his book on jokes, though full of ingenious foresight, reveals some difficulties. The discoverer of the noncommunicating language of the unconscious was now tackling phenomena and problems of communicating speech that had not yet been scientifically elucidated. Nevertheless Freud gives extensive proof that the internal logic of the joke has something in common with that of, for instance, the dream and therefore with the unconscious generally.

I shall mention only in passing the overwhelming importance for the mechanism of jokes of the *letter* of the words, the corpus of syllables, vowels, and consonants making up the words—in linguistic and semiotic terms, the "signifier" as independent from the "signified." A similar *predominance of the letter* characterizes in various ways all the languages of the unconscious described by Freud. Fortuitous points of contact between signifiers favor the manifestation of hidden signifieds. They determine the development of the symbols which clothe dreams, the point of least resistance at which the parapraxis is produced, the behavioral trait whose obsessive repetition makes it a symptom. Yet who could fail to notice that the predominance of the letter, the dominance of the verbal signifier, though now controlled by the conscious ego, equally decisively characterizes poetic language? This is why I believe that *Jokes and Their Relation to the Unconscious,* along with *The Interpretation of Dreams,* is much more valuable to the literary scholar than any of Freud's subsequent writings dedicated to art, to artists and writers, and to their work. All these studies share the limitation mentioned above: they are based on the psychology of the creator and his creation, rather than on the language which constitutes the works. It may be stated, as above, that these psychological problems never become historical problems, and only in a relatively disappointing way do they become semiotic problems. We are faced therefore with this paradox: if a specific semiotic lesson may be learned from the works of Freud, it must depend more on his analyses of dreams, parapraxes, jokes, and even neurotic symptoms than on those of literary and artistic works, of which, nonetheless, he undertook more than one.

Beyond the bounds thus marked off by Freud's work itself, and which all too often have been slavishly respected by subsequent research into psychoanalysis and art, there does seem to be a problem which arises from his discoveries and is still open today. How much does the language of poetry, like that of jokes, have in common with the inner logic of the unconscious? And how far does the relation between poetry and history, or, rather, that which poetry expresses of history (if it is true, as I believe, that it expresses some of its most profound values), remain incomprehensible when an attempt at understanding it is made without taking into account the logic of the unconscious? Alternatively, while we may differentiate and characterize poetic language as much as we like, should we consider it among the languages through which the unconscious manifests itself and is recognizable? The enormous complexity of the problem could lead me even to doubt the usefulness of facing it in a theoretical form. Nevertheless I should like to contribute to its solution in the only way possible at present—experimentally. This entails formulating a working hypothesis, inconceivable without the logic of the unconscious, and verifying it in the text of a poetic masterpiece by means of arguments that depend on the same logic.

2
Definition of Freudian Negation

Tout nous trahit, la voix, le silence, les yeux;
Et les feux mal couverts n'en éclatent que mieux.
      RACINE, *Andromaque*

After what I have just said about the importance of the semiotic compo-
nent of psychoanalysis, the Freudian text on which I have chosen to base
my hypothesis should come as no surprise. It is a very brief but extremely
fruitful essay published by Freud in 1925, which sheds light on the
particular meaning that a phenomenon of language—of the most common,
everyday language—may assume in psychoanalysis. The phenomenon is
negation, and it provides the title of the essay (*Die Verneinung*). I shall
first give an exact definition of the most important technical term to be
found in it, *repression,* which will form the basis of the whole series of
arguments that I am about to develop. In psychoanalysis, repression
refers to the operation by means of which an individual attempts to
exclude from the conscious ego, or even to keep within the unconscious,
a content of images, or thoughts, or memories connected with an instinct.
Here are the first few paragraphs of Freud's essay on negation:

> The manner in which our patients bring forward their associations during the
> work of analysis gives us an opportunity for making some interesting observations.
> "Now you'll think I mean to say something insulting, but really I've no such
> intention." We realize that this is a rejection, by projection, of an idea that has
> just come up. Or: "You ask who this person in the dream can be. It's *not* my
> mother." We amend this to: "So it *is* his mother." In our interpretation, we take
> the liberty of disregarding the negation and of picking out the subject-matter
> alone of the association. It is as though the patient had said: "It's true that my
> mother came into my mind as I thought of this person, but I don't feel inclined to
> let the association count."
>
> There is a very convenient method by which we can sometimes obtain a piece
> of information we want about unconscious repressed material. "What," we ask,
> "would you consider the most unlikely imaginable thing in that situation? What
> do you think was furthest from your mind at that time?" If the patient falls into
> the trap and says what he thinks is most incredible, he almost always makes the
> right admission . . . .
>
> Thus the content of a repressed image or idea can make its way into conscious-

ness, on condition that it is *negated*. Negation is a way of taking cognizance of what is repressed; indeed it is already a lifting of the repression, though not, of course, an acceptance of what is repressed. We can see how in this the intellectual function is separated from the affective process. With the help of negation only one consequence of the process of repression is undone — the fact, namely, of the ideational content of what is repressed not reaching consciousness. The outcome of this is a kind of intellectual acceptance of the repressed, while at the same time what is essential to the repression persists.[1]

Of course, one should not think that the interpretation suggested to Freud by these negations of his patients is applicable every time one denies something in writing or in speech; but neither should we deceive ourselves into believing that its field of application is restricted to psycho-analytical treatment. Who in everyday life has not used or heard used similar ways of negating while affirming, of affirming while negating? We need only think of all the times we have told someone (just as with Freud's patient) "not that I wish to offend you," precisely because we are about to tell him something that cannot fail to offend him. Or, "not that I wish to upset you," because we shall do just that in what we are about to say; or, "it's not that I am shocked," when we are about to condemn something. Examples such as these could easily be multiplied, while remaining at a level that does not imply repression in the true sense of the word, that is, without involving thoughts kept within the unconscious and revealed only behind a screen of negation. Let us now move closer to the level of repression and imagine a longing, a desire, a sympathy, a passion which is *unavowable* because moral, religious, ideological, or political reasons, or motives of dignity, pride, or education, and so on, prevent the conscious ego from accepting it. In a situation of this kind, it is easy to conceive that the word *unavowable* can have a strong or weak meaning: weak when the inclination in question is clearly known to the conscious ego, which cannot, however, bear its being perceived by others; strong when the inclination does not cross the threshold of the uncon-scious and cannot even be confessed by the conscious ego to itself, when, in other terms, the game of hide-and-seek is not so much played between the individual and others, but inside the individual's own subjectivity. Often it is difficult to distinguish clearly between the two cases; and in both, since there is nothing unavowable that does not tend implicitly toward being avowed, the only way to avow the unavowable is to negate it. All that can be said about something that is secretly pleasing therefore is: I DO NOT LIKE IT.

1. All quotations from Freud are taken from *The Standard Edition of the Complete Psychological Works of Sigmund Freud* (hereafter cited as *Standard Edition*), trans. and ed. James Strachey, in collaboration with Anna Freud, assisted by Alix Strachey and Alan Tyson, 24 vols. (London: Hogarth Press, 1953-74). The essay in question is in vol. 19: 235-36.

Such a sentence may be taken as an extremely simple example of the linguistic manifestation of the phenomenon. It may be analyzed equally simply by dividing it into two parts: (I) DO NOT / LIKE IT. Of these two parts, DO NOT is the camouflage exposed to censure and, if repression is actually involved, will in a sense be the passport of the repressed. (I) LIKE IT is repressed which expresses itself, will protected and neutralized by that negative, especially since the conscious ego of the individual uttering the sentence will not break it down, as we do when referring to the unconscious, but will think only of the whole—I DO NOT LIKE IT. Let us now reread Freud's words: "Negation...is already a lifting of the repression, though not, of course, an acceptance of what is repressed." In its linguistic manifestation the *lifting of the repression* is equivalent to the presence of the fragment (I) LIKE IT, the *nonacceptance of the repressed* is assured by the presence of the fragment DO NOT. With the lifting of the repression, owing to the fragment (I) LIKE IT, a kind of affirmation or return of the repressed takes place. The fragment DO NOT, because of which this affirmation remains unaccepted, ensures that repression is essentially maintained. In the final analysis, DO NOT represents the repression and (I) LIKE IT the repressed according to the following outline of equivalents:

$$I \left\{ \begin{array}{l|ll} \text{DO NOT} & = \text{nonacceptance of repressed} & = \text{REPRESSION} \\ \hline \text{LIKE IT} & = \text{lifting of repression} & = \text{REPRESSED} \end{array} \right.$$

Before explaining what relation all this might have to one of Racine's tragedies, I should observe that my illustrative sentence could be progressively augmented and emphasized as a negation according to means available in the language. But if the negation is not just any negation, but what I shall from now on call a "Freudian negation," what would determine this emphasis?—first of all, the strength of the moral, religious, and other similar prohibitions that weigh heavy on the repressed desire, but also the strength of the desire itself, thus the strength of both the repressed and the repression. If a desire of a certain kind or intensity can be expressed through negation only by the declaration I DO NOT LIKE IT, an even more unavowable or greater desire will give rise, for example, to I DO NOT LIKE IT AT ALL. A still more unavowable or greater desire might be rendered as I HATE IT, I DETEST IT, or other, similar expressions that remain clear negations though incorporated into a verb without a negative particle. We could compare this to a container whose contents exert a more or less strong explosive pressure on its walls; the greater the pressure, the more resistant or numerous the walls must be. Thus the greater the danger posed by the repressed to the consciousness, the more energetically it will be denied by the Freudian negation.

3
The Model of Freudian Negation and *Phèdre*

...because he was a true Poet and of the Devil's party without knowing it.

BLAKE, *The Marriage of Heaven and Hell*

The time has come to discuss *Phèdre*. Anyone who has read the tragedy knows that its subject is bold and disquieting with regard to moral values that are still valid today and that undoubtedly had a far more terrible force in the society in which Racine lived. The play deals with an adulterous and incestuous relationship (or one at least explicitly considered as incestuous by the characters), which leads to a false charge and in turn to the death of an innocent man. This would all be relatively inoffensive if the person responsible for the relationship and the false charge were presented to us as loathsome or awe-inspiring or, at least, unable to conquer our possible feelings of solidarity. All readers of *Phèdre* know, however, that they inevitably sympathize with the protagonist; that is, when confronted with the situations and events, they generally adopt her point of view and emotionally *identify themselves* with her in particular. There exists an anecdote on the genesis of the play, the truth of which is by no means certain; and, in fact, it seems unlikely that things went exactly in this way. Nevertheless the circulation of this story illustrates two points: first, that people at the time were very well aware of the scandal constituted by the subject matter of *Phèdre,* especially considering that for at least three decades playwrights in France had observed the so-called *bienséances* by not depicting actual forbidden love affairs; second, that the focal point of the scandal was precisely the emotional identification with Phaedra, which the poet did not wish the spectator to avoid. According to a third party Madame de la Fayette had taken part in a conversation in which

Racine claimed that an accomplished poet could make the greatest crimes forgivable and even inspire compassion for the criminals. He added that all that was needed was inventiveness, delicacy, and a sense of propriety to reduce the horror of Medea's and Phaedra's crimes and render them pleasing to the audience to the point of arousing pity for the protagonists' woes. When the others present said this was impossible, and some even tried to ridicule such a singular opinion, the resentment he felt led him to undertake the tragedy *Phèdre,* in which he succeeded so well in arousing compassion for her troubles that the spectator feels more pity for the wicked stepmother than for the virtuous Hippolytus.[1]

Of course, no work of art springs from a wager, but even if the anecdote were pure invention, what a significant invention it would be: a wager made on art against morality, and won *through art* in spite of morality! It may be said that in the play the rights of morality are safeguarded by the tragic catastrophe that punishes evil and by the feelings of remorse that go hand in hand with it. This, indeed, is the thesis (and how could it have been otherwise) that Racine put forward in his preface to the tragedy. It matters little for our purposes whether he did so out of a particular concern for the Jansenists, or the influential prelates at the court of Louis XIV, or any other moral or political authority. He states that out of the many tragedies that he has written,

Ce que je puis assurer, c'est que je n'en ai point fait où la vertu soit plus mise en jour que dans celle-ci. Les moindres fautes y sont sévèrement punies. La seule pensée du crime y est regardée avec autant d'horreur que le crime même. Les faiblesses de l'amour y passent pour de vraies faiblesses. Les passions n'y sont présentées aux yeux que pour montrer tout le désordre dont elles sont cause; et le vice y est peint partout avec des couleurs qui en font connaître et haïr la difformité. C'est là proprement le but que tout homme qui travaille pour le public doit se proposer.

[I can safely say that I have not written any other play where virtue is given greater prominence. The slightest errors are severely punished. The very thought of crime is considered with as much horror as crime itself. The weaknesses of love are shown to be real weaknesses. Passions are represented only in order to show all the chaos which they cause; and vice is portrayed everywhere in a light which makes its hideousness known and hated. This is precisely the goal at which any man, working for the public, should aim.][2]

There is truth in more than one of these statements, but I need not add that compared to the much more complex reality of the text, they seem one-sided, oversimplified, and self-interested. They are expressed as though the problem of emotional identification did not exist, yet Racine had in his own way faced this problem in the first paragraph of the same preface. They also disguise the essential fact that the solution given to the

1. Jean Racine, *Œuvres,* ed. Paul Mesnard, vol. 3 (Paris: Hachette, 1923), p. 263. All English translations, here and throughout the book, are by the translator, except where otherwise indicated.
2. I have taken all quotations of Racine's texts from the *Œuvres complètes,* Bibliothèque de la Pléiade, vol. 1 (Paris: Gallimard, 1956), where the preface is on pp. 763-65 and the text on pp. 767-821 (the lines are not numbered, though it will be indispensable for me to use line numbering later on).

problem in *Phèdre* sets up a relationship between the spectator and the criminal protagonist that is hardly limited to moral condemnation. Finally, for the most clear-sighted rejection of this feigned moralizing intention in the tragedy, let us turn to the voice of perturbed morality and religion in Racine's day, the authoritative and stern voice of Bossuet who seventeen years after *Phèdre* was written persisted in the age-old, generalized condemnation of the theater formulated by the Fathers of the Church:

On se voit soi-même, dans ceux qui nous paraissent comme transportés par de semblables objets: on devient bientôt un acteur secret dans la tragédie; on y joue sa propre passion, et la fiction au dehors est froide et sans agrément, si elle ne trouve au dedans une vérité qui lui réponde.

[We see ourselves in those who seem to be enraptured by such objects: we soon become secret actors in the tragedy; we act out our own passions, and fiction outside is cold and pleasureless if it finds within no response of truth.][3]

It would be difficult even in our day to describe better in as few words the spectator's or reader's emotional identification with the theatrical persona, a phenomenon which, through the sympathy or compassion aroused by the character, causes the spectator or reader to become a sort of accomplice to everything in the text. If the contents of the text are morally and socially unacceptable, involving, for example, incest, adultery, and murderous slander, the complicity will be fictitious, the acceptance temporary—this brings to mind the model of Freudian negation. We have observed that behind the screen of Freudian negation an individual may confess more than he might otherwise wish or dare. What comparable process takes place behind the screen of poetic fiction?

In order to answer this question correctly and to specify the comparison on which my working hypothesis is based, we shall need the distinctions permitted by adopting the terms addresser, addressee, message. With reference to a work of art, I believe that the model of Freudian negation may be applied to the relationship between message and addressee, as well as to that between message and addresser. The confusion which may arise from failing to distinguish each case is connected to the fact that both in Freud's examples and in my own, the sentence I DO NOT LIKE IT, only an addresser and a message were taken into consideration and not an addressee. The analyzed phenomenon remained completely enclosed within the sphere of an individual psychology. If we wish, however, to derive a comparison from it concerning the phenomenon of art, we must temporarily isolate the relationship between the message and its addresser, or argue within the sphere of the individual and the psychological. This

3. *Maximes et réflexions sur la comédie, par messire J.-B. Bossuet, évesque de Meaux* (Paris, 1694), pp. 12-13. I have modernized the spelling.

is because art is a social institution and as such is preexistent to the author's act of beginning a work.

Let us consider the relationship between the message and its addresser, in our case that between *Phèdre* and Racine. It would be a commonplace to observe that the illicit content of the play would never have been declared acceptable by the man Jean Racine in real life, or that he would never have defended incest. A proof of this, however superfluous, is to be found in the show of irreproachable moral sentiment which we observed in the preface, outside the actual text of *Phèdre* and where the man, not the poet, is speaking. Within the text of *Phèdre,* behind the screen of poetic fiction, Racine has taken the liberty of showing solidarity with the illicit. Therefore if we consider the psychology of artistic creativity, that screen must have functioned as a Freudian negation primarily for Racine as an individual, no doubt allowing him to project, sublimate, and perhaps calm his innermost conflicts in the creative process. The result of this process was a product still compromising enough to induce Racine, the man, the Christian, the courtier, to disavow it in part. That moralizing passage in the preface, which seems to increase in severity when measured against the tragedy's surpassing audacity is, as we observed, just such a partial disavowal. From the outside, that passage in the preface stands in approximately the same relationship to the work as a whole as the DO NOT in my example of Freudian negation to (I) LIKE IT. But the real equivalent of DO NOT in the relationship between message and addresser cannot be this, which is so extraneous to the message. It is clear from all that has been said that this equivalent consists principally of the *very fact of poetic fiction* acting as a screen, and it therefore involves the institution of art (here poetic and dramatic art) as something socially accepted. Racine was able in his tragedy to speak of particular things in a particular way just because he was speaking about them in a tragedy.

It goes without saying that the same conditions apply on the spectator's or readers' side. They in turn are willing to be told particular things in a particular way only because this is happening in a certain type of literary work. If, however, the model of Freudian negation, when applied to the relation between message and addresser, cannot illustrate the psychology of creativity without involving art as a social institution it leads even more unavoidably from the psychology of artistic enjoyment to a social and historical problem when applied to the relation between message and addressee. The latter is not an individual always identical to himself like the addresser, but rather a constantly changing plurality of individuals which may be loosely defined, in a particular period, as a social class, or as all the people above (or below) a particular cultural level. If we consider the first set of addressees of *Phèdre,* the historical problem emerges as a paradox that may be formulated as follows. How is it possible that in the midst of a monarchic, Catholic civilization, there was performed a tragedy, written by a poet who was preferred above all others by the ruling powers, including the king himself, in which the spectator's compassion and sympathy are directed toward a character burdened with some of the worst violations of contemporary morality? The addressee is, in fact, not free in confronting the characters but is committed to specific reactions *by the text.* That is, if in hearing or reading the text he ignores the prevailing emotional identification with the protagonist, all the meanings of the text will be lost on him. Bossuet realized this when writing the passage that we read about the theater in general; so did the author of the wager anecdote, in which the poet appears stimulated only by the technical matter of winning over the spectator to Phaedra's side.

Thus the case in hand confirms that the entire historical problem must in turn become a semiotic problem. What is there in the composition of *Phèdre* that permits so dangerous an emotional identification and imposes it on the audience or reader? Is it only the screen of poetic fiction that renders it harmless, or is there something else in the text that facilitates and protects such an identification, while the text enforces it at the same time? In this case, what and how many are the equivalents of the negating element with respect to the model of Freudian negation? Before I begin to develop these problems, a terminological definition is called for. I have so far been able to use the terms "repression" and "repressed" in a narrow or technical sense, in accordance with the strict usage of Freud's English translators, even though I have already mentioned, in referring to Freudian negation, the shifting boundary between the true repression of thoughts kept back within the unconscious and the repression of conscious thoughts unacceptable to the ego or concealed from others. Because of the difficulty of finding suitable alternative terms in English (as may, however, be found in German, French, and especially Italian), I shall continue to use the same terms. This I do despite the fact that, when applied to my working hypothesis, the model of Freudian negation will undergo two parallel extensions: one is from the individual to the social dimension, the other is that which no longer makes necessary the exclusion of particular contents from the conscious level, an exclusion which, when transferred to the social dimension, would lead to the non-Freudian concept of a "collective unconscious." Repression and repressed may also refer only to the prohibition by which some contents are officially censured in a society, whether excluded from the conscious level, or from that of speech, or perhaps only from that of decent speech.[4]

4. Chapter 11 is partly given over to the theoretical problems arising from this choice of terminology as is, even more particularly, Appendix 1, "The Compromise-Formation as a Freudian Model."

According to Freud's theory of the Oedipus complex, incest, which in the tragedy is the essential cause of Phaedra's guilt, is the prime object of prohibition. It is the object of that original desire, whose prohibition is the original law and which, when interiorized, leads to all the other rules and prohibitions that organize human civilizations. According to Lévi-Strauss, the variety of historical forms in which the prohibition of incest has articulated itself on earth, in time, and in space, only serves to confirm its universality. It has been the minimum and ever-present condition for the passage of any community of men from a state of nature to one of culture. Psychoanalysis and anthropology agree in considering a prohibition on sex as the very basis of what we call civilization. Freud had clearly evaluated the price of repression, the dangers of the return of the repressed, in effect all the contradictions and tension that are implicit in such a conception of civilization:

We believe that civilization has been created under the pressure of the exigencies of life at the cost of satisfaction of the instincts; and we believe that civilization is to a large extent being constantly created anew, since each individual who makes a fresh entry into human society repeats this sacrifice of instinctual satisfaction for the benefit of the whole community. Among the instinctual forces which are put to this use the sexual impulses play an important part; in this process they are sublimated—that is to say, they are diverted from their sexual aims and directed to others that are socially higher and no longer sexual. But this arrangement is unstable; the sexual instincts are imperfectly tamed, and, in the case of every individual who is supposed to join in the work of civilization, there is a risk that his sexual instincts may refuse to be put to that use. Society believes that no greater threat to its civilization could arise than if the sexual instincts were to be liberated and returned to their original aims.[5]

In the light of these elementary yet immense problems (which are developed in an optimistic and progressive way in Marcuse's famous essay *Eros and Civilization*), two points in my previous arguments take on added importance. In the first place, the dialectic between repression and repressed contained in the model of Freudian negation, also or especially when the meaning of the terms is extended as I have done, may be extended farther until it emerges as the dialectics of human civilization itself; yet it remains recognizable in even the smallest concrete example. This prompts one to think of the juxtaposition of myths in *Phèdre*, apparently unmotivated, if not contradictory, and yet certainly not attributable to the sources alone. In the spotlight is a myth of forbidden love, but there is also, in the background of the tragedy, the myth of Theseus' heroic deeds, emphasized precisely as a myth of the foundation of civilization. We realize then that if there is a desperately

5. Sigmund Freud, *Introductory Lectures on Psycho-Analysis*, pt. 1, *Standard Edition*, 15: 22-23.

subversive need within the character of Phaedra, it is not only because her desire conflicts with the incest taboo, but is especially because her desire has all the characteristics of a refusal to let herself be subordinated and sacrificed to sublimated aims, and of the socially dangerous liberation mentioned by Freud. Despite the extreme discretion with which Racine's style handles this aspect of Phaedra, we feel that her desire knows no bounds in the physical dimension as it knows none in the emotional. It is total, absolute, gratuitous, existing entirely for its own sake. Precisely in this sense is it perverse according to Freud's definition of the term ("We actually describe a sexual activity as perverse if it has given up the aim of reproduction and pursues the attainment of pleasure as an aim independent of it.");[6] precisely for this reason is it so completely unacceptable ("these sexual perversions are subject to a quite special ban.... It is as though no one could forget that they are not only something disgusting but also something monstrous and dangerous—as though people felt them as seductive, and had at bottom to fight down a secret envy of those who were enjoying them").[7] Phaedra is the first to reject her own desire. The opposing demands of a particular repressive society make themselves felt most purely and severely in the character's inflexible moral conscience, so that the social repression is interiorized. It is the basic conflict between the two terms in the dialectic of civilization according to Freud that, favored by historical and literary conditions, emerges so clearly in this tragedy and makes death the only possible outcome of love. In the text, therefore, the negating element in the model of Freudian negation is undoubtedly as important as the negated element (though we must still ask ourselves what form it will take). The voice of repression is heard no less forcefully than that of the repressed.

Phèdre, in fact, belongs to an age in which neither the religious tradition of Western civilization nor its political organization had yet undergone that radical intellectual reexamination known as the Enlightenment. More precisely (and we shall see the importance of this), the tragedy dates from the very threshold of this phenomenon (1677), only a few years before the fundamental works of those generally considered to be the earliest writers of the Enlightenment (Fontenelle, Bayle). In a very broad historical perspective, it should be observed that the Enlightenment, by providing the first example of a systematic challenge to established order, forever modified the relation between the phenomenon of art and the model of Freudian negation. It made it possible for a work of art to become voluntarily the instrument of such a challenge and to adopt openly contents forbidden by an established order or, at least, not conforming to that order when not actually threatening it directly. Not only does

6. Ibid., pt. 3, *Standard Edition*, 16: 316.
7. Ibid., p. 321.

Enlightenment literature, with its characteristic collaboration between art and ideology, presuppose this change, but also inconceivable without it is Romantic literature, which completely assimilates the change and institutionalizes it almost to the point, for example, of making a favorite theme of socially forbidden passion, in which the author's and the audience's sympathies may converge with nothing left hidden. Obviously, even in the literature of this period, socially forbidden passion is usually at odds with society and comes off worse in the conflict. But mostly, it is society that is held to be in the wrong by these authors and their works; and in the texts, defeats, catastrophic deaths, punishment, or remorse no longer counterbalance the reader's emotional involvement. The only remaining counterpoise, the only real distinction, for example, between adultery presented to the reader's sympathies and adultery actually experienced is the fact of poetic fiction itself. The same applies if we substitute for involvement in a forbidden passion the countless other attitudes of rejection of the established order, or, to be more precise, the established order of the bourgeoisie: these are all the attitudes that, following the Romantic period, have manifested themselves either in the various forms of the antibourgeois concept of "art for art's sake" from 1848 onward or in the various forms of ideologically committed literature up to Surrealism and even to the present day. If the model of Freudian negation can somehow correspond to so many of art's phenomena, it must do so in a single, though still extremely generalized, way:

DO NOT	= nonacceptance of repressed	= REPRESSION	= poetic fiction
LIKE IT	= lifting of repression	= REPRESSED	= solidarity with contents that do not conform to established order

I { (bracket spanning DO NOT / LIKE IT)

This may be defined as a minimal application of the model, in the sense that it credits only the socially negated element, the repressed, with valid or sympathetic equivalents in the text of a work. On the contrary, the negating element, the repression, which is in the wrong even when victorious in the conflict, lacks similar equivalents in the text. It tends to be reduced to the conditions of existence of the text itself, or to the institutional unreality of art, which practically neutralizes the repressed. According to this model, art in modern times has lent itself to such an obvious and frequent return of the repressed that it has become conventional and inflated. According to this model, so-called committed art has been able to collaborate with revolutionary ideologies in attacking an established order, but without ever being able to identify itself with political practice.[8]

If I dared further to generalize a working hypothesis, which instead I propose to verify in a manner restricted to a single text, I would simply say this: poetry in itself, unlike ideology, much less practice, cannot contribute in any way to changing the world. Yet it has perhaps always been the only force able to lend its voice to all that remains suffocated in *the world as it is,* to any thing in whose name the world ought from time to time to be changed, to any demands that are neither recognized by established order nor favored by public opinion. If this is so, poetry is incorrigibly conservative yet subversive at the same time. I prefer this paradoxical formulation to a more evasive and idealistic one, which consists in the claim that there is no sense in asking whether it is conservative or subversive. A return of the repressed made accessible to a community of men but rendered harmless by sublimation and fiction would deserve both, not just one, of these contradictory attributes; one cannot claim that it deserves neither the one nor the other. Should a revolution ever occur, poetry, which *before* might not have served to hasten its arrival by even an hour, will *afterward* venture to save a voice for all the sacrifices to the new regime, no matter what the authorities might demand. This is not to say that in such a case the authorities would necessarily notice or worry about it any more than Louis XIV was suspicious of *Phèdre.*

We already know that the minimal application of the model is valid in the case of *Phèdre,* but we know also that it is insufficient. Furthermore, to take another example from history contemporary with Racine and preceding the Enlightenment, it would not even be sufficient for Molière's masterpieces, which dramatize a conflict between individual extravagance and social behavioral norms. Frequently in these great comedies the maniacal needs of the individual are equivalent to a negated repressed, while the ridicule that punishes them and sanctions society's arguments is equivalent to an overwhelming negating element. In the text of *Phèdre,* the overwhelming value of the negating element will be recognized at first sight by any reader who agrees to recognize quite varying elements as its equivalents: speeches, situations, intrigues, characters, aspects of a character, and also images, symbols, myths... Since the concept of the

8. It is significant that the most ingenious modern effort at bringing the effectiveness of art close to revolutionary practice, that of Brecht, was accompanied by a theory of permanent demystification of the theatrical illusion. If the political repressed is not to remain practically neutralized in art, the institutional unreality of art must be exposed, displayed, controlled. It seems clear to me that in this way one attempts, on the contrary, to neutralize the repressive function attributed in the above model to the poetic fiction itself.

symbol, within the poetic fiction, can itself assimilate all of these elements, I shall speak generically of *symbolic negations* within the text; and I shall elaborate a second application of the model of Freudian negation for *Phèdre*, making visible a relationship of forces present within the message itself, apart from those (illustrated in the first model) between message and addresser, and between message and addressee:

		= nonacceptance of repressed	= REPRESSION	= symbolic negations
I	DO NOT			
	LIKE IT	= lifting of repression	= REPRESSED	= Phaedra's desire

The internal logic of Freudian negation requires the negating element to continue expressing the negated element in the most indirect way imaginable. Indeed it calls for the strength of the former to be directly proportionate to that of the latter. Thus it is not surprising that, when the negating element reveals itself forcefully within a text, the situation is almost a reversal of that in the Romantic or post-Romantic work of art in which, as I argued, only the negated element forcefully revealed itself. In *Phèdre* the corpus of symbolic negations is infinitely richer and more imposing than the direct expression of Phaedra's desire. The latter actually tends to disappear under the weight of an extremely dense combination of symbols, by means of which the desire is all the more able to affirm its strength, and appears all the more seductive and tormenting, the more it is irremediably negated.

4
The Historical Question of Myth and the Symbolic Negations

...ce que j'ai peut être mis de plus raisonnable
sur le théâtre.
RACINE, Preface to *Phèdre*

The aims of my discourse from now on are clear. I shall present the results of a study conducted according to the following principles: singling out all the possible symbolic negations within the text of *Phèdre* that correspond to the model of Freudian negation expressed in the terms $\frac{\text{REPRESSION}}{\text{REPRESSED}}$,[1] which, as we have seen, are according to Freud the terms of the dialectics of civilization itself; asking what relationship these symbolic negations have with each other; then trying to build them into a system that respects their equivalences or oppositions in the text. The variety of ways in which I shall identify the symbolic negations and specify their relationship will no doubt reflect the prescientific situation, the impossibility of giving up the spontaneous, intuitive hypothesis, which still characterizes literary studies. On the other hand, it will also reflect my premise that the language of poetry has something in common with the logic of the unconscious, as Freud described it in detail on the basis of the discovery and analysis of other languages. From this logic can be derived the concept of *symbolic coherence,* according to which symbols, quite different from one another, may contain relations of equivalence or opposition that are difficult to bring immediately to consciousness, though they can be proved to exist. Moreover, this justifies the indifference I shall show toward the literary sources of *Phèdre* (except where a comparison with these can help me prove a point). Whether, in fact, an element of the play was invented by Racine or derived in some way from ancient works by Euripides (*Hippolytus*), Seneca (*Phaedra*), Ovid (*Heroides* IV, *Metamorphoses* VII, XV), or Plutarch (*Life of Theseus*), its

1. For a theoretical justification of the model and its visual translation into fraction form, see the final pages of Appendix 1, "The Compromise-Formation as a Freudian Model."

true significance comes only from the complex of symbolic coherences belonging exclusively to the work by Racine. The same applies should the element in question be endowed a priori with certain meanings by myth, folklore, or dreams, and perhaps even by the interpretations of psychoanalysis. Freudian psychoanalysis does not ignore recurrent or, so to speak, traditional symbols, but its constant recognition of the *predominance of the letter* forces it above all to be respectful of anything historically individualized. In this sense the literary scholar may draw from it only a lesson in submissiveness toward the text. Even if, for example, the symbol of the Labyrinth, about which I shall be speaking at length, may itself be traced back to the form of human entrails or to the experience of childbirth, as far as I am concerned only the letter of the text will determine its precise significance within the corpus of *Phèdre's* symbolic coherences. Finally, I believe it quite vain to ponder the poet's degree of consciousness and calculation of each of the symbolic coherences as they were formed in his work through a logic akin to that of the unconscious. For three reasons I shall seldom dare to answer either affirmatively or negatively such questions as "but did Racine know this, is this what he wanted?" with any degree of verisimilitude: Racine is dead, levels of consciousness are unequal and changeable even among the living, and, finally, no scholar has so far been able to tell us very much about the dynamics of artistic creativity.

A single example will suffice to open the discussion. The most famous line in the tragedy is perhaps that which identifies Phaedra the second time she is mentioned, a few lines from the beginning, creating an effect of fear and mystery by using a genealogical periphrasis instead of her name (l. 36):

> La fille de Minos et de Pasiphaé.
> [the daughter of Minos and Pasiphaë.]

In order that this effect of fear and mystery should occur, one need not reflect on it but rather know (notwithstanding all that has been written about the pure sonorous beauty of this line) that: (1) according to the myth, Minos, king of Crete and an extremely just lawgiver, had been made a judge in the underworld after his death; (2) according to the myth, his wife Pasiphaë had conceived a monstrous passion for a beautiful bull and had borne a child by this animal. Both these mythical parents are mentioned again at highly significant points in the tragedy, as is also Phaedra's monstrous half-brother, the Minotaur. We shall then understand that the father, a symbol of the law's unerring severity, and the mother, a symbol of unbridled, unlimited, perverse desire, burden Phaedra's conscience and her blood; that Phaedra is thus truly the daughter of both

Law and Desire; that her internal conflict is projected into her mythical genealogy and vice versa. We may already perceive the outline of a symbolic negation straddling a moral situation and myth, and corresponding perfectly to the Freudian model:

REPRESSION	LAW	MINOS
REPRESSED	DESIRE	PASIPHAE

The parallel existence of this relationship of negation in the character's moral consciousness and in the myth that she bears brings me first to confront a problem of the greatest importance both for the interpretation of the work and for setting it against its historical background. In so doing, I am only apparently deferring the task of singling out the symbolic negations: in fact, I am beginning to move decisively toward its fulfillment. The problem I wish to discuss stems from the amazing consistency and fascination of *Phèdre*'s mythical, archaic, and fabulous aspects. The result of this is a curious duplicity of levels, since in other respects the characters rather obviously recall the gentlewomen and gentlemen of Racine's day. Well aware of this are producers, who today can choose or seek various compromises, between the original staging in the costume and milieu of the seventeenth-century French court and a mise-en-scène in Greek or even Minoan dress and settings: between Versailles and Troezen or Crete. The stratification and conciliation of two seemingly incompatible dimensions, introduced into the text of this tragedy from myth, was evocatively described by Jules Lemaître at the beginning of this century:

This Christian Phaedra of the seventeenth century and of our day is the daughter of Minos and Pasiphaë and the granddaughter of the Sun. This coquettish and lively Aricia, so witty and wise, and who will only flee with Hippolytus once she has a ring on her finger, is the great-granddaughter of the Earth. Both allude calmly to their forefathers. We are told of Sciron, of Procrustes, of Sinis, and of the Minotaur. We are reminded that one day Phaedra's husband entered Tartarus to "dishonor Pluto's bed." We are in a world where the gods keep monsters for their friends to dispose of and where the sea spews up enormous serpents with bulls' heads. Some lines suddenly inform us that these characters, who had only just seemed so close to us, belong to an extraordinarily distant age, filled with the memory of great natural disasters and in which there perhaps lived species of animals now extinct; this was the age of the earliest cities, of monsters and heroes. The poignant drama, which could easily belong to our age, carries with it remnants of legends that are thirty or forty centuries old.[2]

I do not believe, however, that literary historians have sufficiently asked why or how it was possible for such an ancient myth to be revived so

2. Jules Lemaître, *Jean Racine* (Paris: Calmann-Lévy, 1908), pp. 252-53.

formidably in *Phèdre*, even though they have stressed the obvious exceptionality of this case, even in Racine's dramatic work almost unique. Of his four tragedies on Greek subjects, *Iphigénie* alone contains a vaguely similar, though much less successful, compromise between a sense of the wonder of myth and seventeenth-century "modernity." Furthermore, *Iphigénie* immediately precedes *Phèdre*, so that this problem, to the extent that it is treated here, can be considered identical to the problem as it appears in *Phèdre*: we shall see to what extent.

From the viewpoint of literary history, the so-called Classical period in which Racine wrote stands between an age conventionally called Baroque and one conventionally called pre-Enlightenment (the age of the "crise de la conscience européenne," 1680-1715, as it is labeled in the title of Paul Hazard's famous book). Neither of these literary periods, however, seems to have offered any fertile ground for an authentic revival of Greek myth. Of course, it is well known that both used and abused all kinds of references to Greco-Roman mythology: gods, demigods, and heroes, the legends, prodigies, and monsters of pagan antiquity furnished par excellence the materials and embellishments of literature for an even longer period of time, stretching, in effect, from the Renaissance to Neoclassicism. But this prolonged phenomenon only rarely involved the genuine and deeper meaning of myth. As early as the Baroque period, the body of mythical evocations consecrated by ancient literary tradition had gradually been reduced to a stock repertory of rhetorical figures, of allusions that could be pleasurably understood by the ordinary reader. The result of this progressive draining of mythology's original vital force was already taken for granted by Racine's contemporaries. In a famous text like Boileau's *Art Poétique,* the indispensability of pagan mythology in literature is extolled with conviction, almost affectionately (in opposition to the supporters of the so-called *merveilleux chrétien*). Yet at the same time the decorative and rhetorical function attributed to ancient names is naïvely stressed (chant III, for example: "Chaque Vertu devient une Divinité./Minerve est la Prudence, et Vénus la Beauté").

In spite of the *querelle des Anciens et des Modernes*, the pre-Enlightenment period failed to eliminate this function from mythology in literature and the arts. However, in another area, the ideological, there arose an open, clear, and severe, intolerance, of myth's irrationality, something which for a century had lain hidden beneath the reduction of myth to a purely rhetorical system. It is well known that the case that Enlightenment reason tried to bring against myth as being absurd, childish, contradictory, coarse, indecent, senseless, at the time of Fontenelle and Bayle, was nothing less than an early, disguised phase of an open attack against religion. Pagan supernatural beliefs could be discussed with greater impunity than could those of Christianity, although, to the eyes of

Enlightenment reason, they were just as scandalous. In a short essay by Fontenelle entitled *Sur l'histoire,* whose exact date is uncertain but is either that of *Phèdre* or some ten years later, the advantages of studying and handing down "fantastic history" — that is, mythology — are questioned in the following terms:

Pourra-t-on croire qu'on puisse tirer quelque chose de bon de cet amas de chimères qui compose l'Histoire des Dieux et des Héros du Paganisme? Ne semblerait-il pas plutôt que pour l'honneur du genre humain, la mémoire de ces impertinences devrait être abolie à jamais?

[Can one really believe that some good may be derived from that mass of illusions that comprise the History of the Pagan Gods and Heroes? Would it not be better for the honor of the human race if the memory of this indignity were forever erased?][3]

Fontenelle's answer, that the human spirit is nevertheless still interested in knowing the history of its own errors, is less important to us than the question itself. Let us return to the text of *Phèdre.*

At the point where Phaedra is about to confess her guilty passion, she begins unexpectedly to recall her mother's monstrous relationship and elicits this response from her astonished nurse (ll. 251-52):

Oublions-les, Madame. Et qu'à tout l'avenir
Un silence éternel cache ce souvenir.
[Let us forget them, my Queen. And may eternal silence conceal this memory forevermore.]

This appeal to forget a scandalous story for modesty's sake is not an isolated instance in the tragedy, but one of a series of distichs scattered through the text having not only a common theme but also the same characteristic of exclamation or horrified exhortation. We shall consider each of them at the proper time. For the moment let us confine ourselves to examining the last of the series. It follows the final line uttered by the dying Phaedra and contains the announcement of her death and Theseus' comment on it (ll. 1645-46):

Elle expire, Seigneur. — D'une action si noire
Que ne peut avec elle expirer la mémoire!
[She is dying, my Lord. — Oh, that the memory of such terrible deeds could die with her!]

No sooner is Phaedra dead than an appeal is made that her story be

---

3. B. Le Bovier de Fontenelle, *Œuvres,* vol. 9 (Paris, 1758), p. 359. I have modernized the spelling. An accessible reprint of this text is in the "Bibliothèque 10/18" following the *Histoire des oracles* (Paris, 1966), pp. 149-68. For the date of the text, see Arnaldo Pizzorusso, *Il ventaglio e il compasso: Fontenelle e le sue teorie letterarie* (Naples: Edizioni Scientifiche Italiane, 1964), p. 100, n. 36.

forgotten, the same appeal made for her mother before her. Culminating in death, her story has at once become no different from her mother's, a myth: in both cases a myth of shame, a memory that, unfortunately, cannot (but ought to) fade. It can surely be no accident that Racine has here subverted the text of one of his principal sources. In Euripides' *Hippolytus*, the goddess Artemis gently consoles the dying Hippolytus and reassures him: "nor shall Phaedra's love/Forgotten in thy story be unhymned" (ll. 1429-30). The appeals to Racine's characters to forget seem rather to have something in common with Fontenelle's question: in both cases, myth is basically *scandalous*. The difference lies in the fact that Fontenelle viewed it as a rational scandal, a scandal to reason, and Racine's characters view it instead as a moral scandal. Nevertheless the scandal dwells in the remembrance, in the survival of a memory of something deserving oblivion as almost a punishment. The two men belonged to the same age, and Racine, like all poets of this age, was concerned with *vraisemblance*. For this reason, he was not too far removed from the kind of rationalistic diffidence expressed in exemplary fashion in Fontenelle's two sentences on mythology quoted above. A few passages from the prefaces of *Iphigénie* and *Phèdre* would suffice to prove this, revealing Racine's caution and his maneuvers in approaching myth; so, too, would the corresponding passages from the texts, even from *Phèdre*. All these are subjects to which I shall need to return.

The fact is, however, that in *Phèdre* the moral scandal assimilates the rational scandal, with which it is in direct contact. If Phaedra's love is equated to Pasiphaë's by such an appeal for oblivion, uniting them in what we might call mythical shame, their moral monstrousness on both occasions gives rise to monsters at the physical level. The Minotaur is born of Pasiphaë; Theseus' curse, provoked by Phaedra, produces the sea monster, which brings about the catastrophe. I am certainly not the first to notice that the word *monstre* is one of the most important in the tragedy, and that it recurs in two usages that are distinct but always apt to be placed in contact with each other. One is the physical-literal usage, where monster means the sea monster (ll. 1515ff.), the Minotaur (l. 649), or the numerous prehistorical monsters that infested the earth and that Theseus exterminated (ll. 79, 99, 938, 948, 963, 970, 1444). The other is the moral-figurative usage, whereby an intolerably guilty person may be called a monster, as happens to Hippolytus (ll. 520, 884, 1045), to Oenone (l. 1317), and, as could be expected, to Phaedra. In both passages in which Phaedra is called morally monstrous (ll. 700-703, and 1444-46), there is an explicit reference to the fact that she deserves to be killed like one of the prehistoric monsters exterminated by Theseus, among which is included her mother's son, the Minotaur. Thus the circle of monstrousness is closed, containing within itself and linking together two essential elements:

on one hand, the entire complex of the tragedy's truly mythical aspects, without any exceptions; on the other, all the moral horror that can be generated by the tension between an overbearing repression and an overbearing return of the repressed. The monstrousness which on the one hand is a part of the mythical dimension is on the other the dimension of nature itself, in conformity with the Jansenist view, shared by Racine, of human nature as damned without any hope for salvation other than divine grace.[4] A monstrous, bestial supernatural employs its forms to reveal something like the *subnatural* aspect of nature degraded by original sin. In the final analysis it is this latent ideological conception that has revived the deeper meaning of the myth, creating from its materials powerful symbolic equivalences. It is Phaedra's predestination to guilt that is painfully symbolized by a kind of monstrous inheritance from her maternal ancestors.

At this point one can understand what Racine held in common historically with a Fontenelle and what separated them. For both myth, when it is not just a harmless rhetorical device, is scandal by nature, the scandal of the irrational, of non-sense. Nevertheless, for Fontenelle, the unbeliever, there is nothing left to do but cast this non-sense into oblivion or keep it as a monument and a warning against innate human gullibility. On the contrary, Racine, the Jansenist, can poetically transform mythical scandal into a much greater scandal, but one endowed with sense: the supreme scandal of divine will and human predestination to evil. What I had presented as the historico-literary problem of the force of myth in *Phèdre* comes unexpectedly to coincide with the other historical problem that I raised earlier on: the boldness of the incest theme and of the emotional identification associated with it. Racine has dared to represent incest on the strength of the same moral-religious and repressive horror that enabled him to succeed in having monsters and myth, symbolic vehicles of the repressed, taken seriously. For him to succeed in this, however, the symbolic vehicles also had to be adequate to their awesome content. The monsters and myth, if taken seriously, were bound to offend the essence of the mind of his age: reason, a reason which included decency and morality. Yet, since myth in its milder sense was expected by the literary code, its use as part of the poetic fiction itself actually contributed simultaneously to the neutralization of the return of the repressed in the work of art. A character in Phaedra's emotional situation

---

4. In order to understand how Jansenist ideology lent itself to the workings of the poet by repressively eliminating any intermediate value between man and God and viewing nature as a repressed with an incurable return, the most illuminating pages seem to me to be those of Paul Bénichou, *Morales du grand siècle* (Paris: Gallimard, 1967), pp. 121-213; Eng. trans. as *Man and Ethics: Studies in French Classicism*, trans. Elizabeth Hughes (Garden City, N.J.: Doubleday & Co., 1971), pp. 116-67.

who was not a well-known mythological heroine would undoubtedly have been far less feasible at that time. Nevertheless, if Racine has here been able to use the literary code profitably, it is especially by crossing its rationalistic bounds from within—a literal interpretation of the myth was sufficient—and by making this violation expressive of something. The problem appears to solve itself, as do many problems, provided that the conjunction expressing its logical formulation is changed from *even though* to *because.* In substance I had asked myself: why is it that in *Phèdre* myth has such a profound vitality, *even though* the tragedy was written between two eras which found myth disgusting unless used superficially? I am able to reply: myth has such a profound vitality in *Phèdre* precisely *because* the tragedy was written between two eras that found it disgusting unless used superficially. The rational abhorrence of myth in the pre-Enlightenment period, exploited symbolically as moral horror, is at the base of this tragedy, filled with monsters and the gods that arouse them. And, in the form of an appeal to forget the story of Phaedra as a shameful myth, it also stands at the conclusion of the tragedy to excuse and, in a way, to negate the work itself.

5

A System of Symbolic Negations

Besides, I don't see any connection... — You can leave the
connection to me.
FREUD, *The Psychopathology of Everyday Life*

The appeal to forget the myth I shall consider as the first obviously
recognizable symbolic negation in *Phèdre*. It is, without doubt, the one of
greatest possible importance within the work, the one according to which,
if repressive rationality had prevailed over the repressed, there would
have been in place of the play only silence:

$$\frac{\text{REPRESSION} \mid \text{OBLIVION}}{\text{REPRESSED} \mid \text{MYTH}} \qquad (7)$$

The work exists, however, with the license of the repressive rationality
that has modeled it step by step, and it tells of moral and physical
monsters. The myth = repressed is actually the set of aspects in the work
in which physical monsters manifest themselves; I have already said
enough to be able to articulate within this set the various symbolic
negations that subdivide it.

One is that which corresponds to the theme of Theseus' deeds,
frequently recalled from one end of the tragedy to the other. In this the
monsters appear as a submissive repressed, as the primordial and
ferocious irrationality that the civilizing hero has progressively eliminated
from the earth, thus strengthening, if not actually founding, the reign of
humanity. This violent rationalization of the world seems related to the
consolidation or foundation of Theseus' political power, which required
no less violence: the massacre of Aricia's brothers, the Pallantids. Political
insubordination tends to be assimilated into the archaic anarchy of the
monsters, and established order results at the expense of both. The
symbolic negation in question may thus be summarized as follows:

$$\frac{\text{REPRESSION} \mid \text{HERO} \mid \text{KING}}{\text{REPRESSED} \mid \text{PREHISTORIC MONSTERS} \mid \text{REBELLIOUS RELATIONS}} \quad (6)$$

More difficult to explain in a synthesized form is the presence of
another symbolic negation, in parts of the text where the occurence of

evocations of the far-off myth must be evaluated in a very close connection with what occurs in the present tragic action. These are evocations of myths from the island of Crete, Phaedra's homeland, or rather of myths of her family, particularly the Minotaur. The latter's story would fit simply into the cycle of the deeds of Theseus, who slew him, if it were not also drawn toward different symbolic meanings by the equation set up between two elements: the Minotaur had to be reached in the depths of the Labyrinth, where he was kept hidden by its impenetrable windings; he was Phaedra's half-brother, and she too hides a secret and cannot reveal it without resistance and hesitation. Racine has evoked the Cretan myths twice, both occasions coinciding with moments in which Phaedra's secret is about to be laboriously brought into the open. The reference to the Minotaur's birth occurs at the point where Phaedra strays from the subject to delay her imminent confession to her nurse (l. 250). The lengthy and tortuous fantasy about the Labyrinth is nothing less than Phaedra's struggle to declare herself to Hippolytus (ll. 634-62). In at least this second case the Labyrinth not only provides a theme, it is at the same time a labyrinth of verbal hesitation, a labyrinthic verbal structure. The hidden monster becomes Phaedra's vainly repressed secret, whose scandalous nature is worthy of her mother's perverse race incarnated by the Minotaur. Since the verbal labyrinth holds back, or represses, the secret and corresponds therefore to the strict moral conscience which Phaedra has inherited instead from her father, we can now also retrieve the symbolic negation that we had perceived earlier in discussing the two parents, by means of the following equations:

$$\frac{\text{REPRESSION}}{\text{REPRESSED}} \left| \frac{\text{LABYRINTH}}{\text{MINOTAUR}} \right| \frac{\text{MINOS}}{\text{PASIPHAË}} \qquad (5)$$

The third and final symbolic negation linked to a mythical aspect is the only one in which a monster appears in the present, rather than in the distant past, and is the only one in which the position of the monster, a destroyer before being destroyed, corresponds to the negating element of the Freudian model rather than to the negated. I am referring to the sea monster that brings about Hippolytus' death. Obviously, it is provoked by Phaedra, through a series of deadly mediators such as Oenone, Theseus, the god Neptune; it is Phaedra herself, her monstrous desire or rather its aggressive revenge. In this sense I could almost equate it to the negated element of the preceding symbolic negation, the Minotaur, and it is no accident that it has the same horned brow of a bull while its back bears the winding folds of the Labyrinth (ll. 1517-20). Nevertheless it represents the complete transformation of the repressed desire into aggression. The object of this homicidal aggression, and thus the element actually negated, is Hippolytus' body, the handsome body that Phaedra desired and which, after the monster has burst upon the scene, is concretely and cruelly slaughtered. Here the relationship of symbolic negation is between death and physical beauty, thus remaining entirely within the physical dimension (in which only the sea monster is actually described), and now also entirely within the realm of guilty desire, which negates itself by causing the destruction of its own object:

$$\frac{\text{REPRESSION} \mid \text{SEA MONSTER}}{\text{REPRESSED} \mid \text{HIPPOLYTUS' BODY}} \tag{4}$$

So far I have pointed out four symbolic negations, of which the last three are in turn negated by the first, $\frac{\text{OBLIVION}}{\text{MYTH}}$, in the sense that each of the three is derived from within its negated element: myth. At this point, if only that which involves the supernatural may be termed mythical, as I have assumed from the start, have we exhausted the mythical aspects of *Phèdre?* Yes, with one apparent exception, represented by a myth that seems to take shape before our eyes during the first half of the tragedy, only to be given the lie around the middle and restored to a nonsupernatural version. Theseus' death, feared at first and then confirmed during Act 1, takes on a mythical character in the second act because it is rumored to have been caused by the impossibility of returning from the kingdom of the dead, into which the hero supposedly descended alive (ll. 383-88). When Theseus reappears, however, in the third act, he himself reduces his apparent stay in hell to a long underground imprisonment at Epirus, though saying that he was kept in caverns so deep that they were actually near the kingdom of the dead (ll. 965-66). Thus the rational solution, the denial of the nascent myth, is ultimately insufficient to dispel retrospectively the supernatural aura created by the poet around this apparent death. If we take this into consideration and try to include it among the mythical aspects that I formulated as symbolic negations, we soon realize that it is impossible to derive from it a negation parallel to the others. The imaginary disappearance of the hero, who brought about the triumph of rational repression on earth and founded established order, will rather have exactly the opposite value: a suspension of rational repression, an eclipse or crisis of established order, in effect, *a negation of the negation*, which will return to the advantage of the repressed. Indeed, in the tragic action, it is the news of Theseus' death, skillfully exploited by Oenone, which is decisive in encouraging Phaedra to make her declaration. The contradictory function of this half-myth, which is positive because it is a negation of the negation, will be kept in mind as we now go on to consider which nonmythical aspects of *Phèdre* correspond to the mythical ones examined so far. In fact, if we follow for the former the same succession already adopted for the latter, it will confront us immediately.

According to this succession, we must ask ourselves what corresponds at the nonmythical level, and in the present, to the symbolic negation $\frac{\text{HERO}}{\text{PREHISTORIC MONSTERS}}$, situated in discussions of the distant past. The answer would be easy were we to consider abstractly that in the play the character of Theseus accumulates all the possible designations of political, social, and family authority. He is king, father, and husband, and circumstances inevitably endow him with the duty of judge. Standing by himself, he should therefore embody a symbolic negation of the type:

$$\frac{\text{REPRESSION}}{\text{REPRESSED}} \,\bigg|\, \frac{\text{AUTHORITY}}{\text{TRANSGRESSION}}$$

But what relation does the real character bear to his titles and duties? It would be tempting to answer that he seems perfectly capable of fulfilling these just as long as he *remains unreal.* I am referring to those two and a half acts in which he is feared or believed dead, is absent, and yet the number of speeches concerning him would, but for the compensation of their extraordinary variety, seem quite obsessive. In this first half of the tragedy, the other characters either admire or blame him but without ever compromising the prestige surrounding his image. They seem unable to avoid speaking about him: as dead or alive, as the hero of countless great deeds, as the seducer in countless affairs, as the tyrant who has placed an erotic ban on Aricia, after having done away with her brothers, as the handsome young man of earlier days whose memory is revived for Phaedra in his son. Everything is overturned, however, in the second half of the tragedy. When the man believed dead is replaced by one restored unexpectedly to life, the aging seducer must immediately consider himself a deceived husband and father, the tyrant soon discovers that he is being disobeyed, the hero who exterminated monsters is transformed into a provoker of monsters, into the hasty and blind judge easily duped by Oenone. The real father betrays his previous, ideal image of Father, to which he shows himself to be so inadequate that his failure serves only to prolong his absence and is, in effect, equivalent to it. The mythical irrationality of the rumors about Theseus' death was literally correct: one cannot return from the underworld. If the character was absent in the first half of the tragedy, in the second half things are worse still, or, if one likes, the same, for he utterly fails to perform his functions. In reality, at the nonmythical level, in place of the symbolic negation that Theseus should incarnate and that remains void, we have only a negation of the negation, which may be expressed as follows:

$$\frac{\text{(REPRESSION)}}{\text{REPRESSED}} \,\bigg|\, \frac{\text{(AUTHORITY)}}{\text{TRANSGRESSION}} \tag{3}$$

The fact that at least one of the symbolic negations in the series I am outlining should be missing or negated was, on close consideration, an indispensable premise for the tragic action itself. If all the negations conspiring against Phaedra's desire existed and held out, if the repressed could not find a point of least resistance through which to surface, we should have not a plot in movement but a static situation, or only a single event: Phaedra would die alone, in darkness and silence, consumed by her own unavowed desire. The confession of her forbidden desire to others, however, first to Oenone, then to Hippolytus, makes way for the events which defer Phaedra's death up to the moment when her secret is no longer such for anybody, for it has been avowed to the representative of repressive authority itself — Theseus. At that moment, when the secret has definitively ceased to be, the myth of shame, which Theseus wishes were forgotten, arises in its place. Until that moment the tension between confession and secret, silence and speech, corresponds at the nonmythical level, as we perceived earlier, to the symbolic negation of a mythical character $\frac{\text{LABYRINTH}}{\text{MINOTAUR}}$. Moreover, in an early phase, indeed at the beginning of the tragedy, the tension between silence and speech is actually preceded by a choice which Phaedra has had to make between a hidden state and the light of day, reluctantly appearing on stage and explicitly qualifying it as the place of light as well as speech. Stage and dialogue, the two basic constituents of a dramatic production, both seem endowed with the symbolic value of the seat of the return of the repressed. The new symbolic negation will include the following equations:

$$\frac{\text{REPRESSION}}{\text{REPRESSED}} \left| \frac{\text{HIDDEN STATE}}{\text{STAGE}} = \frac{\text{DARKNESS}}{\text{LIGHT}} \right| \frac{\text{SECRET}}{\text{CONFESSION}} = \frac{\text{SILENCE}}{\text{SPEECH}} \quad (2)$$

Finally we may assume that to the last symbolic negation of a mythical character, $\frac{\text{SEA MONSTER}}{\text{HIPPOLYTUS' BODY}}$, there corresponds at the nonmythical level another entirely within the physical dimension. This is not for the sake of a preconceived symmetry, but because the two physical realities of death and desire do not oppose each other only in the ultimate catastrophe, nor only through the destruction of the desired object. It is primarily within its subject that desire gets twisted into death. Phaedra has not yet come on stage when, as our first news of her, we learn about the state of agony in which she is languishing. This is identical to the hidden state that I discussed for the previous symbolic negation. Here the physical affirmation of desire is negated from within by the defensive-punitive tendency toward death, before an entrance is made into the circle of light and speech and there arises the temptation to confess it to the outside world. Solitary and entirely within silence and darkness, this initial negation seems to consist less of a voluntary decision to die than of a spontaneous transformation of desire into consumption of the body.

Eventually Phaedra will die equally alone, having repudiated the nurse who constantly personifies her instinct of self-preservation and, as such, also plays a part in the plot—parallel to Theseus' imaginary death and then his real inadequacy—as a negation of the negation. Having run out of detailed arguments for protecting Phaedra's desire and her life, Oenone then dared to appeal to an absolute argument: the legitimation of the desire in the name of the human condition. We might say that here the negation of the negation momentarily becomes an affirmation (ll. 1295-1306). This affirmation is in turn immediately punished by death, for Phaedra's repudiation is followed by Oenone's suicide, after which Phaedra's own death cannot be long in coming. The final symbolic negation of the whole series, ideally before or more immediate than all the others, will therefore be:

$$\frac{\text{REPRESSION}}{\text{REPRESSED}} \left| \frac{\text{PHAEDRA'S DEATH}}{\text{PHAEDRA'S DESIRE}} \right| \frac{\text{OENONE'S SUICIDE}}{\text{PROTECTION AND LEGITIMATION OF DESIRE}} \qquad (1)$$

In this way I have formulated seven symbolic negations in all. It is my belief that in these the themes of the tragedy, and thus the text, are all abstractly summarized. In the following chapters I shall go through the entire series again, inverting the order in which I arrived at them, moving from the most immediate negation, the one of least consequence, to that of the greatest importance, from which I had started out. I shall proceed in this order to comment on passages scattered throughout the text, whose relation to what has been observed so far will be like that of an analysis of something concrete to an abstraction of its results. However the order in which the symbolic negations will be reexamined requires some further comment. I singled out three of a mythical character, to which I made three of a nonmythical character correspond. In doing this, I noted that these six negations divide themselves into groups of two. If we straightaway adopt the descending numeration in parentheses that I have been using to identify them, the first corresponds to the fourth, the second to the fifth, the third to the sixth. This correspondence between the nonmythical and mythical level joins together the first negation and the fourth within the *physical* dimension ($\frac{\text{PHAEDRA'S DEATH}}{\text{PHAEDRA'S DESIRE}}$ = $\frac{\text{SEA MONSTER}}{\text{HIPPOLYTUS' BODY}}$). The second negation and the fifth also have a common dimension, the reason for which I shall not repeat, which is the *verbal* dimension ($\frac{\text{SECRET}}{\text{CONFESSION}}$ = $\frac{\text{LABYRINTH}}{\text{MINOTAUR}}$). I shall also observe that the common dimension of the third and sixth negation is the *institutional* one ($\frac{\text{(AUTHORITY)}}{\text{TRANSGRESSION}}$ = $\frac{\text{HERO}}{\text{PREHISTORIC MONSTERS}}$). While the first pair of symbolic negations remained entirely within the subject of desire and its unique object, the second pair involved other subjects through speech, and this third pair implies the social order as a preexistent institution, outside the subject. The preferable order for re-examining the first six negations will therefore be 1-4, 2-5, 3-6. Finally, the seventh negation $\left(\dfrac{\text{OBLIVION}}{\text{MYTH}}\right)$ dominates and in turn negates the negations of a mythical character, and through these the others too. Thus, paradoxically, it negates the whole work.

Let us schematize all these relationships in a way that shows how the symbolic negations are distributed over the two levels, mythical and nonmythical, and correspond to each other in the three orders, physical, verbal, and institutional:

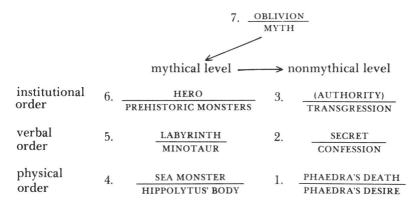

7. $\dfrac{\text{OBLIVION}}{\text{MYTH}}$

mythical level ⟶ nonmythical level

institutional order	6.	$\dfrac{\text{HERO}}{\text{PREHISTORIC MONSTERS}}$	3.	$\dfrac{\text{(AUTHORITY)}}{\text{TRANSGRESSION}}$
verbal order	5.	$\dfrac{\text{LABYRINTH}}{\text{MINOTAUR}}$	2.	$\dfrac{\text{SECRET}}{\text{CONFESSION}}$
physical order	4.	$\dfrac{\text{SEA MONSTER}}{\text{HIPPOLYTUS' BODY}}$	1.	$\dfrac{\text{PHAEDRA'S DEATH}}{\text{PHAEDRA'S DESIRE}}$

A further diagram will show more clearly the ideal hierarchy of the three orders within the two planes, and the virtual negation of the work above them all. Phaedra's desire, which is almost lacking in any expression that is not contradicted and, thus, in any autonomous space in the text, will be represented by the point which is enclosed within the seven semicircles; the dotted semicircle represents the inadequacy of one of the symbolic negations:

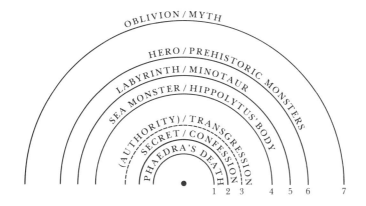

I am well aware that any abstraction violates the reality of things to a greater or lesser degree. Besides, I have simplified these diagrams by deliberately leaving out some of the pairs of elements that I had already placed among the symbolic negations as I went along. If I must refer, however, to the analysis of the text that is to follow, for all other necessary specifications or nuances, I must still deal synthetically with one aspect beforehand. This concerns the character of Hippolytus and with it those of Aricia and Theramenes which, unlike those of Phaedra, Oenone, and Theseus, seem not to have found a place in the series of symbolic negations. Hippolytus appears in these only as the object of Phaedra's desire, by virtue of his physical beauty, and therefore not as an actual subject or character. It is precisely Hippolytus' place in this tragedy that offers an excellent occasion to dispel the concept of substantial characters, seen more or less improperly as independent beings, which I had rejected from the first. It is a concept that has proved particularly damaging in criticism of *Phèdre,* afflicted by the tendency to exalt the protagonist at the expense of the other characters as a poetic or psychological or moral creation: an aberrant effect, in an individualistic sense, of the main emotional identification. Leo Spitzer's masterly essay on Theramenes' narration[1] marks a turning point with respect to this tendency (which even reappears, in ideologized form, in a work as untraditional as Lucien Goldmann's *Le Dieu caché*[2]). Thus my interpretation owes more to Spitzer's essay than I have acknowledged in passing. If we wish to make room for the character of Hippolytus in this already schematic interpretation, we must first of all note that he is defined as a subject only in being distinguished, by similarity and opposition, from other subjects, and particularly because a double series of similarities and oppositions distinguishes him from Theseus and Phaedra respectively.

The basis of similarity against which his opposition to Phaedra stands out, is obviously transgression: Hippolytus loves Aricia in spite of his father's ban. The symmetry of construction between the first act, in which Hippolytus' confession to Theramenes precedes that of Phaedra to Oenone, and the second, in which Hippolytus' declaration to Aricia precedes that of Phaedra to Hippolytus, in effect sets up a comparison between their respective transgressions. The opposition, however, springs from this comparison and consists in the measure and quality of the two transgressions (it would be much more apparent if, in each of the first two acts, the weaker transgression were to follow instead of to precede

1. Leo Spitzer, "The 'Récit de Théramène,'" in *Linguistics and Literary History: Essays in Stylistics* (Princeton: Princeton University Press, 1948), pp. 87-134.
2. Lucien Goldmann, *Le Dieu caché* (Paris: Gallimard, 1955), pp. 416-40; Eng. trans. as *The Hidden God: A Study of Tragic Vision in the "Pensées" of Pascal and the Tragedies of Racine,* trans. Philip Thody (London: Routledge and Kegan Paul, 1964), pp. 371-91.

the stronger, whose overwhelming effect almost makes us forget it). Phaedra's transgression is unpardonable, endangering one of the bases of established order, the morality which controls sexuality. Hippolytus' transgression is entirely pardonable and comprehensible within the bounds of established order; it endangers only the authority of the individual in command, Theseus—indeed, just one, questionable, order of his. It would therefore cease to be a transgression were Theseus really dead and Hippolytus to inherit his authority, were it possible to transform transgression into succession. The similarities and oppositions between Hippolytus and Theseus appear in turn in the relationship of royal succession. The continuation of the order established by the father, which the son would assure by succeeding him, is a sufficient basis of similarity, but the order which Hippolytus promises is, with regard to his father's, nevertheless modified by sufficient oppositions for them not to be considered identical. The son's promised order would appear to be at once less violent, more just, and sexually more repressive; it implies a more advanced stage, so to speak, of rationalization of the world, of civilization. Spurred on by a burning desire to emulate his father, Hippolytus no longer has the need or the possibility of taming monsters with their own blood, for Theseus has already dealt adequately with this rudimentary civilizing task. His son can only tame horses, a bloodless exercise that curbs a much lesser bestiality. His very disobedience to the king, his father, is transformed into making reparations for the injustices which Hippolytus believes him to have committed (ll. 475, 494), in annulling the ban on Aricia's marrying and in yielding to her a throne that is dynastically hers. With the permissiveness and fickleness of the heroic seducer, in whose habits the uncontested use of pleasure seemed almost a prerogative of authority, is contrasted the moral censure and chastity of his son, who has a first and only love.

It will be useful to set up a comparison between Theseus, Hippolytus, and Phaedra based on the respective attitudes of their desires. Two pairs of meanings in opposition are enough to distinguish the three characters: pardonable desire versus unpardonable desire (in a social, moral sense, etc.); faithful desire versus unfaithful desire (in the sense of the uniqueness or plurality of its object). Theseus' desire is unfaithful but pardonable, since his affairs, though countless, do not infringe any really fundamental prohibitions. Phaedra's desire, which on the contrary is unpardonable, is nevertheless faithful (as Spitzer has observed) in that it superimposes the image of Hippolytus onto that of the young Theseus, and it is as though by identifying them with each other Phaedra remained faithful to one object only. Only Hippolytus' desire is both pardonable and faithful; but that which with respect to Theseus' desire it gains in intensity because of its constancy, it pays for in the terrible confrontation with Phaedra's desire because of its innocence. The monogamous integrality of the perverse desire causes not only the superficiality of the frivolous affairs to pale by comparison, but does so still more obviously (and this not the least of *Phèdre*'s boldnesses) to the chastity of regular monogamy, embellished by a touch of the illicit. Hippolytus essentially represents a dual alternative, as a transgressor with respect to Phaedra and as a successor with respect to Theseus. Far from threatening established order, Hippolytus' passing transgression would actually strengthen it, if it were to become a lasting succession. Rationality and sexual repression would go forward together. The genius of the poet, who lived during the reign of Louis XIV, appears to have sensed something of the dialectics which is in civilization according to Freud, causing the catastrophic suppression of this particular new order by the return of the repressed that Phaedra introduces between the reign of the father and that of his son. The physical beauty of the repressive Hippolytus, which kindles her desire, comes to represent the accidental point at which opposites meet, where the repressed is vindicated and rational order succumbs. For this reason the character requires two very different interpretations according to whether he is considered as object or subject. For this reason, too, I would place him (and his confidant, and Aricia who mirrors him on the feminine side) among the symbolic negations principally in the vacant space of the third negation, $\frac{\text{(AUTHORITY)}}{\text{TRANSGRESSION}}$, where Hippolytus unsuccessfully offers an alternative to his father during the latter's absence.

I cannot end this discussion without observing that *Phèdre* describes for us an established order at a time of the transfer of power, before it has been shaken by the catastrophe which marks its failure. It is depicted neither as immovable in the face of the impending catastrophe nor as left intact by the possible succession from one generation to another on the throne, but rather as dedicated in such circumstances to an evolution whose essential features I have attempted to define. Historically speaking this is an aspect of the work which is all the more interesting in that, as we have seen, it hinges above all on the character of Hippolytus in love—a modern innovation as regards the extremely chaste hunter of the classical sources. As an explanation of his development in *Phèdre*, I consider as satisfactory neither Racine's statement in the preface that he wished to avoid creating too perfect a character nor the anecdote according to which Racine was afraid that the dandies might joke about a Hippolytus who was hostile to women. The need for Hippolytus' love in the work goes much deeper: it qualifies the presence of a new generation beyond the character himself, and introduces a sense of change beyond the tragic action. What politico-social development in reflected or even anticipated historical reality could have corresponded to this tangible aspect of the poetic text? If the imaginary order established by Theseus had a connection with the real order established by the young Louis XIV, for they must be connected in some way and to some extent, with what might be connected the order announced by Hippolytus? I do not feel competent to attempt an answer to this question, but only to point out its importance. A nonextrinsic Marxist interpretation might perhaps start out from this very question. Reluctantly I must hand it over to the historians, since for me there remains only the task of firmly approaching the letter of the text.

6

Symbolic Negations of the Physical Order (First and Fourth)

The verses of Racine that I shall be quoting in the course of my analysis will not appear in the order that they occupy in the text. This is because my analysis, bringing them together according to the greatest number of oppositions and similarities from among the infinite possibilities by which each passage derives from others its precise sense, will attempt to reconstruct an *alternative order,* which is immanent and partly hidden within the text. My reconstruction of this alternative order not only involves an unavoidable margin of arbitrariness, as did the preceding diagrams, which will guide it, but it must in any case be considered an essentially provisional operation. It is intended solely to be inserted between one reading of the text and another, as a moment of reflection. After this moment, one must return to reading the text, though, I hope, with increased understanding and enjoyment. The complexities of my analysis are justified by the wealth of coherent relationships of meaning, of oppositions and similarities, in the text. Whether we say that *Phèdre* is an exceptionally great, or important, or beautiful work, I would tend to make the object of our judgment of value coincide entirely with this inexhaustible wealth and perfect coherence of meaning.

I.

Forbidden desire cannot impose itself without upsetting repressive rationality: the return of the repressed induces in Phaedra a permanent crisis of reason. *Raison, esprit* have ceased to reign, while *désordre, trouble, fureur,* and a tendency to *s'égarer* have taken their place:

147   Un désordre éternel règne dans son esprit.
      [An eternal confusion reigns within her mind.]

179   Insensée, où suis-je? et qu'ai-je dit?
      Où laissé-je égarer mes voeux et mon esprit?
      Je l'ai perdu: les Dieux m'en ont ravi l'usage.
      [Madness, where am I, and what have I said? Where have I let my desires and my reason stray? I have lost it: the Gods have seized it.]

282   Je cherchais dans leurs flancs ma raison égarée.
      [I sought my deranged reason in their flanks.]

675   Ni que du fol amour qui trouble ma raison
      [Nor the madness of this love which disturbs my reason]

792   Sers ma fureur, Oenone, et non point ma raison.
      [Serve my madness, Oenone, and not my reason.]

1264 Que fais-je? Où ma raison se va-t-elle égarer?
      [What am I doing? Where is my mind straying?]

1470 Le trouble semble croître en son âme incertaine.
      [The confusion seems to grow in her wavering heart.]

The submission which rages within the subject in this way prefigures the external repercussions that it will have as a setback to the established institutions. These are all the greater because the protagonist is a queen, and the two senses, public and private, of the verb *régner* inevitably coincide in the incapacity that forces her to lay aside the responsibilities of state:

759   Moi régner! Moi ranger un Etat sous ma loi,
      Quand ma faible raison ne règne plus sur moi!
      [*I* reign! *I* place a state under my rule, when my weakened reason no longer reigns over me!]

In Phaedra's relating of her past conflicts to Oenone and Hippolytus, after her confession to the former and her declaration to the latter, four exclamations, two in each account, form a symmetrical arrangement. All four deplore the routing of the forms of resistance which reason had successively opposed to love; remedies, precautions, cures, plans have each time proved powerless, vain, useless, weak:

283   D'un incurable amour remèdes impuissants!
      [Powerless remedies for an incurable love!]

301   Vaines précautions! Cruelle destinée!
      [Vain precautions! Cruel destiny!]

687   De quoi m'ont profité mes inutiles soins?
      [What did I gain from my useless troubles?]

697   Faibles projets d'un cœur trop plein de ce qu'il aime!
      [Feeble plans made by a heart too full of what it loves!]

II.

Lines 147 and 1470, which open and close the first set of quotations, are the only ones in the set not pronounced by Phaedra. They come from two scenes in the first and fifth acts (I,2 and V,5) which correspond to each other on the basis of many elements. Both are opened by a messenger bringing news of Phaedra, who has never been seen by the audience in the first case and has disappeared from sight in the second. This news is in both cases of impending death and prepares the entrance of Phaedra, worn out by sleeplessness and fasting in the first case, already infiltrated by the poison in the second. Oenone in the first instance and Panope in the second ignore the reasons for the impending death; they announce it but cannot explain it. Let us compare the openings of these two speeches, in which Phaedra is observed from without and the terror of the return of the repressed reverberates in the others, who are unaware and bewildered; the only symptoms they can see, apart from the crisis of her reason, are the physical signs of death:

143   Hélas! Seigneur, quel trouble au mien peut être égal?
La Reine touche presque à son terme fatal.
En vain à l'observer jour et nuit je m'attache:
Elle meurt dans mes bras d'un mal qu'elle me cache.
[Alas, my Lord, what troubles can equal mine? The Queen has almost reached the hour of her death. I strive in vain to watch over her day and night: she is dying of an illness she keeps hidden from me.]

1461   J'ignore le projet que la Reine médite,
Seigneur. Mais je crains tout du transport qui l'agite.
Un mortel désespoir sur son visage est peint;
La pâleur de la mort est déjà sur son teint.
[I do not know what the Queen is meditating, my Lord, but I greatly fear her state of distraction. A mortal despair is revealed by her face and death's pallor is already on her cheeks.]

III.

The body negated by death because it is the seat of desire seems in turn to reject an upright position, movement, and light, when Phaedra arrives on the scene:

154   Je ne me soutiens plus: ma force m'abandonne.
Mes yeux sont éblouis du jour que je revoi,
Et mes genoux tremblants se dérobent sous moi.
[I can no longer stand upright: my strength is failing me. My eyes are dazzled by the light of day and my trembling knees give beneath me.]

The annoyance that Phaedra feels at her clothing and hairstyle is intolerance of the body, as well as a vindictive rejection by the body of the demands of social life (ll. 158-61). Nevertheless, all references to her agony in the following dialogues, whether uttered by Phaedra or Oenone, are related to the latter's insistence on salvation, which negates the negation. If the amount of life remaining in Phaedra is described as a "remnant," it is still enough to warrant the nurse's appeal to live, whether successful or not:

214   Réparez promptement votre force abattue,
        Tandis que de vos jours, prêts à se consumer,
        Le flambeau dure encore, et peut se rallumer.
        [Quickly regain your weakened strength while the flame of life, though
        ready to expire, still burns, and may be rekindled.]

315   Et que tes vains secours cessent de rappeler
        Un reste de chaleur tout prêt à s'exhaler.
        [May your vain help cease trying to kindle a remnant of the flame that is
        about to expire.]

364   Vivons, si vers la vie on peut me ramener,
        Et si l'amour d'un fils en ce moment funeste
        De mes faibles esprits peut ranimer le reste.
        [I'll live, if I can still be brought back to life and if my love for my son can
        revive what remains of my feeble strength in this fatal hour.]

With these last words the situation is already modified; but they are belied by Phaedra's recollection and accusation two acts later. It is not love for her son that has revived her in her moment of agony, but another love:

769   Toi-même rappelant ma force défaillante,
        Et mon âme déjà sur mes lèvres errante,
        Par tes conseils flatteurs tu m'as su ranimer.
        Tu m'as fait entrevoir que je pouvais l'aimer.
        [You yourself, by rallying my failing strength, knew how to revive me
        with your advice, when my soul was already wandering on my lips. You
        let me think that I could love him.]

                IV.

It could be said that Oenone's words of advice best suit the utterer just when they are *flatteurs* to desire; but if a choice becomes necessary their fidelity is not to desire but to Phaedra's life. Oenone personifies an instinct of preservation which speaks from this side of the desire itself. It is only when she is faced with the impending risk of Phaedra's death that her moral pretexts yield:

239   Et que me direz-vous qui ne cède, grands Dieux!
        A l'horreur de vous voir expirer à mes yeux?
        [Tell me, by the Gods, what could be more terrible than to see you perish
        before my eyes?]

773   Hélas de vos malheurs innocente ou coupable,
       De quoi pour vous sauver n'étais-je point capable?
       [Alas, whether you were innocent or guilty of your troubles, what would I
       not have done to save you?]

897   Mais puisque je vous perds sans ce triste remède,
       Votre vie est pour moi d'un prix à qui tout cède.
       [But since I shall lose you without this unhappy remedy, your life is
       worth more than anything else to me.]

903   Mais le sang de l'innocence dût-il être versé,
       Que ne demande point votre honneur menacé?
       [But even if innocent blood must be shed, what does your threatened
       honor not demand?]

The safeguarding of threatened honor cannot be distinguished from that of life. Oenone's relative indifference to the morality of the means, the perpetually instrumental nature of her kind of persuasion, which because of this is all the more tenacious and passionate, even includes orthodox arguments about established order where these seem appropriate:

196   De quel droit sur vous-même osez-vous attenter?
       Vous offensez les Dieux auteurs de votre vie;
       Vous trahissez l'époux à qui la foi vous lie;
       Vous trahissez enfin vos enfants malheureux...
       [What right do you have to dare to take your own life? You offend the
       Gods who have given you life; you betray your husband to whom you are
       bound by your vows; and finally you betray your unhappy children...]

755   Ne vaudrait-il pas mieux, digne sang de Minos,
       Dans de plus nobles soins chercher votre repos,
       Contre un ingrat qui plaît recourir à la fuite,
       Régner, et de l'Etat embrasser la conduite?
       [Would it not be better, oh noble daughter of Minos, to seek repose
       through more worthy deeds? Flee from an ungrateful youth, to whom
       you are attracted, reign, and take on the leadership of the State?]

825   Il faut d'un vain amour étouffer la pensée,
       Madame. Rappelez votre vertu passée.
       [My lady, you must stifle any thought of this vain love and remember
       your past virtue.]

I should point out the solemn and untimely evocation of Minos in line 755, and I might also add that it is Oenone who utters the appeal to cast Pasiphaë into oblivion (ll. 251-52). As soon as she hears Phaedra's confession, Oenone is horrified (ll. 265-68) and struck dumb. Her silence is all the more eloquent, coming at the end of a scene of which two thirds has been carried along by such a compact dialectic between the two speakers.

V.

Oenone remains silent not only during but also after Phaedra's account, that is after Phaedra has drawn the consequences of what she has related in terms of her inevitable death. *At this point* Oenone has nothing else to say against the necessity of death: the negation of the negation can no longer find a spokesman. In Euripides' *Hippolytus*, the nurse undertook the legitimation of Phaedra's love immediately after the account (ll. 437-76), where it had a function in both Phaedra's and the plot's interests. Anything similar in Racine has been moved to much later on, to a point at which it may no longer have such a functionality at all. At the end of the first act, Oenone speaks again at length only after the news of Theseus' death has arrived. This is equivalent to saying that the only decisive negation of the negation in *Phèdre* is the lack of paternal authority and not an instinct of preservation that had found the time to yield for an instant when confronted by the unpardonability of incest:

337 Madame, je cessais de vous pressez de vivre;
   Déjà même au tombeau je songeais à vous suivre;
   Pour vous en détourner *je n'avais plus de voix* . . .
   [My Lady, I had already given up urging you to live. I already imagined I would follow you to the grave; I no longer had words to turn you back . . .]

This is not to say that Oenone's voice does not complement that lack, that it does not fill the gap to the advantage of the repressed. She quickly provides Phaedra's love with a legitimation of a relative nature, by interpreting the consequences of the death of him who was both husband and father:

349 Vivez, vous n'avez plus de reproche à vous faire:
   Votre flamme devient une flamme ordinaire.
   Thésée en expirant vient de rompre les nœuds
   Qui faisaient tout le crime et l'horreur de vos feux.
   [Live, for you no longer have anything for which to reproach yourself: your passion becomes a normal passion. Theseus' death has untied the knots that made your love a crime and an abhorrence.]

Oenone's voice will once again make up for the absence of the character of Theseus, when at the time of his return Phaedra will wish no longer to let herself die as at the beginning, but rather to commit a deliberate suicide (ll. 857-59). This plan Oenone opposes with that of slandering Hippolytus in order to save Phaedra, a plan which presumes, and will in fact exploit, Theseus' blindness, just as her earlier encouragement of

Phaedra presumed that he was dead. Since it is linked to forbidden desire, the preservation instinct can only move onto other ground when it is temporarily abandoned by an interrupted or blind law.

VI.

There is one law which cannot be interrupted or blinded. It rests in a Father who cannot die for the categorical reason that he is already dead; and his death is not an outside event like Theseus' supposed death, but rather a profound interiorization of the Law into the consciousness. I am, of course, referring to Minos, the father of the myth. The confrontation with him, in the great hallucination of the fourth act, marks the point at which the violence of Phaedra's sense of guilt, breaking the equilibrium with that of desire, breaks the alliance between desire and the preservation instinct; by eliminating all means of escape for Phaedra, even in the afterlife, it eliminates all of Oenone's practical arguments. Yet Oenone still has something to say. The Jansenist ideology that has just inspired the terroristic paroxysm of the hallucination contains a virtual reverse side, for it acknowledges the inextinguishability of desire in human nature, even if it is evil and weak. A similar reverse side may be exploited in an indulgent sense in deriving the indirect homage to nature from this repressive pessimism. This is why contemporaries of *Phèdre* observed a Jansenist tone most of all in its only ideologically licentious passage, where the negation of the negation becomes an affirmation, an absolute legitimation of desire:

1297 Vous aimez. On ne peut vaincre sa destinée.
   Par un charme fatal vous fûtes entraînée.
   Est-ce donc un prodige inouï parmi nous?
   L'amour n'a-t-il encor triomphé que de vous?
   La faiblesse aux humains n'est que trop naturelle.
   Mortelle, subissez le sort d'une mortelle.
   [You are in love. One cannot overcome one's destiny. You were led astray
   by a fatal enchantment. Is that so strange or so unheard of among men?
   Has love ever triumphed only over you? Weakness is quite natural to
   mankind. You are mortal and must suffer a mortal's fate.]

The example of the illegitimate love affairs of the Gods which immediately follows, sounds in this desperate context both like an accusation and an appeal. Both are aimed at an established order in which pardonable transgressions may be freely practiced at the level of the sovereign, and in which there are nevertheless some unpardonable transgressions:

1304 Les Dieux même, les Dieux, de l'Olympe habitants,
   Qui d'un bruit si terrible épouvantent les crimes,
   Ont brûlé quelquefois de feux illégitimes.

[Even the very Gods themselves, who dwell in Olympus and who keep crime at bay with their awesome thunder, have sometimes burned with illicit passion.]

VII.

Before we heard these lines another confidant had convincingly legitimized another relationship. The task was easier and less audacious; but the succession of arguments, from the essential innocuousness of the feeling to the examples of its most illustrious victims, was initially the same. Only Hippolytus' immediately preceding condemnation of his father's affairs prevented Theramenes from pointing the way to his absolution in Theseus himself and made him resort to the superior mythical model of Hercules:

119   Enfin d'un chaste amour pourquoi vous effrayer?
       S'il a quelque douceur, n'osez vous l'essayer?
       En croirez-vous toujours un farouche scrupule?
       Craint-on de s'égarer sur les traces d'Hercule?
       [Why fear a chaste love? Why not taste it if it is at all sweet? Will you
       always be timid and have qualms about it? Can one fear to go wrong when
       following in Hercules' footsteps?]

The reasoning that followed was appropriate for Hippolytus, in love with Aricia, but Oenone could never take it up before Phaedra. The perpetuation of the race, to which his Amazon mother has contributed and to which Hippolytus owes his existence, is a goal so fitting for a chaste passion that it seems irreconcilable with the much more passionate shamelessness of a desire without goals:

123   Quels courages Vénus n'a-t-elle pas domptés?
       Vous-même où seriez-vous, vous qui la combattez,
       Si toujours Antiope à ses lois opposée,
       D'une pudique ardeur n'eût brûlé pour Thésée?
       [What hearts have not succumbed to Venus' powers? Where would you
       be, you who now fight her, if Antiope, who was always opposed to her
       ways, had not burned for Theseus with a chaste passion?]

VIII.

The repudiation of Oenone, Phaedra's curse, the nurse's suicide, these negate the negation of the negation. They punish without a moment's delay that affirmation which Phaedra never allows herself, and which has the intolerable overtones of heresy (doubly so if it is overturned Jansenism). Between the death of Oenone, who disappears head first into the waves, and Phaedra's final agony, which prolongs that of the entire tragedy, the letter of the text confirms an antithesis: quick death versus slow death. Even in the first act, as she spoke to Phaedra, Oenone was unwittingly prophesying:

229   Quoiqu'il vous reste à peine une faible lumière,
        Mon âme *chez les morts descendra* la première.
        Mille *chemins* ouverts y conduisent toujours,
        Et ma juste douleur choisira les plus *courts.*
        [Although your light has almost faded, my soul will go down to the
        Underworld before yours. A thousand roads lead there always, but my
        grief will choose the shortest.]

In the fifth act, with identical but opposite words, Phaedra says that she had wanted:

1636   Par un *chemin* plus *lent descendre chez les morts.*
        [To go down to the Underworld by a slower road.]

The delaying of Phaedra's death is a conflict, a moral conflict between secret and confession, between silence and speech, within a sense of shame: the final delay serves the purposes of the final confession. The promptness of Oenone's suicide is negatively coherent with the physical immediacy of the preservation instinct she embodies. Yet it is still too sweet a punishment for such shameful haste, as well as for such monstrous affirmations which, if acted upon, would tend to cancel out the very meaning of that conflict:

1317   Je ne t'écoute plus. Va-t'en, monstre exécrable.
        [I will no longer hear you. Go away, vile monster.]

1629   La perfide, abusant de ma faiblesse extrême,
        S'est hâtée à vos yeux de l'accuser lui-même.
        Elle s'en est punie, et fuyant mon courroux,
        A cherché dans les flots un supplice trop doux.
        [The treacherous woman took advantage of my extreme weakness and
        hurried before you to accuse him. She has punished herself and, fleeing
        my anger, sought too gentle a death beneath the waves.]

The social conformity of the preface, which considers the baseness of slander less unworthy of a nurse than of a princess, is echoed in the text by the imprecations against flatterers (ll. 1320-26), which would attempt to find a social motivation for that existence apart from Phaedra that the character of Oenone hardly possesses. This is perhaps the point at which the text makes the greatest concession to the external necessities that had dictated the preface. Yet the context is such that this concession eventually cancels itself out. Though the condemnation of bad counsellors as being equally responsible for the guilt of princes was a commonplace of the baroque theater, no spectator could entirely sympathize with the enormous injustice and ingratitude that Phaedra shows Oenone. By exaggerating these, Racine largely ends up by having proposed them to no purpose, and the greater part is thus surreptitiously appropriated for the repressed. In the violent repressive division, the spectator's sympathy might even be concentrated for a moment on Oenone alone, if there were not among the other lines that tremendous one in which Phaedra prepares to be left alone:

1318   Va, laisse-moi le soin de mon sort déplorable.
       [Go, and let me take care of my pitiable fate.]

IX.

Phaedra's slow death at the end is the slow entry of the poison into her heart. The line that announces it appears to be scanned on the basis of a much earlier line, which announced instead the flow of blood into her heart as an effect of desire, an immediate swoon at the mere sight of the young man she loves:

1639   Déjà / jusqu'à mon cœur / le venin / parvenu
       [The poison has already reached my heart.]

581   Le voici. / Vers mon cœur / tout mon sang / se retire.
       [Here he is. My blood rushes into my heart.]

Poison in place of blood. Thus the letter of the text confirms the correspondence by negation between death and desire in the physical dimension. In this dimension Phaedra's desire asserts itself. Love springs from sight, and its effects indiscriminately upset both parts of the person, the soul and the whole body, to the extent that one seems to be a part of the other, or that there no longer appear to be any parts at all:

273   Je le vis, je rougis, je pâlis à sa vue;
       Un trouble s'éleva dans mon âme éperdue;
       Mes yeux ne voyaient plus, je ne pouvais parler;
       Je sentis tout mon corps et transir et brûler.
       [I saw him, I blushed, I grew pale at his sight; my distracted heart was confused; I could no longer see nor speak; I felt my whole body freeze and burn at the same time.]

The importance of Hippolytus' physical resemblance to the young Theseus in Phaedra's eyes may suggest problems with the character's history: problems of age, chronology, psychology. Did Phaedra ever really love the father before the son? Since it is stated that the adulterous feeling arose immediately after the wedding (l. 269), such a love could only be placed hypothetically in a period sometime before Theseus came to Crete and before his affair with Ariadne. It is not hypothetical, however, that in the text Phaedra passionately identifies herself with the image of her sister, through compassion, erotic emulation, and solidarity in a condemned line of ancestors:

253 Ariane, ma sœur! de quel amour blessée,
   Vous mourûtes aux bords où vous fûtes laissée!
   [Oh my sister, Ariadne! From what wounds of love did you die on the shores where you were abandoned!]

652 Ma sœur du fil fatal eût armé votre main.
   Mais non, dans ce dessein je l'aurais devancée . . .
   [My sister would have armed you with the fatal thread. No, for in this plan I would have forestalled her . . .]

It is this imaginary substitution of herself for her sister that, integrating that of Hippolytus for Theseus, sets off the labyrinthic avowal of love in the final phase of disclosure. The resemblance between father and son provides the indispensable premise for the entire declaration, allowing such a prolongation of its ambiguity and at the same time stressing both its aura of unavowable incest and the essential fidelity to a single image by which adultery is redeemed. Phaedra's desire owes to the coincidence of its unpardonable with its faithful nature, the totality, which much more than incest and adultery, makes it the "greatest of horrors." The same coincidence makes it the very "height of misery":

261   Tu vas ouïr le comble des horreurs.
   [You are about to hear the greatest of horrors.]

289 Je l'évitais partout. O comble de misère!
   Mes yeux le retrouvaient dans les traits de son père.
   [I avoided him everywhere. Oh height of misery! My eyes picked him out in his father's face.]

X.

The modern reader may have some difficulty in recognizing Phaedra's children behind the periphrasis by which their mother refers to them at the point of least tension in the relating of her story of love:

299 Soumise à mon époux, et cachant mes ennuis,
   De son fatal hymen je cultivais les fruits.
   [Obedient to my husband and concealing my woes, I raised the fruit of our ill-fated union.]

Periphrases in the noble style, however, which require many words to express a single concept, permit these words to be selected deliberately. Often in Racine they are veiled revelations, concealed accusations. In fact, Phaedra seems far less capable of showing fondness for these as yet immature fruits, in which her union had realized its purpose, than she would have shown, without or in opposition to any definite sexual aims for the blooming Hippolytus:

657   Que de soins m'eût coûtés cette tête charmante!
       [What attention I would have paid to that beautiful head!]

In the game in which Racine has won his bet on Phaedra, he has surely not played a rasher card than this: to have made her a bad mother, or at least to have placed her children at a permanent disadvantage in their contrast with her desire for love or her desire for death. Maternal responsibility for her runs the risk of being totally confused with dynastic responsibility, and of being given up in the same gesture of mortal fatigue (ll. 759-63). In Act 1 the children are merely an argument for persuading her to live spoken by Oenone, and always with reference to dynastic responsibility. It is in this context that we hear the only note of affection toward her first-born:

345   Sur qui, dans son malheur, voulez-vous qu'il s'appuie?
       Ses larmes n'auront plus de main qui les essuie...
       [On whom can he lean in his misery? There will be no more hand to wipe
       away his tears...]

The ambiguity, already noted in Phaedra's reference to the "love for my son" in the penultimate line of the act, prepares for a further ambiguity of far graver consequences in the next act. It is the motion of pity for her son that provides Phaedra with an excuse both to request the conversation with Hippolytus and to slip quickly and imperceptibly into the motion of pity for herself. She will appeal too late for her good intentions to be believed:

695   Tremblante pour un fils que je n'osais trahir,
       Je te venais prier de ne le point haïr.
       [Fearing for my son whom I dared not betray, I came to beg you not to
       hate him.]

In the third act, at the moment of greatest weakening of Phaedra's resistance there is a corresponding impulse to exploit quite voluntarily her own maternal and dynastic responsibility, to entice Hippolytus with the kingdom:

803   Cédons-lui ce pouvoir que je ne puis garder.
       Il instruira mon fils dans l'art de commander.
       Peut-être il voudra bien lui tenir lieu de père.
       Je mets sous son pouvoir et le fils et la mère.
       [I will yield him the power I cannot keep. He will instruct my son in the
       art of commanding. Perhaps he will be willing to act as his father. I
       commend both the son and the mother to him.]

Once again the children are an obstacle to her renewed decision to die, this time because of the shame they would inherit (ll. 860-61), and the obstacle only leads to greater shame. Phaedra's last gesture toward her children, at the moment of her suicide, turns her remorse into a horrified rejection, which is at the same time a rejection of herself inasmuch as she too had inherited such shame before handing it down. Pasiphaë's daughter, after having wept over her children for an unavowable grief, renounces maternal love, the chain of guilt and the perpetuation of the species:

> 1471   Quelquefois, pour flatter ses secrètes douleurs,
> Elle prend ses enfants et les baigne de pleurs;
> Et soudain, renonçant à l'amour maternelle,
> Sa main avec horreur les repousse loin d'elle.
> [To placate her hidden grief she sometimes takes hold of her children and showers them with tears; then suddenly, renouncing her maternal love, she pushes them far away with a shudder.]

Oenone's viscerally maternal feelings toward Phaedra are also at the expense of her own maternal duties:

> 235   Mon pays, mes enfants, pour vous j'ai tout quitté.
> [For you I gave up everything, my country, my children.]

XI.

There is for Aricia as well the possibility of sorrowfully soliciting the spectator's emotional identification. The enormous bias in favor of the bearer of perverse desire is asserted alongside the impartiality of the poet, who can provide even her rival with moving lines:

> 417   O toi qui me connais, te semblait-il croyable
> Que le triste jouet d'un sort impitoyable,
> Un cœur toujours nourri d'amertume et de pleurs,
> Dût connaître l'amour et ses folles douleurs?
> [You who know me, does it seem possible that the wretched victim of a ruthless fate, a heart that has always lived on bitterness and tears, should know love and its pain?]

Aricia's love for Hippolytus, just like Hippolytus' for Aricia, derives its chastity from having arisen as an exception to a previous attitude, that of being "forever" averse to love. Aricia admits that which Phaedra confessed, and that about which Hippolytus is most reticent (ll. 522, 543), thus according to feminine beauty correspondingly less space in the tragedy—that love stems from sight:

> 433   Tu sais que de tout temps à l'amour opposée,
> Je rendais souvent grâce à l'injuste Thésée

Dont l'heureuse rigueur secondait mes mépris.
Mes yeux alors, mes yeux n'avaient pas vu son fils.
[You know that I was always opposed to love and often thanked unjust Theseus, whose fortunate harshness favored my contempt. But then my eyes had not beheld his son.]

This admission is followed a line later by its negation, explicit and, moreover, conforming to that of Hippolytus himself, who naturally despises and ignores his own beauty:

437   Non que par les yeux seuls lâchement enchantée,
J'aime en lui sa beauté, sa grâce tant vantée,
Présents dont la nature a voulu l'honorer,
Qu'il méprise lui-même, et qu'il semble ignorer.
[Not that I was charmed by my eyes alone; I love his beauty, his much praised grace, gifts with which nature has honored him and that he himself despises and seems to ignore.]

But is Aricia's a true Freudian negation, as its linguistic form here might lead us to believe? Usually we are not so much interested in the character's psychology as in its opposition to others. In saying this Aricia becomes the symbolic negator of the value of beauty, which is recognized by Phaedra, and beyond this of the physical totality or completeness or gratuitousness, and thus potential perversity, of desire. The actual opposition set up between the two women coincides with that between pardonable and unpardonable desire. We are not deceived by Aricia's ignorance: by believing that Phaedra is loved by Theseus, she hopes, in the following lines, to vie with her victoriously according to the other opposition, that is, as the object of faithful instead of unfaithful desire:

445   Phèdre en vain s'honorait des soupirs de Thésée:
Pour moi, je suis plus fière, et fuis la gloire aisée
D'arracher un hommage à milles autres offert,
Et d'entrer dans un cœur de toutes parts ouvert.
[In vain Phaedra gloried in Theseus' sighs: I have more pride in myself and avoid the easy glory of snatching a compliment offered to a thousand others, and of entering into a heart open to all.]

The catastrophe punctually reserves a retaliatory torment for chaste Aricia, in which I cannot refrain from pointing out the play of symbolic negations, which has imperceptibly become cruelly precious. She will be the one who refuses to recognize as a corpse the very body of Hippolytus whose beauty she had failed to appreciate and, in some ways, had repudiated:

1578   Elle voit (quel objet pour les yeux d'une amante!)
Hippolyte étendu, sans forme et sans couleur.
Elle veut quelque temps douter de son malheur,

Et ne connaissant plus ce héros qu'elle adore,
Elle voit Hippolyte et le demande encore.
[She saw a terrible sight for a lover's eyes! Hippolytus stretched out, disfigured and pale. She tried to ignore her misfortune for a while and, no longer recognizing the hero she adored, she saw Hippolytus, yet still asked for him.]

XII.

Thus we have passed inadvertently from the first symbolic negation to the fourth. It will be recalled that the relationship between these two negations did not only imply an opposition between nonmythical and mythical, but also between death of the subject and death of the object of desire. Nevertheless the death of the subject also contains a mythical element in the evocative name of the unnatural sorceress who provided the poison used in Phaedra's suicide—Medea:

1637   J'ai pris, j'ai fait couler dans mes brûlantes veines
        Un poison que Médée apporta dans Athènes.
        [I have taken into my burning veins a poison which Medea brought to Athens.]

Inversely, Aricia's failure to recognize physical beauty is, on a nonmythical level, a negation of that object of desire which will be destroyed by the intervention of a monster. Only Aricia actually refuses for an instant to recognize the corpse, but for the objective Theramenes who recounts this it was already no more than

1568   un corps défiguré,
        Triste objet, où des Dieux triomphe la colère,
        Et que méconnaîtrait l'œil même de son père.
        [a sad object, a disfigured body in which the anger of the Gods has triumphed, and that even his father's eyes would not recognize.]

XIII.

If this outcome is a triumph of the anger of the Gods, whom Aricia reproaches with her gaze (l. 1584), the earthly responsibility for it rests with Phaedra. Phaedra's secret identity with the sea monster is not only assured, through a kind of transitive quality, by the Minotaur, who is related to the former and resembles the latter; the letter of the text identifies them, for they both deserve to suffer at the hands of Hippolytus the fate reserved for monsters, inflicted by his father on the Minotaur as well as many others. In fact:

1527   Hippolyte lui seul, digne fils d'un héros...
        [Hippolytus alone, a hero's worthy son...]

faces the sea monster while everyone else flees. Nevertheless Phaedra had told him, as she passionately threw herself into the path of his attack:

700   *Digne fils du héros* qui t'a donné le jour,
        Délivre l'univers d'un monstre qui t'irrite.
        [Worthy son of the hero who gave you life, free the world from a troublesome monster.]

The monster was incest itself:

702   La veuve de Thésée ose aimer Hippolyte!
        Crois-moi, ce monstre affreux ne doit point t'échapper.
        [Theseus' widow dares love Hippolytus! Believe me this frightful monster must not escape.]

The punishment she begged for was, however, difficult to separate from a torment of love:

704   Voilà mon cœur. C'est là que ta main doit frapper.
        Impatient déjà d'expier son offense,
        Au-devant de ton bras je le sens qui s'avance.
        Frappe. Ou si tu le crois indigne de tes coups,
        Si ta haine m'envie un supplice si doux...
        [Here is my heart. Here must your hand strike. I feel it move forward to meet your blow, impatient to pay for its crime. Strike; or if you believe it to be unworthy of your blows, if your hatred feels this is too mild a punishment...]

Death, which the subject is here denied, becomes the death of the object. The attack that Hippolytus denies Phaedra and that is soon turned against him by Phaedra becomes the monster that attacks Hippolytus and that Hippolytus hardly has time to strike (l. 1530) before being overcome. The phases through which Phaedra's attack passes (Oenone's slander, Theseus' appeal to Neptune) are somehow symbolically reproduced in Theramenes' narration, in which it is not the monster that kills Hippolytus directly, but rather the horses, who are terrified and blinded by the monster:

1531   De rage et de douleur le monstre bondissant
        Vient aux pieds des chevaux tomber en mugissant,
        Se roule, et leur présente une gueule enflammée,
        Qui les couvre de feu, de sang et de fumée.
        [Leaping up with rage and pain, the monster fell moaning at the horses' feet, rolled over and showed them his flaming jaws, which covered them with fire, blood and smoke.]

The monster arose from the sea, from beyond those shores which Theseus' courage had delivered from heinous murderers (ll. 1065-66), just as Phaedra's desire has arisen outside of moral and rational order. But the horses that kill Hippolytus had been tamed by him, and the order of civilization immediately wipes itself out in their savage disobedience, just as it does in Theseus' blind rage. Theramenes' narration is the mythical moment par excellence, as it is the only passage in the tragedy in which a physical monster became inevitable if Racine was to adopt this myth. Not surprisingly, this was the object of much discussion on taste in Racine's lifetime and throughout the eighteenth century; not surprisingly, in our day, the exhaustive analysis of the work begun by Spitzer took this as its starting point. We shall encounter this again several times in the course of the analysis; it repeats and translates the entire tragedy into an augmented density of symbols. If, in this, the monster negates the object of Phaedra's desire with a repression-destruction, the myth of Theseus' heroic deeds has reminded us sufficiently that a monster is by nature the repressed, here by a tragic inversion victorious not as love but at least as death. Even the most criticized line of the narration adheres admirably to the logic of the Freudian negation, which is terrified by what it produces. Into the baroque figure of speech, which links the ebb of the waves to the horror of all nature at the sight of the monster, is projected the same impulse of fear that the protagonist has felt from the outset toward her own repressed (l. 307), and perhaps even the author toward his own work:

1524   Le flot qui l'apporta recule épouvanté.
       [The wave that brought it recoiled in horror.]

XIV.

Phaedra's desire waited neither for the hour of slander nor for the fatal meeting with Hippolytus to transform itself into aggressiveness. Hippolytus' exile, obtained by her from his father, his alleged persecution of a stepmother in whom love disguised itself as hatred, are presented by Phaedra as practical means of moral self-defense but in the unambiguous terms of one who "worships" her enemy, who "exposes" herself to enmity, who "seeks" hatred:

291   Contre moi-même enfin j'osais me révolter:
       J'excitai mon courage à le persécuter.
       Pour bannir l'ennemi dont j'étais idolâtre,
       J'affectai les chagrins d'une injuste marâtre...
       [Finally I dared revolt against myself. I rallied my courage to persecute him. I simulated the sorrows of an unjust stepmother to banish the enemy I worshipped...]

599   A votre inimité j'ai pris soin de m'offrir.
       Aux bords que j'habitais je n'ai pu vous souffrir.

En public, en secret, contre vous déclarée,
J'ai voulu par des mers en être séparée...
[I took pains to expose myself to your enmity. I could not tolerate you in
the land where I lived. Declaring myself your enemy, in public and in
private, I sought to be separated from you by the oceans...]

683   Toi-même en ton esprit rappelle le passé.
C'est peu de t'avoir fui, cruel, je t'ai chassé.
J'ai voulu te paraître odieuse, inhumaine.
Pour mieux te résister, j'ai recherché ta haine.
[Recall the past yourself. I did not flee you, cruel one, I drove you away. I
wanted to seem hateful, inhuman to you. I sought your hatred to resist
you better.]

Is this a spontaneous aggressive instinct that projects itself toward the
outside, in the same way that it rages inside the subject? Or is it instead a
distortion imposed upon the desire by the repressive consciousness or by
the frustration of the desire itself by the denial of its object? The most
important theoretical question left open, or, rather, answered incon-
clusively by Freud, that of the existence of a death or destructive instinct
independent of the erotic instinct, can surely not be more easily resolved
on the basis of *Phèdre* than on the basis of experimental material provided
to psychoanalysis by living beings. Phaedra's plea to be spared the horrors
of remorse and the cries of blood, at the moment in which she fears that
the destructive effects of her desire have already come to pass, is perhaps
all the more heartrending because it echoes the desire's irresistible fear
of itself:

1167   Seigneur, je viens à vous, pleine d'un juste effroi.
Votre voix redoutable a passé jusqu'à moi.
Je crains qu'un prompt effet n'ait suivi la menace.
S'il en est temps encore, épargnez votre race,
Respectez votre sang, j'ose vous en prier.
Sauvez-moi de l'horreur de l'entendre crier;
Ne me préparez point la douleur éternelle
De l'avoir fait répandre à la main paternelle.
[My Lord, I come to you full of terror. Your dreadful voice has reached
me. I fear that your threats may receive a prompt effect. I dare beg you, if
there is still time, to spare your son, respect your flesh and blood. Spare
me the horror of hearing him cry out; do not prepare me the eternal grief
of having caused a father to shed his own blood.]

The tremendous diverting of this fear by jealousy does not prevent
Phaedra from again finding herself face to face with it inside of a hundred
lines, with remorse now heightened by a true bloodthirsty passion:

1271   Mes homicides mains, promptes à me venger,

Dans le sang innocent brûlent de se plonger.
[My murderous hands, ready for revenge, cannot wait to plunge into innocent blood.]

It is too late, however, for trembling with horror at this passion to be of any use. We shall learn from Theramenes' narration to what extent the bloodshed and the tearing to pieces of the handsome beloved's body becomes reality; the classical sources provided Racine with an ample choice of hair-raising details:

1550   Tout son corps n'est bientôt qu'une plaie.
. . . .
1556 De son généreux sang la trace nous conduit:
   Les rochers en sont teints; les ronces dégouttantes
   Portent de ses cheveux les dépouilles sanglantes.
   [His whole body was soon a single wound. . . . The traces of his generous blood led the way: the rocks were stained by it, from the thorns dripped the bleeding remnants of his hair.]

Furthermore, the letter of the text makes an accurate statement some distance away that it does not forget. In Act 1, Phaedra's frenzy nostalgically shifted her desire for Hippolytus, as yet unavowed, onto an object that was intimately connected with the young athlete's body, his chariot:

176 Dieux! que ne suis-je assise à l'ombre des forêts!
   Quand pourrai-je, au travers d'une noble poussière,
   Suivre de l'œil un char fuyant dans la carrière?
   [Oh Gods, I wish I were sitting in the shade of the forest! When will I be able to follow, through the dust, a chariot racing along the course?]

In the last act, we learn that Hippolytus' chariot has suffered an exemplary destruction, immediately preceding that of its driver's body:

1542 L'essieu crie et se rompt. L'intrépide Hippolyte
   Voit voler en éclats tout son char fracassé . . .
   [The axle groaned and broke. Intrepid Hippolytus saw his chariot shattered to pieces . . .]

The desire literally shatters into tiny pieces the image that it had dared to long for.

7
Symbolic Negations of the Verbal
Order (Second and Fifth)

I.

That the bed in which Phaedra lies at the beginning is in darkness is never directly stated. The darkness in which Phaedra hides has no linguistic expression of its own, as the silence does, except in the negation of daylight that has been her lengthy refusal to face it, which was in turn the premise for her desire to see it again. The meaning of *jour* fluctuates between that of "light" and of "life," and in any case always implies both:

45   Phèdre, atteinte d'un mal qu'elle s'obstine à taire,
       Lasse enfin d'elle-même et du jour qui l'éclaire...
       [Afflicted by a malady she refuses to reveal, Phaedra is tired of herself
       and the light that shines on her...]

148   Son chagrin inquiet l'arrache de son lit.
       Elle veut voir le jour...
       [Her restless sorrow tears her from her bed. She wants to see daylight...]

155   Mes yeux sont éblouis du jour que je revoi...
       [My eyes are dazzled at seeing the light...]

166   Vous vouliez vous montrer et revoir la lumière.
       Vous la voyez, Madame, et prête à vous cacher,
       Vous haïssez le jour que vous veniez chercher?
       [You wished to come out and see the light. You have seen it, my Lady,
       and are ready to hide, hating the light that you sought?]

The shame felt for a monstrous repressed does not call the entire work into question only at the point at which Phaedra dies, and the poet who has ensured that she will be remembered seems to regret this through Theseus' words: Phaedra's reluctance to come on the scene opens her parable with an effort, whose origin is the same as that of the modesty with which the appeal to forget concludes it. Her first speech denies, tries to halt, her way toward light and makes her presence before the spectators tantamount to an enormous effort at the very moment in which it is fixed:

153   N'allons point plus avant. Demeurons, chère Œnone.
      [Let us go no further. Stay here, dear Oenone.]

Although the only reference to the scenery in the entire text is to "walls and vaults" (l. 854), in accordance with surviving evidence from the seventeenth-century stage director ("Théâtre est un palais voûté"), the stage must be sufficiently bright for Phaedra to identify it with light. Her third speech is a salute to the sun:

169   Noble et brillant auteur d'une triste famille,
      Toi, dont ma mère osait se vanter d'être fille,
      Qui peut-être rougis du trouble où tu me vois,
      Soleil, je te viens voir pour la dernière fois.
      [Oh noble and shining founder of a wretched race; you, whom my mother boasted as a father, who probably blush at my distress; oh Sun, I am coming to see you for the last time.]

Into the sun that illuminates inside her the conflict between Law and Desire, Phaedra seems to project them both. Perhaps the sun blushes at her humiliation, as though the Law shone in it, yet her mother, who had ignored all the limits of Desire, boasted of being its daughter. The sun is the vital principle, noble and brilliant, from which life has sadly degenerated, and it is to the sun that Phaedra directs a final glance before paying the penalty of death. For an instant this glance transcends the contradictions in a nostalgia ignorant of the conflict, as if Law and Desire could cease from the eternal implication and exclusion of one another. When Oenone states a little later that Phaedra has not slept for three nights or eaten for three days, the noble style obliges her to negate or conceal in a periphrasis these needs of the flesh, which Phaedra negates by allowing herself to die. However, the periphrasis betrays its function in fulfilling it, as do all the symbolic negations in *Phèdre*, and it nostalgically opposes the innocence of a natural rhythm of sunsets and dawns to the remorse that causes Phaedra to destroy nature within herself:

191   Les ombres par trois fois ont obscurci les cieux
      Depuis que le sommeil n'est entré dans vos yeux;
      Et le jour a trois fois chassé la nuit obscure
      Depuis que votre corps languit sans nourriture.
      [The shadows have covered the sky three times since sleep last entered your eyes, and daylight has driven away dark night three times since your body has languished without nourishment.]

II.

A bed in the shadows is to Phaedra what the depths of the woods are to Hippolytus. The lover's inactivity and his disobedience toward his father are hidden in the place where he used to pursue his emulation as a horse tamer or a hunter (ll. 133, 176, 543, 782, 933). The alternation of day and night is also evoked with regard to his transgression, but against a background of the forest's half-light, whose relationship to Phaedra's darkness is the same as that of his love for Aricia to incest:

543   Dans le fond des forêts votre image me suit;
        La lumière du jour, les ombres de la nuit,
        Tout retrace à mes yeux les charmes que j'évite...
        [Your image follows me into the woods; the light of day, the shadows of
        night, everything conjures up the charms I avoid...]

Unjustly accused of incest, at the end of a lengthy self-defense, in which the heroic silence he keeps should pardon the exaltation of his own virtue, he himself dares to compare the depths of his heart to the light of day:

1112   Le jour n'est pas plus pur que le fond de mon cœur.
       [The daylight is no purer than the bottom of my heart.]

III.

Yet the absolute innocence for which Phaedra longs is quite different from the relative innocence of Hippolytus' real love. It is something glimpsed entirely on this side of, or entirely beyond, all feelings of guilt, and has so few chances of becoming reality that it may be yearned for, from afar, only in the image of others. Perhaps in Phaedra's eyes Hippolytus' beauty is nothing more than this. Deprivation and despair have the greatest power to increase such a longing, and thus Phaedra will be able to drink deeply of it only when seized by the pangs of jealousy. That the two requited lovers should hide in the depths of the forest seems at first as plausible to her as it is in the reality of Hippolytus and Aricia, which is certainly not immune from feelings of guilt. Then this gives way to a dream of complete license, approved innocence, love without remorse, which is her own dream of freedom from repression, and it is imagined in the light of a never-ending series of calm mornings:

1236   Dans le fond des forêts allaient-ils se cacher?
       Hélas! ils se voyaient avec pleine licence.
       Le ciel de leur soupirs approuvait l'innocence;
       Ils suivaient sans remords leur penchant amoureux;
       Tous les jours se levaient clairs et sereins pour eux.
       Et moi, triste rebut de la nature entière,
       Je me cachais au jour, je fuyais la lumière.
       [Did they hide deep in the forest? Alas! They could meet each other with
       complete license. The sky approved the innocence of their desires; they
       followed their love's whims without remorse; every day dawned clear

and calm for them, and I, a wretch rejected by all nature, I hid from the daylight and fled the light.]

The spectator or reader for whom Phaedra provokes the greatest emotion at this point is the one who feels how Phaedra must consider herself rejected by all nature, must hide from daylight, must flee the light, precisely because a nature and a light, imagined as free from any veil of repression, are repressed within her. Only the moment of death will allow her to feel *shut out* as absolutely as the violence of her jealousy had been able to do. It is this same sublime misunderstanding that in fact inspires Phaedra's dying words. The light of day, which death steals from her eyes and which was soiled by them, was and will remain, according to her, the light that all others deserve. Instead, the total purity that the closing of her eyes should restore to daylight, is precisely that which no eye will ever be able to see or even be able to dream of after her:

1643   Et la mort, à mes yeux dérobant la clarté,
        Rend au jour, qu'ils souillaient, toute sa pureté.
        [But death, by stealing the light from my eyes, will restore the total
        purity, which they soiled, to the daylight.]

                IV.

In the initial conflict between between darkness and light, bed and stage, Phaedra was, so to speak, hiding twice: she was concealing herself and her secret. At a certain point in her dialogue with Oenone (from l. 217), a second conflict definitively takes the place of the first: that between secret and confession, silence and speech. Definitively, because after this second conflict has been concluded with the declaration to Hippolytus, any illusion or pretense of returning to the terms of the earlier one by hiding herself would be a useless expedient for Phaedra, as it would for Oenone:

713   Venez, rentrez, fuyez une honte certaine.
       [Come, let us go inside to avoid certain disgrace.]

740   Cache-moi bien plutôt, je n'ai que trop parlé.
       [You must rather hide me, for I have said too much.]

920   Je ne dois désormais songer qu'à me cacher.
       [From now on I must think only of hiding.]

Phaedra's words to Oenone, which taken out of context could only sound like gratitude, express in this context the cruelest reproach:

1310   Au jour que je fuyais c'est toi qui m'as rendue.
        [You restored me to the daylight I shunned.]

V.

In the conflict between silence and speech, the first word that must yield to silence is the name of the beloved. Just as the mere sight of Hippolytus upsets Phaedra to the point of its being an involuntary violation of modesty, so his very name threatens unwittingly to violate her secret if it is uttered by her or by others:

206 Malheureuse, quel nom est sorti de ta bouche?
     [Wretch, what name have you uttered?]

261 J'aime...A ce nom fatal je tremble, je frissonne.
     [I love...I tremble and shudder at this fatal name.]

264 Hippolyte! Grands Dieux! — C'est toi qui l'as nommé.
     [Hippolytus! Ye Gods!—You have uttered his name.]

288 J'offrais tout à ce Dieu que je n'osais nommer.
     [I offered everything to this God whom I dared not name.]

603 J'ai même défendu, par une expresse loi,
     Qu'on osât prononcer votre nom devant moi.
     [By an express decree, I even forbade your name to be uttered in my presence.]

When Oenone incites, goads, and even blackmails, by threatening suicide, Phaedra's need to confess, it seems that it is to this need, more than to the latent existence of the secret, that Phaedra in resisting sacrifices her life. The confession is in itself horror and guilt, and the responsibility of the person predestined to evil seems greater in this act than in the actual evil to be avowed or kept silent:

225 Je t'en ai dit assez. Epargne-moi le reste.
     Je meurs, pour ne point faire un aveu si funeste.
     [I have told you enough. Spare me the rest. I am dying so as not to make such a grim confession.]

237 Quel fruit espères-tu de tant de violence?
     Tu frémiras d'horreur si je romps le silence.
     [What fruit do you expect to reap from this violence? You will shudder in horror if I break my silence.]

241 Quand tu sauras mon crime, et le sort qui m'accable,
     Je n'en mourrai pas moins, j'en mourrai plus coupable.
     [Even when you know my crime and the fate which oppresses me, I will still die, I shall die all the guiltier.]

The person who has caused a scandal is guiltier than one who dies in silence, because scandal immediately involves others in the inner criminal process, in the return of the repressed. The involvement of others in turn encourages the inner process, making it irreversible. Oenone is *another* with respect to Phaedra only to the extent that the confession made to her creates this first opening to the outside for the repressed. It is then but a short step to bring the scandal to the *other* in the fullest sense of the word, to the object of love. The criminal nature of speech appears evident after the declaration to Hippolytus:

741   Mes fureurs au dehors ont osé se répandre.
       J'ai dit ce que jamais on ne devait entendre.
       [My passions have dared reveal themselves. I have said that which no one
       should ever have heard.]

Irreversibility, however, has a first name which is hope. This means that the way outside for the repressed opened up by speech cannot be closed again, and hope is that which takes advantage of this to slip inside. To admit shame, or rather merely to stop concealing it, means for Phaedra abandoning herself to the gaze of others, which goes hand in hand with the occurence of a *malgré moi* within her, that is, with the assertion of an emotion that eludes the repressive consciousness. Naturally it is after the declaration to Hippolytus, the consummation of the conflict, that this final meaning of the entire conflict becomes apparent:

765   Il n'est plus temps. Il sait mes ardeurs insensées.
       De l'austère pudeur les bornes sont passées.
       J'ai déclaré ma honte aux yeux de mon vainqueur.
       Et l'espoir, malgré moi, s'est glissé dans mon cœur.
       [It is too late. He knows my mad desires. The bounds of austere modesty
       have been crossed. I have revealed my shame to my conqueror and hope,
       despite myself, has slipped into my heart.]

What the last two lines reveal, however, was prefigured in two lines addressed to Oenone even before the confession to her, and in which was established the same relationship between the disclosure of shame and the *malgré moi:*

183   Je te laisse trop voir mes honteuses douleurs,
       Et mes yeux, malgré moi, se remplissent de pleurs.
       [I have allowed you to see my shameful grief all too clearly, and my eyes,
       despite myself, are filled with tears.]

Until then the complete repression of her secret had, in fact, meant succumbing to the joy of weeping only when she was not observed. Though a silent, physical vent for the repressed, tears were still too much nearer words than silence for Phaedra to feel free to abandon herself to them, or to experience them without trembling, and not to be frequently forced to deprive herself of them:

1245   Me nourrissant de fiel, de larmes abreuvée,
       Encor dans mon malheur de trop près observée,
       Je n'osais dans mes pleurs me noyer à loisir;
       Je goûtais en tremblant ce funeste plaisir,
       Et sous un front serein déguisant mes alarmes,
       Il fallait bien souvent me priver de mes larmes.
       [Feeding on gall, drinking tears, my sorrow was still too closely watched
       and I did not dare give free rein to my tears; trembling I enjoyed this
       baleful pleasure, and hiding my woes behind a calm expression, I was
       often forced to deprive myself of my tears.]

The letter of lines 184 and 768, where the two *malgré moi* are in the same
central position in each line, surrounded, so to speak, by the repressed,
confirms that coming out of the dark and breaking one's silence are
essentially the same fault. Phaedra does not commit any other. The total
innocence, as far as deeds are concerned, of this sinner in thoughts and
words (and, with regard to the slander, in omissions), allowed Racine to
boast of the morality of his tragedy in the preface in the terms that we
observed: "La seule pensée du crime y est regardée avec autant d'horreur
que le crime même" [The very thought of crime is considered with as
much horror as the crime itself]. Phaedra says exactly the same thing at
one point, but, in her words, any boasting is given the lie by the cry of
regret from desire transformed into crime and shame, *even though* forever
thwarted:

1291   Hélas! du crime affreux dont la honte me suit
       Jamais mon triste cœur n'a recueilli le fruit.
       [Alas, my sad heart never reaped the fruits of the crime, whose shame
       haunts me.]

VI.

Hippolytus' reticence toward his pardonable secret is in contrast with the
conflict between silence and speech within Phaedra, as is the obedience
to or transgression of a social norm with the fear of that Law from which
all social norms are derived. Verbal similarities occur in the symmetry
between the two confessions and the two declarations in the first and
second acts. Hippolytus never directly gives in to his confidant, who
would make him confess his love for Aricia, but he allows him to draw
the inevitable conclusions:

136   Vous périssez d'un mal que vous dissimulez.
       [You are dying of a sickness which you conceal.]

Ten lines later Oenone practically repeats these lines, though substituting
two simple and powerful verbs for Theramenes' more elegant ones, and

adding the rending contrast between intimacy and silence: Phaedra hides her illness from her while dying "in her embrace:"

146   Elle meurt dans mes bras d'un mal qu'elle me cache.
       [She is dying in my embrace of an illness she keeps hidden from me.]

In Act 2, Aricia provides the occasion for Hippolytus' declaration when she praises his generosity, stating that it would have been presumable for him to have hated her:

516   N'était-ce pas assez de ne me point haïr?
       Et d'avoir si longtemps pu défendre votre âme
       De cette inimité . . . — Moi, vous haïr, Madame?
       [Was it not enough that you did not hate me and were able to keep your heart from such enmity . . . What, *I* hate you, Madam?]

For Phaedra, on the other hand, Hippolytus' hatred is so foreseeable that there is nothing to do but to excuse and accept it, whereas it is not acceptable that he himself, incapable of seeing into her heart, should take for granted the idea of being hated by her:

596   Quand vous me haïrez, je ne m'en plaindrais pas,
       Seigneur. Vous m'avez vue attachée à vous nuire;
       Dans le fonds de mon cœur vous ne pouvez pas lire.
       A votre inimité j'ai pris soin de m'offrir.
       [I would not complain if you were to hate me, my Lord. You have seen me strive to harm you; you could not read what lay at the bottom of my heart. I took pains to expose myself to your enmity.]

In both declarations the transgression is effected verbally at a certain point, because a limit has been crossed beyond which it is no longer possible to assume that the other has not understood. In spite of the five lines of lively verbal abandon in which this happens to Hippolytus (ll. 519-23), his moving on to the declaration remains an explicit and voluntary choice:

524   Je me suis engagé trop avant.
       Je vois que la raison cède à la violence.
       Puisque j'ai commencé de rompre le silence,
       Madame, il faut poursuivre: il faut vous informer
       D'un secret que mon cœur ne peut plus renfermer.
       [I have gone too far. I see that reason is yielding to violence. Since I have begun to break my silence, my Lady, I must go on: I must tell you a secret that my heart can no longer contain.]

On the other hand, after a verbal abandon which is incomparably longer, more tortuous, and languid, Phaedra's moving on to the declaration is much briefer, violent, and forced; but the words closely recall each other so that the two situations may be better opposed:

670   Ah! cruel, tu m'as trop entendue.
        Je t'en ai dit assez pour te tirer d'erreur.
        Hé bien! connais donc Phèdre et toute sa fureur.
        [Ah, cruel one! You have heard too much. I have told you enough to
        clear up all your doubts. Know Phaedra, then, and all her madness.]

Even during the course of the declarations the words again come close
together:

547   Moi-même, pour tout fruit de mes soins superflus...
        [Myself, as the only fruit of my useless suffering...]

687   De quoi m'ont profité mes inutiles soins?
        [What did I gain from my useless suffering?]

The third revelation of the secret transgression, following those to the
confidant and the beloved, is the only one left for both Hippolytus and
Phaedra:

1119   Non, mon père, ce cœur (c'est trop vous le celer)
        [No, father, this heart (for it would be too much to conceal)]

1617   Non, Thésée, il faut rompre un injuste silence...
        [No, Theseus, I must break this unjust silence...]

This is the revelation to Theseus as father or husband and, in any case, as
king and judge. Given the authority and power of the person hearing it,
it has a kind of public value in which the secret is finally used up. By
Hippolytus this revelation could be attempted with such relative impunity
(if only the attempt had not come too late) as to serve as an alibi for the
unpardonable act that has calumniously been attributed to him. Phaedra,
on the contrary, can only carry it out at the moment when she has made
sure that she will not survive physically. The slow struggle of her
preceding revelations is followed by the haste of one disposing of the few
moments of her final agony:

1622   Les moments me sont chers, écoutez-moi, Thésée.
        [Listen to me, Theseus, my moments are precious.]

        VII.

Thus, the correspondence I postulated between the second symbolic
negation and the fifth, between the scandal related to speech and the
myth of the Labyrinth, finds a first basis in the very irreversibility of
speech. The *trop* in the verbal transgression (*Je me suis engagé trop avant*,
l. 524; *tu m'as trop entendue*, l. 670; *je n'ai que trop parlé*, l. 740) is equivalent
to a more or less blind step forward along a path on which one remains a
prisoner because it allows no turning back. It would not be unapt to

recall that in a classical text as famous as the *Aeneid,* the Labyrinth was defined as *inremeabilis error* (V, 591): a wandering that cannot be repeated in the opposite direction. It may be said that as they unfold both the scene containing Phaedra's confession and that containing her declaration (Act 1, scene 3 and Act 2, scene 5) follow a labyrinthic verbal pattern, though in different ways and to different extents. This occurs, leaving aside the references to the Labyrinth, to the extent that any approach in words to the secret can never be annulled—it is irreversible—though one may attempt to correct it afterwards by moving away, hence the turning, the winding, the meandering that traces the path of speech. In the scene of confession this winding course is characterized by a fragmentary revelation: in Oenone's presence, Phaedra at first seems to be monologizing or thinking of unconnected things aloud (ll. 158ff.). The only other signs of her secret that she gives away are those that each time should help preserve it, in the course of a discussion led not by her but by Oenone (ll. 185ff.). For obvious reasons the scene of the declaration to Hippolytus is the one in which the identity of the spoken word with the guilty act is closest to reality. The secret of Phaedra, no longer on the defensive but on the offensive, tends to emerge with no other invitation than the internal compulsion to attempt the seduction of the other. Overcome at the same time from opposite directions by this compulsion and by the responsibility of secrecy, her words become ambiguous, as well as timid and tortuous.

VIII.

The sentences conceal an unpardonable sense, behind an acceptable though enigmatic one:

605   Si pourtant à l'offense on mesure la peine,
       Si la haine peut seule attirer votre haine,
       Jamais femme ne fut plus digne de pitié,
       Et moins digne, Seigneur, de votre inimité.
       [If the punishment fits the crime, if only hatred can arouse your hatred, then there was never a woman who deserved pity more and your enmity less, my Lord.]

615   Ah! Seigneur, que le Ciel, j'ose ici l'attester,
       De cette loi commune a voulu m'excepter!
       Qu'un soin bien différent me trouble et me dévore!
       [Ah, my Lord, I dare attest that Heaven wished to exempt me from this universal law! For a much different care agitates and gnaws at me!]

The ambiguity of words open to two different meanings, which nevertheless direct the hearer toward the false one, offers Phaedra its morally unfruitful resources even at the moment in which she agrees to the slander by preparing it (ll. 914-20). Oenone, too, will avail herself of a somewhat similar ambiguity in carrying it out:

1029   Seigneur, souvenez-vous des plaintes de la Reine.
Un amour criminel causa toute sa haine.
[My Lord, remember the Queen's complaints. A criminal passion was the cause of her hatred.]

The ambiguity of Phaedra's words in the declaration scene, however, does not follow any haphazard meanderings, but rather those that have been laid out by the very definition of the unavowable that it is aimed at concealing—incest. For her, Hippolytus is an object of forbidden love because he is her husband's son. Phaedra, speaks to him, ambiguously, first only about her own son, then about her husband. She justifies the meeting in the name of her son; and begging for her ɔ n the pity for which she herself yearns, warding off from her son the hatred which she fears for herself, she borrows from her remarks about her son the victimized and grieving maternal affection that she seems to have taken away from him to direct at Hippolytus (ll. 586-94). Subsequently the ambiguity takes advantage of the physical resemblance between her husband and Hippolytus; this enables Phaedra to withhold her secret behind the ever more precarious likelihood of a verbal turning point, at the very moment in which she is forced to admit that she has gone astray:

627   Que dis-je? Il n'est point mort, puisqu'il respire en vous.
Toujours devant mes yeux je crois voir mon époux.
Je le vois, je lui parle, et mon cœur. . . je m'égare,
Seigneur; ma folle ardeur malgré moi se déclare.
[What am I saying? He is not dead since he lives in you. I believe that I am still seeing my husband. I see him, I speak to him and my heart. . . I am going astray, my Lord; my frenzied passion reveals itself despite myself.]

The line in which her husband's name justifies Phaedra's beginning to speak of love also contains a dual literal truth, owing to that physical resemblance:

634   Oui, Prince, je languis, je brûle pour Thésée.
[Yes, Prince, I languish, I burn for Theseus.]

With this line, however, the ever more intricate labyrinth that the words are beginning to create takes us into the theme of the Labyrinth.

IX.

Phaedra's words have pretended to move away from the declaration of her wild passion for Hippolytus, claiming that it is for Theseus. But she immediately reapproaches it by rejecting Theseus' present image as both dissolute and mortuary, and even more by treasuring an image that is Hippolytus' present one, modeled by faithful desire:

635   Je l'aime, non point tel que l'ont vu les enfers,
       Volage adorateur de mille objets divers,
       Qui va du Dieu des morts déshonorer la couche;
       Mais fidèle, mais fier, et même un peu farouche,
       Charmant, jeune, traînant tous les cœurs après soi,
       Tel qu'on dépeint nos Dieux, *ou* tel que je vous voi.
       [I love him, not as the Underworld saw him, a fickle worshipper of a thousand different objects, who goes to dishonor the bed of the God of the dead; but faithful, proud, and even a little shy; charming, young, attracting all hearts, just as the Gods are depicted, *or* as you are now.]

In this final line the declaration is virtually complete. Among words laden with such a degree of ambiguity, the conjuction *ou*, which mediates a relationship of substitution, is particularly compromising. It is no accident that this reappears in the last line of the speech with the same underhand and swift revelatory function. The law governing labyrinthic speech, however, requires that this point of maximum approximation to the secret be followed by a deviation moving away from it. Phaedra brings this about by projecting the image into the past and quickly causing it to become that of Theseus once again. Hippolytus' identity, saved by the very identification by resemblance that pretends to deny it, is thus brought into the Cretan myth, the imperfect tense:

641   Il *avait* votre port, vos yeux, votre langage,
       Cette noble pudeur colorait son visage,
       Lorsque de notre Crète il traversa les flots,
       Digne sujet des voeux des filles de Minos.
       [He had your bearing, your eyes, your voice, a noble modesty covered his face when he crossed the waves to my land of Crete, a worthy object for the vows of Minos' daughters.]

The approach to the secret, which here begins again, much more slowly and relentlessly as it no longer marks any clear turning points but rather lingers in sweeping curves, will merely undermine that swift return into the past. The myth, in whose remoteness Hippolytus' image should have sacrificed its present reality to that of Theseus, will be reelaborated or regretted in the conditional tense, thereby becoming a present reality that is fantastically accessible to desire:

645   Que faisiez-vous alors? Pourquoi sans Hippolyte
       Des héros de la Grèce assembla-t-il l'élite?
       Pourquoi, trop jeune encor, ne pûtes-vous alors
       Entrer dans le vaisseau qui le mit sur nos bords?
       Par vous aurait péri le monstre de la Crète,

Malgré tous les détours de sa vaste retraite.
Pour en développer l'embarras incertain,
Ma sœur du fil fatal eût armé votre main.
[What were you doing then? Why did he gather together the best heroes
of Greece without Hippolytus? Why could you, still too young, not have
embarked on the vessel that brought him to our shores? The monster of
Crete would have been killed by you, despite the windings of its vast lair.
My sister would have armed you with the fatal thread to lead you through
its confusing maze.]

The undermining of the myth does not consist only in this actualization
that modifies it at will but also in the very meaning of this modification.
The victory over the monster, reached in the depths of his vast hiding
place despite all its meanderings, is evoked at the moment in which
Phaedra's perverse desire unswervingly comes out of its hiding place of
secrecy despite all the meanderings traced by her words. A line in Seneca's
Phaedra (l. 122) says this about the Labyrinth, or rather about its architect,
Daedalus: *qui nostra caeca monstra conclusit domo,* he has enclosed the
monsters of our family in a gloomy dwelling. The mythical Labyrinth
was a prison that concealed a monster, and the aggressor had to proceed
through it toward its interior, where the repressed to be struck down was
hidden. The labyrinth of Phaedra's words is a prison which delays but
does not prevent the monstrous secret from escaping; and it must be
traversed moving toward the exterior, toward a point which the repressed
aspires to reach in order to cease being a repressed. The myth of beneficient
repression, of civilizing violence, is subverted into a myth of the verbal
liberation of Desire, which Law has silenced, the once passionless myth
of glory into a moving myth of shame. Never, perhaps, as in these lines
of Racine, has the poetic word complicated itself with richer and more
contradictory meanings in order to embrace and overturn the terms of a
more profound conflict. By substituting herself for Ariadne, after having
substituted Hippolytus for Theseus, Phaedra finishes by replacing with a
kind of erotic initiation the combative task for which the hero entered
the Labyrinth. It is this dream of showing him through its meanderings
which renders uncontainable her sigh of physical admiration:

653   Mais non, dans ce dessein je l'aurais devancée:
       L'amour m'en eût d'abord inspiré la pensée.
       C'est moi, Prince, c'est moi dont l'utile secours
       Vous eût du Labyrinthe enseigné les détours.
       Que de soins m'eût coûtés cette tête charmante!
       [No, for in this plan I would have forestalled her: love would have
       inspired me first with the idea. It is I, Prince, it is I whose useful aid
       would have revealed the windings of the Labyrinth to you. What attention
       would I not have paid to that beautiful head!]

While the secret thus escapes from the last windings of the verbal labyrinth, the centripetal direction of the path through the mythical Labyrinth moves into the depths, from which the monster may be said to have disappeared. The danger in which Phaedra would like to have shared seems to be feared so little, that the function of the thread is abolished in the reworking of the myth which desire permits itself. Her physical presence, which replaces the thread, does not guarantee that they will find their way out, indeed it discloses—by a bold new substitutive, *ou*, which acts as the extreme revelation—that it might be better if they were to lose their way:

658   Un fil n'eût point assez rassuré votre amante.
      Compagne du péril qu'il vous fallait chercher,
      Moi-même devant vous j'aurais voulu marcher;
      Et Phèdre au Labyrinthe avec vous descendue
      Se serait avec vous retrouvée, *ou* perdue.
      [A thread would not have been enough to reassure your lover. Accompanying you in the danger you had to seek, I would have wished to lead the way myself; Phaedra would have gone down into the Labyrinth with you and returned or have perished alongside you.]

X.

Not only because of the distance separating the two parts of the text, but also because of the incalculable difference between the two contexts, few readers would notice that Aricia, like Phaedra, fantasizes about disappearing from the world with Hippolytus. This is by comparison very brief and needs no verbal labyrinths, since the conditional tense in which it is formulated is that of moral scruple. Aricia has had from the exiled Hippolytus a proposal of flight together, but not yet one of marriage:

1376   Hélas! qu'un tel exil, Seigneur, me serait cher!
      Dans quels ravissements, à votre sort liée,
      Du reste des mortels je vivrais oubliée!
      Mais n'étant point unis par un lien si doux,
      Me puis-je avec honneur dérober avec vous?
      [Alas, my Lord, how pleasant would such an exile be! With what delight would I live, linking my fate with yours, forgotten by other mortals! But since we are not joined by such a sweet knot, can I honorably flee with you?]

XI.

At the climax of the confession scene, neither is the theme of the Labyrinth made so explicit nor the verbal labyrinth made so long as at the climax of the scene of declaration. Yet everything that takes place on this second occasion confirms that the same was taking place, though much more fleetingly, on the first. The fact that these two passages turn out to have been derived from two different sources, Euripides (*Hippolytus*, ll. 336-41) and Seneca (*Phaedra*, ll. 646-62) respectively, merely shows toward what degree of literal coherence Racine's marvelous combinatorial skill worked. The labyrinthic course of the confession scene ought to stop at the point at which Phaedra gives in. Oenone is ready to listen to what Phaedra should now be ready to say:

246   Tu le veux. Lève-toi.—Parlez: je vous écoute.
     [It is your wish. Rise.—Speak: I am listening.]

Instead Phaedra hesitates like one who has arrived at the threshold of the most terrible labyrinth, made hopelessly intricate by shame:

247   Ciel! que lui vais-je dire? Et *par où* commencer?
     [Heavens, what shall I tell her? Where shall I begin?]

Her words that follow, estranged from Oenone's and from the spectator's expectations by a semblance of digression, conceal their lasting pertinence beneath their temporary delaying function. The double labyrinth, mythical and verbal, is here condensed into a single verse:

249   O haine de Vénus! O fatale colère!
     Dans quels égarements l'amour jeta ma mère!
     [Oh hatred of Venus! Oh fatal rage! Into what madness did love cast my mother!]

The veiled allusion was intended to spare the audience of this tragedy written in the noble style the most scabrous part of the myth's entire scandal: Pasiphaë's affair with the bull. Elsewhere in the text the Minotaur is mentioned twice (ll. 82 and 649); but in the whole of Racine's text there is nothing that could reveal to anyone who did not know it either the union that produced the monster or that its mother was also Phaedra's. The nurse's clear reply in Euripides ("O hapless mother! what strange love was yours!—Love for the bull, my child? or what would you say?"), is not surprisingly replaced in Racine by Oenone's appeal to forget this, in answer to Phaedra's allusion. Seneca's characters even crudely stress the monstrous relationship. Because of the incest, his Phaedra compares herself (ll. 115-28), and is compared by the nurse (ll. 142-44, 169-77) and by Hippolytus (ll. 688-93), to her mother made pregnant by the bull. In this source, concealed by almost complete silence in the preface to *Phèdre*, Racine could have read such elaborations of the theme as the following:

690   tacitum diu
    crimen biformi partus exhibuit nota
    scelusque matris arguit vultu truci
    ambiguus infans: ille te venter tulit.

[The crime that had long been silent was made known by a birth of a biform nature, and a hybrid child revealed his mother's guilt in his fierce face: this is the womb that bore you.]

Racine's language has no access to this dimension of horrifying sensuality, where, moreover, desire repudiates itself in disgust. Racine's language becomes veiled in the face of the committed crime in order to become all the more transparent with respect to uncontaminated, frightened, and infinite desire: one word suffices to imply all of this: *égarements*. Aberrations of the perverse desire, of course, but how many other aberrations could not be quietly assimilated by the indefinite term chosen to summarize them: those of reason, those of speech itself, and the windings of the Labyrinth. Both the monster and his tortuous prison are implied in it, and implied in both senses, as will be made clear in the second act. The mythical meaning is implied because both the Minotaur and the Labyrinth spring from Pasiphaë's *égarements*, the verbal meaning because Phaedra wanders, strays, and delays by speaking about them. On the verbal thread of the digression will follow immediately Ariadne's name (l. 253), which is of necessity associated with the mythical thread and the Labyrinth. I should note in passing that in *Phèdre* there would be one random mythical recollection if the myth of Daedalus' son, recalled by Theramenes at the beginning of the tragedy, were not also part of the Cretan myths. The flight, which was paid for with his life, was undertaken in order to escape from the Labyrinth:

13   J'ai visité l'Elide, et laissant le Ténare,
       Passé jusqu'à la mer qui vit tomber Icare.
       [I visited Elis and, leaving Tenaros behind me, passed into the sea that
       saw Icarus fall.]

       XII.

Myth, image, verbal structure, symbol of secrecy, of repression, and of the irreversibility of the paths of the repressed, the Labyrinth is so central to the work that at times, if I am not mistaken, it is almost imperceptibly emerges in profile in some of these meanings. In the declaration scene, when Phaedra speaks of her son, Hippolytus replies with elusive generalities (ll. 595, 609-14); when Phaedra speaks of her husband, he answers by assuming that he is not dead, or still present even if dead (ll. 618-22, 631-33, 663-64). In both cases he picks on the most innocent meaning of the ambiguous letter of her words and obliges her to prolong the ambiguity and meandering. Thus, in the following act, Phaedra both rightly and wrongly attributes to him and projects onto him her own verbal wanderings:

743   Ciel! comme il m'écoutait! Par combien de détours
        L'insensible a longtemps éludé mes discours!
        [Heavens, how he listened to me! How long did he, caring nothing,
        change the subject to avoid my words!]

In the final act another speech, of Aricia to Theseus, seems like a labyrinth in that it constantly begins and interrupts itself and because it conceals something that Theseus does not understand but which we know to be the monstrous secret itself:

1451   Quelle est donc sa pensée? et que cache un discours
        Commencé tant de fois, interrompu toujours?
        [What is she thinking? What is concealed behind this speech, so often
        begun and always interrupted?]

Then, during Phaedra's final internal struggle before coming on stage to reveal the secret to Theseus and to die, it is the written word that starts up and interrupts itself. A final glimpse of the labyrinth as a force resisting the secret may be perceived in the disordered course of the steps marked by the haggard Phaedra:

1475   Elle porte au hasard ses pas irrésolus;
        Son œil tout égaré ne nous reconnaît plus.
        Elle a trois fois écrit; et changeant de pensée,
        Trois fois elle a rompu sa lettre commencée.
        [She wanders about aimlessly, irresolutely; her wild eyes no longer
        recognize us. She has begun to write three times; and, changing her
        mind, has three times torn up the letter.]

Finally the sea monster, announced by a tremendous noise (ll. 1507-10) that breaks the general silence (ll. 1499-1500), is nothing less than the catastrophic effect of the labyrinthic word and the monstrous silence; thus it is both Minotaur and Labyrinth. Half bull (in Seneca its equivalence to the Minotaur is underlined by Phaedra, ll. 1170-73), it reproduces the Labyrinth in the other half of its body:

1519   Indomptable taureau, dragon impétueux,
        Sa croupe se recourbe en replis tortueux.
        [Both wild bull and impetuous dragon, its tail curved up into winding
        folds.]

XIII.

The irreversibility of speech in *Phèdre* brings to the fore another irreversibility that precedes and transcends it, being endowed with a hidden theological sense: the irreversibility of the tendency toward evil through one's ancestry. For Racine the Jansenist, this descent, persecuted by the

Gods, can only symbolize the human race, condemned in the eyes of God and whose Pasiphaë is its common mother, Eve. In the character of Phaedra, however, the poet has rendered the inclination toward guilt indistinguishable from the awareness of its fatality. Her own fate follows on from her mother's and her sister's with the rigor (as Spitzer has remarked) of a tragic syllogism:

257   Puisque Vénus le veut, de ce sang déplorable
        Je péris la dernière, et la plus misérable.
        [Since Venus wishes it, I die as the last, the most wretched of this ill-starred line.]

And the most genuine feeling that Phaedra shows for her children is the dread of bequeathing them in turn that heritage of guilt and shame, which will weigh heavily even on a race of divine origin (since man was created in God's image):

861   Pour mes tristes enfants quel affreux héritage!
        Le sang de Jupiter doit enfler leur courage;
        Mais quelque juste orgueil qu'inspire un sang si beau,
        Le crime d'une mère est un pesant fardeau.
        Je tremble qu'un discours, hélas! trop véritable,
        Un jour ne leur reproche une mère coupable.
        Je tremble qu'opprimés de ce poids odieux
        L'un ni l'autre jamais n'ose lever les yeux.
        [What a frightful heritage for my wretched children! Jupiter's blood should swell their hearts; but whatever pride such beautiful blood might inspire, a mother's crime is a heavy burden to bear. I tremble that, alas, too real a report might one day reproach them their mother's guilt. I tremble that, oppressed by this hideous burden, neither will ever dare look up.]

XIV.

Faced with this guilty conscience, Hippolytus' good conscience, which inflexibly defends itself with accusations, is not hypocritical. Although ready to confess his own pardonable transgression after having vindicated his past chastity, Hippolytus will pay the greatest price for the silence he believed himself required by dignity to keep about the truly unpardonable transgression—about this return of the repressed, whose deep appeal to the audience's sympathy nevertheless risks making him unsympathetic. His first attempt at making the accusation rebound without his having to reveal the truth, is to maintain five times in succession, in the abstract form of judgments, the irreversibility of the tendency toward evil:

1093   Quelques crimes toujours précèdent les grands crimes.
        Quiconque a pu franchir les bornes légitimes
        Peut violer enfin les droits les plus sacrés;
        Ainsi que la vertu, le crime a ses degrés;
        Et jamais on n'a vu la timide innocence
        Passer subitement à l'extrême licence.
        Un jour seul ne fait point d'un mortel vertueux
        Un perfide assassin, un lâche incestueux.
        [Small crimes always precede great crimes. Whoever has passed beyond
        the bounds of the law may eventually violate the most sacred rules; like
        virtue, crime has its degrees, and timid innocence has never been known
        to move immediately to extreme licence. One day is not enough to turn a
        virtuous man into a treacherous murderer or an incestuous coward.]

Moreover, once the moral implications of one's ancestry and race have been admitted (in virtue of the underlying dogma of predestination), there is no reason why maternal chastity too should not be hereditary:

1101   Elevé dans le sein d'une chaste héroïne,
        Je n'ai point de son sang démenti l'origine.
        [Reared on the breast of a chaste heroine, I have not betrayed her race.]

It is mother against mother. Faced with Theseus' unyielding blindness which continues to mention the unpardonable, Hippolytus feels it is right for him at least to say where this is more likely, likely from the evidence, to have occurred:

1149   Vous me parlez toujours d'inceste et d'adultère!
        Je me tais. Cependant Phèdre sort d'une mère,
        Phèdre est d'un sang, Seigneur, vous le savez trop bien,
        De toutes ces horreurs plus rempli que le mien.
        [You keep talking about incest and adultery. I will say no more. Yet
        Phaedra is of a mother, she is of a race, as you well know, my Lord, that is
        filled with these horrors much more than mine.]

Bound by Hippolytus to the same silence, Aricia, in order to overcome it without breaking it, can proceed no further than he in that same merciless allusion. Nevertheless her allusion is the only other occasion after Phaedra has pleaded for Hippolytus' death in which are brought together the two meanings of the word *monstre:* one refers to concrete mythical beings on the level of poetic fiction but to nothing plausible on the level of reality, and the other is a figurative use with regard to the characters of poetic fiction, but refers to plausible moral turpitude in reality. The spark that issues from this verbal short circuit is the monosyllable, violently separated by the famous enjambment with which Aricia is forced to break off her sentence:

1443   Prenez garde, Seigneur. Vos invincibles mains
Ont de monstres sans nombre affranchi les humains;
Mais tout n'est pas détruit, et vous en laissez vivre
Un...Votre fils, Seigneur me défend de poursuivre
[Beware, my Lord. Your invincible hands have freed mankind from
countless monsters; but all are not destroyed, and you still let live one...
Your son, my Lord, forbids me to go on.]

       XV.

There is only one other term in the text of *Phèdre* that possesses a
frequency and variety of meanings or references as significant as that of
the noun *monstre:* the verb *cacher* or *se cacher,* and its numerous synonyms.
This is no surprise. Although the union of the two words, which would
give *monstre qui se cache* or *monstre caché,* never occurs in the letter of the
text, we know that it would sum up perfectly the central theme of moral
and mythical shame. In the course of our analysis, we have already
encountered the term *cacher* referring to the memory of Pasiphaë's love
affair (l. 252) and to Phaedra's passion (ll. 146, 299, 1451). I may also add
the lines 305, 846 and 1345-46 to this second reference, as well as the
synonyms *dérober, ensevelir, étouffer, déguiser,* all of which are verbs of
repression:

310   'Et dérober au jour une flamme si noire...
       [And hide this dark passion from the light of day...]

720   Cet horrible secret demeure enseveli.
       [This horrible secret must be buried.]

825   Il faut d'un vain amour étouffer la pensée...
       [You must stifle all thoughts of a vain love...]

1194   Quel feu mal étouffé dans mon cœur se réveille?
       [What smouldering passion awakes in my heart?]

1249   Et sous un front serein déguisant mes alarmes...
       [And concealing my woes behind a calm expression...]

We have already come upon the other synonyms, *dissimuler, renfermer,
celer* (ll. 136, 528, 1119) used in referring to Hippolytus' love, either by
himself or his confidant, while Phaedra alone refers once to Hippolytus'
and Aricia's affair with the stronger *se cacher* (l. 1236). Otherwise we have
encountered the verb in this reflexive form only in referring to Phaedra
herself (ll. 167, 740, 920, 1242). I then observed that from a certain point,
no longer being able to hide her feelings, Phaedra would no longer be
able to hide herself. When it comes to expressing this impossibility, as a
consequence of the irreversibility of speech and guilt, she conjugates the
verb *se cacher* desperately one last time.

XVI.

To Phaedra the sun seems to shine over the contradiction between Law and Desire, and therefore it can lavish its light only on the guiltless love of which she is jealous; thus she must now shun the sunlight, less because she fears the Law than because she is torn by Desire that has turned into jealousy and vindictive rage. In a similar torture, Law and Desire, remorse and regret again become identical, rather than inseparable; and their identity, like the light of the sacred sun, cannot be endured while one remains alive. Whether her divine ancestors, who suddenly seem to fill the heavens and the universe, symbolize moral authority or vital forces remains unexplained, but, in any case, their omnipresent and omniscient familiarity renders the whole of illuminated space uninhabitable for Phaedra. She then attempts to hide by escaping into death as if into a remote dark space:

1273 Misérable! et je vis? et je soutiens la vue
   De ce sacré Soleil dont je suis descendue?
   J'ai pour aïeul le père et le maître des Dieux;
   Le ciel, tout l'univers est plein de mes aïeux.
   Où me cacher? Fuyons dans la nuit infernale.
   [Wretch! and I go on living and endure the sight of the sacred Sun from whom I am descended? My ancestor is the father and lord of all the Gods. The sky, the universe are filled with my forebears. Where can I hide? Let us flee into infernal night.]

But if all this crescendo is derived from the horror of having sought to appeal for help in her adulterous jealousy to the very authority of her king and husband (ll. 1259-65), Phaedra will meet as judge in the infernal night a king who will not be resurrected like Theseus and who cannot be deceived like him:

1278 Mais que dis-je? Mon père y tient l'urne fatale;
   Le Sort, dit-on, l'a mise en ses sévères mains:
   Minos juge aux enfers tous les pâles humains.
   [What am I saying? My father holds the fatal urn there; it is said that Destiny placed it in his ruthless hands: Minos judges all the shades of men in the Underworld.]

Minos was alive and still ruling in Seneca (*Phaedra*, ll. 149-52) and in Ovid (*Heroides* IV, l. 157). In selecting the myth that would have him as a dead Father, immortal dispenser of Law in the depths of Phaedra's consciousness and that of all men grown pale from feelings of guilt, Racine's poetic genius grasped another of those truths to be revealed one day by psychoanalysis. According to the Freudian myth in *Totem and*

Taboo, in which the slaying of a primeval father is at the basis of the incest prohibition and thus at the basis of law and civilization, "The dead father became stronger than the living one had been—for events took the course we so often see them follow in human affairs to this day."[1]

1281   Ah! combien frémira son ombre épouvantée,
Lorsqu'il verra sa fille à ses yeux présentée,
Contrainte d'avouer tant de forfaits divers,
Et des crimes peut-être inconnus aux enfers!
Que diras-tu, mon père, à ce spectacle horrible?
Je crois voir de ta main tomber l'urne terrible,
Je crois te voir, cherchant un supplice nouveau,
Toi-même de ton sang devenir le bourreau.
[How his horrified shade will tremble on seeing his daughter appear before him, forced to confess so many sins and crimes that are perhaps unknown to the Underworld! What will you say father, at this terrible sight? I believe I can see the fateful urn drop from your hands; I believe I can see you searching for some new punishment and becoming the executioner of your own flesh and blood.]

So many different sins; crimes which are perhaps even unknown in hell. The shudder of the horrified paternal shade, from whose hands the urn falls, is motivated precisely by the unrestrained and perverse variety of the forms of Desire, and Minos' search for a new punishment must make the Law's subtlety in torture conform relentlessly to this great variety. The dead judge sees his daughter appear before him, hears her confession, and becomes the executioner of his own race. The night, in which hiding is even more difficult than in the light of day, is where a judge is hidden for everyone at a level deeper than the very judgment of one's own consciousness.

1. Sigmund Freud, *Totem and Taboo, Standard Edition,* 13: 143.

8
Symbolic Negations of the Institutional Order (Third and Sixth)

I.

If we ignore some of the uses of the verb *cacher* which are not pertinent to the themes from which my entire interpretation stems (ll. 317, 796, 1361, 1408), in those still to be considered it refers only to the character of Theseus, to his mysterious absence (l. 7), to his eventual new love affairs (l. 20), his presumed death (l. 468) and to his wish to hide and the difficulty in hiding himself after the catastrophe (l. 1611). It is Theseus who substantially shares with Phaedra the implications of this verb that is so important in the text. The potential *pendant* of the *monstre caché* might be said to be a *père caché*. The one most concerned about his being unfindable is in fact his son.

II.

The anxiety that drives Hippolytus to search for his father at the beginning of the tragedy is, however, motivated in a strangely indecisive, and in effect threefold, manner. This has been going on for more than six months:

3   Dans le doute mortel dont je suis agité,
       Je commence à rougir de mon oisiveté.
       Depuis plus de six mois éloigné de mon père,
       J'ignore le destin d'une tête si chère;
       J'ignore jusqu'aux lieux qui le peuvent cacher.
       [I am troubled by uncertainty about the king and begin to be ashamed of my idleness. I have been separated from my father for over six months and ignore the fate of his precious head, I do not even know where he might be hidden.]

The letter of the text informs us some time later, with a barely noticeable precision, that this period coincides approximately with that of Hippolytus' being in love, a transgression of his father's orders:

539   *Depuis près de six mois,* honteux, désespéré . . .
        [Ashamed and in despair for over six months . . .]

Once Theseus has returned, in fact, the duration of his imprisonment is
again measured so as to correspond to that of the love which Hippolytus
is admitting:

967   Les Dieux, *après six mois,* enfin m'ont regardé . . .
        [After six months, the Gods finally looked down on me . . .]

1129   Seigneur, *depuis six mois* je l'évite, et je l'aime.
        [My Lord, for six months I have avoided and loved her.]

Moreover, in the first scene, Hippolytus has at least one motive for
leaving Troezen other than the search for his father:

27   Enfin en le cherchant je suivrai mon devoir,
        Et je fuirai ces lieux que je n'ose plus voir.
        [Finally, by searching for him, I will be doing my duty and fleeing this
        place that I no longer dare see.]

By the end of the dialogue with Theramenes it has been stated several
times that the other motive is indeed his love for Aricia, or rather the
fear of disobeying his father, which this implies:

50   Je fuis, je l'avoûrai, cette jeune Aricie,
        Reste d'un sang fatal conjuré contre nous.
        [I confess, I am fleeing from that youthful Aricia, last of a fatal line that
        plotted against us.]

56   Si je la haïssais, je ne la fuirais pas.
        [If I hated her, I would not flee her.]

137   La charmante Aricie a-t-elle su vous plaire?
        — Théramène, je pars, et je vais chercher mon père.
        [Has fair Aricia been able to charm you? — Theramenes, I am leaving to
        search for my father.]

But this motivation is not immediate. Hippolytus' first reply to his
confidant's shock that Troezen has become uninhabitable for him had
been substantially different, and had the ring of more veiled and passing
sincerity, the sincerity of one who foresees more than he realizes:

34   Cet heureux temps n'est plus. Tout a changé de face
        Depuis que sur ces bords les Dieux ont envoye
        La fille de Minos et de Pasiphaé.
        [Those happy days are no more. Everything has changed since the Gods
        sent the daughter of Minos and Pasiphaë to these shores.]

One would be deaf to the resonance of these words, if, in this verbal
peripetia, in the contradiction that it inadequately conceals, one were to

hear only a device of the poet for imparting all the information of the tragic exposition in a fixed order. Neither can one believe Hippolytus when he tries to eliminate the already avowed connection between his departure and Phaedra's presence:

48   Sa vaine inimitié n'est pas ce que je crains.
      Hippolyte en partant fuit une autre ennemie . . .
      [It is not her vain hostility that I fear. Hippolytus is leaving to escape
      another enemy . . .]

At a deeper level, these three motivations—doubt about his father's death, fear of Phaedra, love for Aricia—are linked so as to resolve all contradictions. His father's disappearance is certainly a necessary condition for the pardonable transgression of which Hippolytus has become the subject, as the chronology confirms. But it is also a favorable condition for the unpardonable transgression, for the true return of the repressed, by which Hippolytus, as its object, feels threatened. The oscillation of his words, in the first scene, between the two women as opposing motives for his leaving to verify his father's disappearance, shows that the pardonable transgression is an alternative to the other, a means of escaping the other. It also shows that both of these assert themselves on the basis of only one *passing,* if this term may be used to describe a death and a succession, each of them feared rather than hoped for by Hippolytus.

III.

The father himself, on leaving, had entrusted to his son the custody of both women. His blindness to Phaedra's unpardonable passion a priori made Aricia the only pardonable alternative for Hippolytus. An unexpected sincerity, slightly inappropriate considering the question, again characterizes his answer to his father regarding his flight from Troezen while Phaedra was living there, and he adds a reference to his responsibility, which is in effect a reproach:

925   Souffrez que pour jamais le tremblant Hippolyte
       Disparaisse des lieux que votre épouse habite.
       —Vous, mon fils, me quitter? —*Je ne la cherchais pas:*
       C'est vous qui sur ces bords conduisîtes ses pas.
       Vous daignâtes, Seigneur, aux rives de Trézène
       Confier en partant Aricie et la Reine:
       Je fus même chargé du soin de les garder.
       [Suffer that a trembling Hippolytus forever leave this place where your
       wife lives. — You, leave me, my son? — I did not seek her. It was you who
       led her to this land. You, my Lord, deigned to commend Aricia and the
       Queen to the shores of Troezen when you left: they were even committed
       to my care.]

By giving the reason a posteriori for his extreme repugnance to meeting with Phaedra (ll. 139-41, 151-52, 565, 580), the shame and horror which Hippolytus cannot help feeling within himself and about himself after her declaration are transformed into an urge to flee, to leave the scene. These are the objective symptoms (and this is not a conjecture about the character's psychology) of his strenuous defense against the appeal with which the return of the repressed disturbs him:

669   Ma honte ne peut plus soutenir votre vue;
        Et je vais...
        [My shame can no longer bear to see you; I am leaving...]

717   Théramène, fuyons. Ma surprise est extrême.
        Je ne puis sans horreur me regarder moi-même.
        [Let us flee, Theramenes. My astonishment is great. I cannot look at myself without shuddering.]

But Phaedra, too, grieves at Theseus' blindness, for he had opened the way to the return of the repressed even before his repressive authority seemed to conceal itself in death:

302   Par mon époux lui-même à Trézène amenée...
        [Brought to the shores of Troezen by my husband himself...]

IV.

La scène est à Trézène, ville du Péloponèse. The unity of place, which is a structural premise of classical tragedy, will prove in this masterpiece to be more than a happy compromise between the characters' entrances and exits. Troezen, as a place, belongs to someone—to Hippolytus. It was peacefully dear to his childhood; he prefers it to the city where his father holds court, Athens (ll. 30-32); it is his inheritance (l. 358) and recognizes him unquestioningly as king on the news of his father's death (ll. 394, 477-79, 505). Yet the arrival *sur ces bords* of the Cretan queen, a foreigner of perverse race just as Hippolytus himself is the son of a proudly chaste foreigner, the Amazon (ll. 204, 489), was enough to dispossess him. It has created a singular relationship of permanent incompatibility between the person and the place. It is through this relationship, which in at least three successive variants presents as a constant the opportunity or necessity for Hippolytus to leave Troezen that the unity of place and the qualifications of the place acquire meaning. The first plan for departure occupies the first two lines of the tragedy, and we have noted the complexity of its motivation:

1   Le dessein en est pris: je pars, cher Théramène,
        Et quitte le séjour de l'aimable Trézène.

[My mind is made up, Theramenes, I am going and leaving the pleasant land of Troezen.]

At the news of his father's death, a second motive for leaving replaces the search for him: the dispute over the throne of Athens, for Hippolytus may truly succeed his father only by disposing of it, either for himself or for Aricia. If one considers that this departure will never take place either, the great number of its announcements deserves noting:

332 Déjà même Hippolyte est tout prêt à partir...
  [Hippolytus is now ready to leave...]

368 Hippolyte me cherche, et veut me dire adieu?
  [Hippolytus is looking for me and wishes to say farewell?]

463 Il vient à vous. — Madame, avant que de partir...
  [He is coming to you. — My Lady, before leaving...]

507 L'Attique est votre bien. Je pars, et vais pour vous...
  [Attica belongs to you. I am leaving and going to...]

564 Phèdre veut vous parler avant votre départ.
  [Phaedra wishes to speak to you before your departure.]

572 Partez, Prince, et suivez vos généreux desseins.
  [Go, Prince, and carry out your generous plans.]

578 Va, que pour le départ tout s'arme en diligence.
  [Go, let everything be carefully prepared for the departure.]

584 On dit qu'un prompt départ vous éloigne de nous...
  [They say that you will soon be leaving us...]

721 Si vous voulez partir, la voile est préparée.
  [If you wish to leave, the ship is ready.]

735 Partons; et quelque prix qu'il en puisse coûter...
  [Let us leave; and at whatever cost...]

Only in the words of Phaedra, for she views Hippolytus in the light of hope and in dreams beyond repression, does the image of this departure negate its irreversibility, turning the prow of the ships toward the open sea and escape, and entrusting its sails to the winds of salvation:

797 Déjà de ses vaisseaux la pointe était tournée,
  Et la voile flottait aux vents abandonnée.
  [The prow of his ships were already heading out, and the sail fluttered freely in the wind.]

Yet it is precisely through Phaedra's guilt that the third motive for leaving will be the exile imposed upon Hippolytus by his father. The departure from Troezen is this time enlarged to become, for the man accused of the nefarious crime whose prohibition forms the basis of civilization, banishment from the whole of the civilized world whose borders have been delimited by the heroic deeds of Theseus and Hercules:

1050   Tu parais dans les lieux pleins de ton infamie,
Et ne vas pas chercher, sous un ciel inconnu,
Des pays où mon nom ne soit point parvenu.
[You appear in this place that is full of your infamy and do not go and seek some unknown land that my name has not yet reached.]

1059   Fuis; et si tu ne veux qu'un châtiment soudain
T'ajoute aux scélérats qu'a punis cette main,
Prends garde que jamais l'astre qui nous éclaire
Ne te voie en ces lieux mettre un pied téméraire.
Fuis, dis-je; et sans retour précipitant tes pas,
De ton horrible aspect purge tous mes Etats.
[Flee; and if you do not wish a sudden punishment to add you to the criminals felled by this hand, take care that the stars above never see you dare to return to this land. Flee, then, hurry away never to return, and purge my land of your terrible presence.]

1141   Fusses-tu par delà les colonnes d'Alcide,
Je me croirais encor trop vóisin d'un perfide.
[Even if you were beyond the pillars of Hercules, I would still feel too close to a traitor.]

And Hippolytus himself wants to leave his own Troezen behind him, as though it were a place that has been profaned, poisoned by the return of the repressed:

1359   Arrachez-vous d'un lieu funeste et profané,
Où la vertu respire un air empoisonné...
[Tear yourself away from a fatal and profaned place, where virtue breathes unclean air...]

At last the departure is actually undertaken, but Hippolytus is unable to go beyond the borders of the tragic place that encloses him. No sooner has he left Troezen than the sound of the catastrophe is heard:

1498   A peine nous sortions des portes de Trézène...
[Hardly had we left Troezen's gates...]

The fact is that Hippolytus not only *possesses* the place where the tragedy unfolds, but that in some ways Hippolytus himself *is* that place, as the unwilling object of unpardonable desire, as an unsuccessful alternative synthesized of Phaedra and Theseus, for he resembles and is contrasted with both of them, and as a proposal for a new established order whose failure is caused by the return of the repressed. The character's youthful fascination lies in the prematurity of this proposal and in the very atrocity of its failure, which is prefigured even in the earliest lines by Hippolytus' lack of self-confidence and his readiness to abandon the place when threatened. Just as a timeless subversive utopia is destroyed for Phaedra, and a past for Theseus, for Hippolytus a future is wrecked. The symbolic failure of the new order, however, presupposes that the old order literally survives itself, not without prestige nor without nostalgia for its past strength. Thus, while Hippolytus' final attempt at departure is in response to his father's error, and his penultimate one is inspired by the ambition to succeed him, the first is merely dictated by a residual hope of finding him alive. The disappointment of this hope at the other end of the tragedy may be symbolized by a detail in Theramenes' narration. The horses that have been dragging Hippolytus stop just next to the ancient tombs, among which Hippolytus had wished to solemnize his wedding vows (ll. 1329-94). In these tombs are cold relics, the bodies of his royal ancestors:

1553 Ils s'arrêtent, non loin de ces tombeaux antiques
   Où des rois ses aïeux sont les froides reliques.
   [They came to a halt near those ancient tombs that contain the cold relics
   of his royal ancestors.]

V.

The death of the king and father is above all the decline of a certain superficial and sovereign way of disposing of pleasure: originally innocent in its dispersiveness, it seems to have been preserved and reserved, as a relic of ancient times, only at the level of the supreme authority. Theramenes has not excluded the country bordering on the kingdom of the dead from his voyage in search of Theseus:

11 J'ai demandé Thésée aux peuples de ces bords
  Où l'on voit l'Achéron se perdre chez les morts...
  [I have sought Theseus among the peoples of the land where Acheron
  descends to the dead...]

Nevertheless, he insinuates to Hippolytus, who demands to know where he is hidden, that it might rather be Theseus himself who wishes to conceal new love affairs:

17 Qui sait même, qui sait si le Roi votre père
  Veut que de son absence on sache le mystère?
  Et si, lorsque avec vous nous tremblons pour ses jours,
  Tranquille, et nous cachant de nouvelles amours,
  Ce héros n'attend point qu'une amante abusée...
  [Who knows even whether the King, your father, wishes the secret of his
  absence to be known? And whether, while we fear with you for his life,

this hero is not concealing some new love affair and merely waiting
calmly for an outraged lover . . .]

This hypothesis and the search undertaken near the river of the Underworld are in no way incompatible. From the moment that Theseus' death
is regarded as certain, the manner of it burgeons into a myth in reiterative
combination with the mythical enterprises of Theseus the seducer. It is
the myth of the insatiability of unfaithful desire, driven to extreme
paradox by a geography that includes the underworld among the places
accessible to the boldness of the living, and Pluto's bed among those
which adultery may dishonor. Phaedra rejects the supreme fickleness in
this image of Theseus:

635   non point tel que l'ont vu les enfers,
   Volage adorateur de mille objets divers,
   Qui va du Dieu des morts déshonorer la couche . . .
   [not as the Underworld saw him, a fickle worshipper of a thousand
   different objects, who goes to dishonor the bed of the God of the dead . . .]

Where unpardonable and faithful desire almost disdains, pardonable,
faithful desire marvels. It is chaste Aricia's confidante who, with a touch
of scandalous curiosity, gives the expurgated account of the fantastic
rumors surrounding this death:

380 On sème de sa mort d'incroyables discours.
   On dit que ravisseur d'une amante nouvelle
   Les flots ont englouti cet époux infidèle.
   On dit même, et ce bruit est partout répandu,
   Qu'avec Pirithoüs aux enfers descendu,
   Il a vu le Cocyte et les rivages sombres,
   Et s'est montré vivant aux infernales ombres;
   Mais qu'il n'a pu sortir de ce triste séjour,
   Et repasser les bords qu'on passe sans retour.
   [There are some incredible rumors about his death. They say that this
   unfaithful husband was drowned while carrying off some new lover.
   They even say, and this rumor is widespread, that he went down into the
   Underworld with Pirithous, saw Cocytus and the dark shores, and pre-
   sented himself alive to the infernal shades. But he could not leave this
   grim land and go back across the frontiers from whence there is no
   return.]

VI.

On dit, on dit même; Ismene does not accept responsibility for what seems
incredible. Unable to settle for the mere absence of a living Theseus, as
in Euripides, neither could Racine risk paying for the subterranean
depths, the shadowy silence of pagan hell from which in Seneca Theseus

actually seemed to return, a price too high for rational verisimilitude. It was already a risky undertaking to ask pre-Enlightenment rationalism to forgive him for using monsters as symbols of unpardonable irrationality. The rationalized version of the myth, which Racine adopted in borrowing from Plutarch's *Life of Theseus*, is correctly presented in the preface as a compromise, owing to which myth and poetry have not had to sacrifice anything to verisimilitude: "Ainsi j'ai tâché de conserver la vraisemblance de l'histoire, sans rien perdre des ornements de la fable, qui fournit extrêmement à la poésie." (I have thus attempted to retain the plausibility of the story without sacrificing any of the ornaments of the legend which contribute greatly to the poetry.) For poetry really to benefit from myth, it was essential that the poet be able to infuse the myth with meaning. In this case one might say, using a modern pun, that the *sens* is a *sens unique*, which consists in the impossibility of returning from *les bords qu'on passe sans retour*. Death, of course, is the prime example of irreversibility, and this was a literary commonplace linked to entering the ancient Underworld. Seneca employed it several times (*Phaedra*, ll. 93-94, 219-21, 625-26) precisely because his Theseus' miraculous return belied it (ll. 222-24, 835-49). Racine's Theseus, however, does not belie any irreversibility, because in his tragedy that of death, as we know, is not the only one. In the *Aeneid*, and this time in a passage that figures with those from Seneca among the classical reminiscences in *Phèdre*, the flow of the infernal river was described by the same adjective used for the Labyrinth — *inremeabilis unda* (VI, 425). The irreversibility of the Labyrinth, which in *Phèdre* becomes the irreversibility of labyrinthic speech, stands in the same relationship to that of death as the theme of the hidden monster to the theme of the hidden father—a relationship linking a phenomenon to its indispensable premise. The condition for the return of the repressed is the disappearance of repressive authority. The monstrous secret spreads irrevocably from the moment that the elimination of the father figure is irrevocable.

VII.

The news of Theseus' death reaches or convinces last of all Phaedra and Aricia respectively, the two women for whom it removes, formally and completely, a prohibition on their desire:

320   Et ce malheur n'est plus ignoré que de vous.
       [And this misfortune is now ignored by you alone.]

392   Thésée est mort, Madame, et vous seule en doutez...
       [Theseus is dead, my Lady, and you alone doubt it...]

However, Hippolytus, who is the first to be informed (ll. 323-24) and given direct responsibility because he is the male heir, shows some hesitation at the news as previously he had done with regard to his motives for leaving in search of his father. The two reasons for this hesitation are the same as before: the love he has vowed to Aricia, the fear inspired by Phaedra. In the presence of Aricia he considers this death as certain, for it alone can explain why his father has remained hidden so long and is a condition for the legitimation of his own transgression in love:

465   Mon père ne vit plus. Ma juste défiance
Présageait les raisons de sa trop longue absence:
La mort seule, bornant ses travaux éclatants,
Pouvait à l'univers le cacher si longtemps.
[My father is dead. My fears proved right in predicting the reason for such a long absence. Only death, by limiting his brilliant deeds, could hide him from the universe so long.]

In the presence of Phaedra, however, the hope that his father might return, might come out of death's hiding place, seems the only defense left to Hippolytus against the emergence, either imminent or just transpired, of the monstrous secret from its hiding place. There is no sense in questioning the character's good or bad faith:

619   Peut-être votre époux voit encore le jour;
Le ciel peut à nos pleurs accorder son retour.
[Perhaps your husband is still alive; may the heavens answer our tears with his return.]

663   Dieux! qu'est-ce que j'entends? Madame, oubliez-vous
Que Thésée *est* mon père et qu'il *est* votre époux?
[Ye Gods! What do I hear? Have you forgotten, my Lady, that Theseus is my father and that he is your husband?]

This hope, this reluctance to admit his father's death, which Hippolytus' immaturity and fear nearly cause to prevail over his love and legitimate ambition, will prove to be justified. Theseus' restoration to life will be announced by that same popular rumor which claimed he had descended into hell. The new report, which makes death reversible, has first a disquieting effect and then a terrifying one, for it comes after Phaedra has been utterly compromised by the irreversibility of speech:

729   Cependant un bruit sourd veut que le Roi respire.
On prétend que Thésée a paru dans l'Epire.
[Meanwhile a vague rumor has it that the King is alive. They say that Theseus has been seen in Epirus.]

827   Le Roi, qu'on a cru mort, va paraître à vos yeux;
Thésée est arrivé, Thésée est en ces lieux.

Le peuple, pour le voir, court et se précipite.
[The King, we thought was dead, is about to appear before you; Theseus
has arrived, Theseus is here. The people are hurrying to see him.]

But the effect of terror produced by what is supernatural in appearance
only, like Theseus' return, cannot derive from a different source than
that produced in *Phèdre* by what is supernatural in substance. Terror
immediately turns into the moral horror that Phaedra feels for herself
(ll. 832 ff.). And because the horror has spread throughout the land,
which is now the symbolic seat of the return of the repressed, the
contagiousness of this terror soon attacks the very person who seemed to
emerge from death, until he actually regrets leaving the place from
which he has emerged:

953   Que vois-je? Quelle horreur dans ces lieux répandue
Fait fuir devant mes yeux ma famille éperdue?
Si je reviens si craint et si peu désiré,
O ciel! de ma prison pourquoi m'as-tu tiré?
[What am I seeing? What horror has spread throughout this land that my
distraught family flees from me? Oh heaven, if my return is thus feared
and unwanted, why did you free me from my prison?]

975   Je n'ai pour tout accueil que des frémissements:
Tout fuit, tout se refuse à mes embrassements.
Et moi-même, éprouvant la terreur que j'inspire,
Je voudrais être encor dans les prisons d'Epire.
[I am welcomed only by shudders: everyone flees, everyone avoids my
embrace. And I, feeling the fear I inspire, would still like to be in the
prisons of Epirus.]

The terror Theseus inspires is the same as that which he feels. The traces
of the apparently supernatural that the character still has about him are
the same as the traces of the disaster that the false report of his death has
unleashed in the place from which he has long been absent. Thus a
shudder of fear still remains in this myth that has been rationalized by a
credible explanation. The prisons of Epirus not only resembled but were
also near to the true realm of death:

965   Moi-même, il m'enferma dans des cavernes sombres,
Lieux profonds, et voisins de l'empire des ombres.
[He imprisoned me in dark, deep caves, close to the realm of the dead.]

VIII.

The terror Theseus feels on his return is the stroke of poetic genius that
prevents the magnitude of his pathetic failure from becoming grotesque,
at a point when the Father or King (with a capital letter) is about to prove

himself a father or king, unsuited to his duties and deceived, and irreversibly dead as an ideal image. Phaedra had confronted the hope for his father's return to which Hippolytus clung with the irreversibility of death, in a somber, convinced, and positive tone very different from that of Aricia's confidante:

623   On ne voit point deux fois le rivage des morts,
       Seigneur. Puisque Thésée a vu les sombres bords,
       En vain vous espérez qu'un Dieu vous le renvoie,
       Et l'avare Achéron ne lâche point sa proie.
       [My Lord, one cannot see the shores of the dead twice. Since Theseus has viewed this grim realm, you wait in vain for a God to return him to you, and avaricious Acheron will not let go his prey.]

Here Phaedra is reading deep within her own self the fatal nature of irreversibility, whether of speech or of death; and thus speaking she is right, wrong, then right again on three different levels. On the most superficial level she is right, because at the moment in which she speaks Hippolytus' hope is unfounded, given the news they have heard. On the level of predicting the future she is wrong, because, as events will prove, Theseus is alive and will return. On the level of divining a truth deeper than the factual, she is again definitively right, for Theseus, the Hero, will never again be worthy of his own self, will never return again. The hidden father is now the *prey* of avaricious Acheron, who will not loosen his grip on him; at the same time and in the same way, Venus will not loosen her grip on Phaedra, the hidden monster, who is her *prey:*

306   C'est Vénus tout entière à sa proie attachée.
       [Venus clings desperately to her prey.]

In these two symmetrical yet incompatible terms, hidden father and hidden monster, the entire system of symbolic negations seems to be summed up at the deepest and most elementary level. Out of methodological interest this may be schematized; a few words will suffice. The monster remained hidden *as long as* the father was not hidden; the monster is no longer hidden *since* the father is hidden. The tragedy begins when the monster is *still* and the father *already* hidden. The irreversibility of speech brings the monster out of its hiding place; the irreversibility of death keeps the father in his. Venus' prey is forced to appear once Acheron's prey has disappeared.

IX.

Just before this Hippolytus had spoken two lines no less loaded with hidden contradiction and destined to be developed much later in the text:

621   Neptune le protège, et ce Dieu tutélaire
           Ne sera pas en vain imploré par mon père.
           [Neptune protects him, my father will not call in vain for this God's aid.]

It is quite true that the appeal to Neptune by Hippolytus' father will not be in vain, but while we shall discover that Theseus had refrained from invoking him during his imprisonment in Epirus (ll. 1069-70), it is against Hippolytus and at the cost of Hippolytus' life that he will appeal to him successfully. Thus this pious and confident phrase, to the letter of the text, belies unknowingly Hippolytus' reasons for hoping in his father's return: by wishing him physically alive he anticipates him as morally dead. The tragedy is full of this blind irony of words that tell the literal truth in a different and invariably much more fatal sense that that understood by the character when uttering them (whether or not the spectator realizes it at the time):

207   Hé bien! votre colère éclate avec raison:
           J'aime à vous voir frémir à ce funeste nom.
           [Your anger may well burst forth: I like to see you tremble at this fatal name.]
           (Oenone to Phaedra after mentioning Hippolytus by name)

580   Me délivrer bientôt d'un fâcheux entretien.
           [Deliver me quickly from this tedious conversation.]
           (Hippolytus while waiting to speak to Phaedra)

1164   Jamais père en effet fut-il plus outragé?
           [Was a father ever more outraged?]
           (Theseus, who believes in Hippolytus' guilt)

1593   Mais j'aperçois venir sa mortelle ennemie.
           [But here comes his mortal enemy.]
           (Theramenes on seeing Phaedra after Hippolytus' death)

Elsewhere, by overturning the truth, whether present or future, words deceive the character who unwittingly utters them:

361   Vous avez l'un et l'autre une juste ennemie:
           Unissez-vous tous deux pour combattre Aricie.
           [You both have a rightful enemy: join forces to fight Aricia.]
           (Oenone to Phaedra on Hippolytus' interests)

790   Je ne me verrai point préférer de rivale.
           [I will see no rival preferred to me.]
           (Phaedra on the fame of Hippolytus' chastity)

913   La fortune à mes vœux cesse d'être opposée...
           [Fortune ceases to go against my wishes...]
           (Theseus to Phaedra at the time of his arrival)

996   Mais l'innocence enfin n'a rien à redouter.
[But surely innocence has nothing to fear.]
(Hippolytus about to be slandered)

1189   Mais je sais rejeter un frivole artifice.
[But I know how to reject a vain pretense.]
(Theseus on the love that Hippolytus has confessed to him)

1351   Sur l'équité des Dieux osons nous confier:
Ils ont trop d'intérêt à me justifier...
[Let us trust in the justice of the Gods: their interest is to render me justice...]
(Hippolytus who refuses to disillusion his father)

X.

Hippolytus trusts in Neptune's protection, in his own innocence, in the fairness of the Gods. But what exactly do the Gods represent in *Phèdre?*

(a) Destiny and order of things (ll. 377, 469, 621, 625, 967, 972, 1244, 1584);

(b) omniscient witnesses of all events (ll. 727, 1165, 1276, 1344, 1411-12);

(c) original supporters of civilization (ll. 131, 360, 550, 1055-66);

(d) superhuman guarantors of human established order (ll. 197, 1158, 1304-6, 1351, 1401-6, 1576);

(e) formalistically blind vindicators (ll. 1160, 1178, 1190, 1484, 1496, 1540, 1569, 1572, 1612);

(f) persecutors who send out irresistible passions (ll. 35, 96, 123, 180, 222, 249, 257, 277, 285, 306, 679-80, 814, 1289);

(g) ideal beauty (l. 640).

Too many alternatives to represent anything. In this tragedy the Gods are nothing and they are everything. Briefly, one could say that, in their manifold and incompatible aspects, they are reality. It would be a mistake to believe that the terrifying seriousness acquired by myth in *Phèdre* contradicts the substantial nonexistence which I am attributing to Racine's Gods. The ornamental, allegorical Gods of so much of other literature of the Baroque or pre-Enlightenment period may exist and, if necessary, even appear, speak, and act just because their existence does not affect any serious sense of the myth: this sense never exists. Racine, who rediscovered the meaning of myth in the diabolical dimensions of the monstrous, has given monsters a body, with bones, blood, scales, and horns, but he has given the Gods no other appearance than that of a pure projection of human fates, passions, and institutions. The fear of them that the characters feel is merely the fear that they feel of themselves, of their individual selves and of each other; their respect is merely for the established order to which they belong. Racine, the last great Christian poet, in effect understood the pagan Gods in exactly the same way that the great Christian historian of the same period, Bossuet, explained idolatry (*Discours sur l'histoire universelle*, II, 25):

...sous le nom de fausses divinités, c'était en effet leurs propres pensées, leurs plaisirs et leurs fantaisies que les Gentils adoraient.
[...though giving them the names of false divinities, it was actually their own thoughts, pleasures and fantasies that the Gentiles worshipped.][1]

As sacred images of Law and Desire, these Gods play with man's language just as Freud has taught us that the human unconscious does, by taking words at their letter, or rather dissociating the letter from the spirit and placing the former before the latter. Both of the prayers that Phaedra and Theseus respectively address to the principal Gods of the tragedy, Venus and Neptune, are fulfilled, but in a strictly, treacherously literal sense, as if the god's omniscience were scoffing at the intentions and interests of the suppliant. Phaedra begs Venus to overcome what she believes to be Hippolytus' unbending chastity:

822   Déesse, venge-toi: nos causes sont pareilles.
        [Goddess, avenge yourself: we share the same cause.]

Theseus appeals to Neptune to punish what he believes to be his son's offense against him:

1073   Je t'implore aujourd'hui. Venge un malheureux père.
        [I implore you now to avenge a wretched father.]

Venus and Neptune, however, do not seem to know or take into account that Hippolytus loves Aricia, or that Hippolytus is innocent. Phaedra will be requited by the torment of jealousy, Theseus by the unjust death of his son. The improvident blindness of Desire and the formalistic blindness of the Law, which in the tragedy are often adumbrated by words that lie unwittingly or tell a truth they do not suspect, may also materialize in a heavenward glance obstructed by the images of the Gods.

XI.

In the preface Racine says that he departed slightly from his ancient sources in order to attenuate in Theseus the sense of being an offended

1. Jacques-Bénigne Bossuet, *Œuvres*, Bibliothèque de la Pléiade (Paris: Gallimard, 1961), p. 898.

husband, which within the framework of the contemporary literary genres was only appropriate for a comic character. Hippolytus shows a similar concern for his father:

1340   Ai-je dû mettre au jour l'opprobre de son lit?
        Devais-je, en lui faisant un récit trop sincère,
        D'une indigne rougeur couvrir le front d'un père?
        [Should I have revealed the outrage to his bed? Should I have told him
        the truth and caused my father to blush unjustly?]

If the aura of a comic husband remains so far removed from Theseus, it is not only because of the play's literary style but particularly because the outrage committed against him burns in Phaedra's consciousness from the moment she learns of his return to the point of death (ll. 832-34, 840-56, 1266, 1642). However, it is also because all the characters long for the prestige and strength of the heroic father figure. This is expressed by the adjectives that so often exalt and honor such a figure, used both in the absence and presence of Theseus himself:

77   Quand tu me dépeignais ce héros *intrépide*
        [When you described that *intrepid* hero to me]

319   La mort vous a ravi votre *invincible* époux...
        [Death has ravished your *invincible* husband...]

467   La mort seule, bornant ses travaux *éclatants*...
        [Only death, by limiting his *brilliant* deeds...]

874   De son époux trahi fuit l'aspect *redoutable.*
        [Fled from the *dreaded* sight of her betrayed husband.]

945   Et moi, fils inconnu d'un si *glorieux* père...
        [And I, unknown son of a *glorious* father...]

1042   quel funeste nuage,
        Seigneur, a pu troubler votre *auguste* visage?
        [what baneful cloud could have troubled your *regal* brow?]

1168   Votre voix *redoutable* a passé jusqu'à moi.
        [Your *awesome* voice has reached me.]

1443   Prenez garde, Seigneur. Vos *invincibles* mains...
        [Beware, my Lord, your *invincible* hands...]

But the only instance of an attempt to invoke his authority as an avenger, apart from the principal action in which Theseus figures primarily as blind judge, is in jealous Phaedra's brief dream of vengeance, where she in turn blinds herself to adultery and incest:

1263   Dans mes jaloux transports je le veux implorer.
        [I wish to implore him in my jealous rage.]

1265   Moi jalouse! Et Thésée est celui que j'implore!
        [I, jealous! And it is Theseus that I implore!]

Perhaps the most moving appeal to the figure of the sovereign, still able
to intervene and bring help at the last moment, is uttered by the humble
Panope, a lady-in-waiting to Phaedra, who has just finished giving
incomprehensible and fatal news of her mistress:

1479   Daignez la voir, Seigneur; daignez la secourir.
        [Deign to see her, my Lord; try to help her.]

        XII.

As blind judge Theseus is open to the explicit reproach of all six of the
principal characters, excluding Oenone who tricks him, but naturally
including himself. To Phaedra the senseless father merely seems to be
the instrument of a potentially deadly attack on her love:

1315   Il en mourra peut-être, et d'un père insensé
        Le sacrilège voeu peut-être exaucé.
        [He may die, and the sacrilegious wish of a senseless father may have
        been granted.]

Aricia's reproof is an insult for his lack of that gift—the knowledge of
men—which should be indispensable to a royal judge:

1429   Avez-vous de son cœur si peu de connaissance?
        Discernez-vous si mal le crime et l'innocence?
        Faut-il qu'à vos yeux seuls un nuage odieux
        Dérobe sa vertu qui brille à tous les yeux?
        [Do you know so little about his feelings? Do you distinguish guilt and
        innocence with such difficulty? Must a hideous cloud hide his virtue
        from your eyes alone when it shines in those of all others?]

Theramenes' reproof is respectfully indirect:

1493   J'ai vu des mortels périr le plus aimable,
        Et j'ose dire encor, Seigneur, le moins coupable.
        [I have seen the finest of mortals die, and I dare to add, my Lord, the
        most innocent.]

Hippolytus' reproof is condensed into an elegiac sigh, at the moment of
his death:

1563   Cher ami, si mon père un jour désabusé
        Plaint le malheur d'un fils faussement accusé...
        [My dear friend, should my father ever find out the truth and feel sorrow
        for the misfortune of a wrongly accused son...]

And Theseus is tormented too late by the instinct for truth in his own pity:

1455   Mais moi-même, malgré ma sévère rigueur,
       Quelle plaintive voix crie au fond de mon cœur?
       Une pitié secrète et m'afflige et m'étonne.
       [But I myself, despite my harshness, what plaintive voice do I hear crying out in my heart? A hidden pity troubles and surprises me.]

The pity was preceded by a confusion that the Gods who have been invoked would have been as incapable of clarifying as the places now devastated by the return of the repressed would have been propitious to Theseus' search for the truth:

1411   Dieux, éclairez mon trouble, et daignez à mes yeux
       Montrer la vérité, que je cherche en ces lieux.
       [Ye Gods, throw a light on my confusion, and deign to reveal to me the truth that I am searching for here.]

Even before, in fact, he rejected the chance offered him by Phaedra's remorse in a rage, in which fear of the truth close at hand only added to his blindness:

1182   Dans toute leur noirceur retracez-moi ses crimes;
       Echauffez mes transports trop lents, trop retenus.
       [Tell me of his crimes in all their heinousness. Arouse my sluggish rage, too long contained.]

The combination of false evidence about Hippolytus, in which Oenone perceived the perfect crime (ll. 888-92), is worsened by the father's swift intuition of the false in misunderstanding his son's welcome (ll. 1023-26) and not acknowledging his past chastity (ll. 1114-18). Except in the experience of terror and error, this character can cry out his sorrowful and bewildered appeal for emotional identification only by taking up that great commonplace of the Baroque theater, the *ubi consistam:*

1003   Avec quelle rigueur, Destin, tu me poursuis!
       Je ne sais où je vais, je ne sais où je suis.
       [How harshly you pursue me, Destiny! I do not know where I am going, nor where I am.]

Once the parable of the blind judge has been completed in disillusion, Theseus is virtually deprived of authority by his own injustice and tormented by the very prestige of his name. All that now remains for him is the regret that he cannot better conceal himself:

1607   Confus, persécuté d'un mortel souvenir,
       De l'univers entier je voudrais me bannir.

Tout semble s'élever contre mon injustice.
L'éclat de mon nom même augmente mon supplice.
Moins connu des mortels, je me cacherais mieux.
[Confused, hounded by a grim memory, I would be banished from the whole universe. Everything seems to rise up against my injustice. The very renown of my name increases my torment. If I were less known among mortals, I could hide myself better.]

The irreversibility of the return of the repressed renders vain Theseus' hopes for a return to his initial state of hidden father, as it was also impossible for Phaedra to return to that of hidden monster. But a hidden father and a failed father are invariably tantamount to a dead father.

XIII.

I have taken into account all those elements in the poetic reality of *Phèdre* that occupy the vacancy of authority in the third symbolic negation: Hippolytus, whom I had already mentioned and shall mention again, the theme of the father's death, the theme of his failure. Thus the sixth symbolic negation, compared with the third, seems somewhat displaced in the tragedy's chronology: with reference to the present time of the action, it was in the distant past that Theseus had freed the civilized world from monsters and brigands, and in a more recent past that he had crushed the dynastic opposition of the Pallantids. Furthermore this symbolic negation stands apart from all those preceding it because of the term it negates. The monsters and brigands overcome by heroic repression, like the political rivals, represent a repressed that is objectively different from the one negated by all the other five symbolic negations — Phaedra's desire. So different, in fact, that the parallelism between the sixth negation and the previous ones must be justified and its meaning must be commented upon. It seems to me that this can only be done on the basis of the Freudian dialectics of civilization, whose logic, lying in human actions, seems to have been completely penetrated symbolically by the seventeenth-century poet. He has recognized in the repression of the perverse (nonreproductive) desire of the individual that collective, recurrent sacrifice which continually forms and recreates society *ex novo.* He has even rediscovered in myth the link between the personal disaster of one who has rejected this sacrifice and the celebration of the defeat of an original asociality. It is no accident that the origins of civilization may be glimpsed on the archaic horizon of the tragedy of love, from the moment that they are deeply involved in the same impossibility, which makes something tragic of this particular love. The tragedy of repressed love, which becomes the tragedy of repression with no limits to its

profoundness, reflects in its own margins a permanent tragedy of civilization and tells what price continues to be exacted by civilization's unexcep-
tionable triumph.

XIV.

Stifled and punished like Phaedra's desire, countless monsters and bandits
seem to have passed through Theseus' hands. Their frightening names
are crowded into a single line, their memorable punishment is briefly
rendered in all its violence by two more:

79   Les monstres étouffés et les brigands punis,
      Procuste, Cercyon, et Scirron, et Sinnis,
      Et les os dispersés du géant D'Epidaure,
      Et la Crète fumant du sang du Minotaure.
      [Monsters suppressed and brigands punished: Procrustes, Cercyron,
      Sciron and Sinis; the bones of the giant of Epidaurus strewn about, and
      Crete steaming in the blood of the Minotaur.]

Was monogamy better consolidated on earth than civilization itself when
such famous and bloody deeds occurred? It would appear not, judging
by the number of victims of love felled by Theseus' uncontainable virility.
Their number is even less specifiable than that of the deserving victims
of his heroism, and both former and latter are placed in an obvious
stylistic parallelism:

84   Sa foi partout offerte et reçue en cent lieux,
      Hélène à ses parents dans Sparte dérobée,
      Salamine témoin des pleurs de Péribée;
      Tant d'autres, dont les noms lui sont même échappés,
      Trop crédules esprits que sa flamme a trompés;
      Ariane aux rochers contant ses injustices,
      Phèdre enlevée enfin sous de meilleurs auspices...
      [His word pledged everywhere and believed in a hundred lands. Helen
      stolen from her family in Sparta, Salamis witnessing Periboea's tears; so
      many more, whose names he has forgotten, people too credulous deceived
      by his passion; Ariadne on the rocks, recalling his injustice, and, finally,
      Phaedra, abducted for more honorable ends...]

The sense of morality opposing these two aspects of his paternal history,
one glorious and the other unworthy of it, is all to be attributed to
Hippolytus who speaks of it, illustrating the viewpoint of another
generation. Yet, in the tragedy, we know that it is Hippolytus who
represents the present or future, just as he holds the scene of the action,
and he is confident that by now his father has adapted to this monogamous
present (ll. 23-26). On the other hand, more recently in the struggle

against the rival house, this same father who had arranged unlimited pleasure for himself, had even though with a political pretext, banned a woman from loving. This is the third point of an exposé contained in Hippolytus' lengthy narrative. Aricia was the sister of the massacred rebels:

105   Mon père la réprouve; et par des lois sévères
       Il défend de donner des neveux à ses frères:
       D'une tige coupable il craint un rejeton;
       Il veut avec leur sœur ensevelir leur nom,
       Et que jusqu'au tombeau soumise à sa tutelle,
       Jamais les feux d'hymen ne s'allument pour elle.
       [My father punishes her, and by strict laws forbids her to give any nephew
       to her brothers: he fears a blossom from this guilty stem; he wants their
       name to be buried with their sister; as his ward until the grave, the
       marriage torch will never be lit for her.]

       XV.

The bounds of Phaedra's experience are ample: one might say that Racine's tragedy contains in reverse the entire Freudian myth of *Totem and Taboo*, to which I referred when speaking of the coincidence between the Law buried in the unconscious and the dead Father. This scientific myth, or rather, this momentous (but not demonstrable, because it is prehistoric) hypothesis requires that the children and brothers one day unite to kill their father, the primitive patriarch who monopolized all the women in the tribe. In the same way Theseus, in *Phèdre*, after having enjoyed countless women, saves both female protagonists, his wife and his enemies' sister, for himself or at least forbids others to possess them. Contrary, however, to Freud's patriarch, it is Theseus who has single-handedly massacred a community of brothers (fifty in Plutarch, reduced to six by Racine), who, according to the mythical family tree, were more or less his nephews and descendants of the primary mother, the Earth. Aricia states:

421   Reste du sang d'un roi, noble fils de la terre.
       Je suis seule échappée aux fureurs de la guerre.
       J'ai perdu, dans la fleur de leur jeune saison,
       Six frères, quel espoir d'une illustre maison!
       Le fer moissonna tout, et la terre humectée
       But à regret le sang des neveux d'Erechthée.
       [Last of a king's race, who was a noble son of the earth, I was the only one
       to escape war's fury. I lost six brothers in the flower of their youth, the
       hope of an illustrious house! The sword cut everything down and the
       drenched earth regretfully drank the blood of Erechtheus' nephews.]

When Hippolytus takes up the theme a little later on, the letter of the text, here the image of a field reeking with blood, distantly recalls line 82 and seems to say that bloodshed is always the basis of rational authority, whether the taming of the ferocity of monsters or the audacity of rebels, or whether concerning Phaedra's half-brother or Aricia's brothers. The blood of the Pallantids has steamed in the furrows of the earth at Athens just like that of the Minotaur in Crete:

503   Assez dans ses sillons votre sang englouti
      A fait fumer le champ dont il était sorti.
      [Your race's blood has flowed too long in this earth and has drenched the fields from whence it sprung.]

XVI.

But Athens, which appears to be contrasted with mysterious Crete as the first clearly human city, though its ramparts are the work of a goddess, has had nothing but cause for rejoicing over Theseus' rational authority:

360   Les superbes remparts que Minerve a bâtis.
      [The high ramparts which Minerva built.]

498   Athènes, par mon père accrue et protégée,
      Reconnut avec joie un roi si généreux...
      [Athens, enlarged and protected by my father, received such a generous king with joy...]

His son's admiration seems justified. The generous king had asserted himself against tyrants as well as against brigands and monsters. He had been able to ensure the safe passage of travelers from one sea to another:

938   Déjà plus d'un tyran, plus d'un monstre farouche
      Avait de votre bras senti la pesanteur;
      Déjà, de l'insolence heureux persécuteur,
      Vous aviez des deux mers assuré les rivages.
      Le libre voyageur ne craignait plus d'outrages;
      Hercule, respirant sur le bruit de vos coups,
      Déjà de son travail se reposait sur vous.
      [Already more than one tyrant, more than one fierce monster had felt the weight of your arm; already the successful scourge of the insolent, you had made safe the shores of the two seas. The traveler, now free, no longer feared attacks; Hercules, resting on the renown of your blows, already looked to you for his labors.]

The name of Hercules, whose work Theseus has carried forward, returns again and again as if to remind us that neither one man nor one generation was enough to establish civilization:

78   Consolant les mortels de l'absence d'Alcide...
       [Consoling mankind for the loss of Alcides...]

470   L'ami, le compagnon, le successeur d'Alcide.
       [Alcides' friend, companion, and successor.]

1141   Fusses-tu par delà les colonnes d'Alcide...
       [Even if you were beyond the pillars of Hercules...]

Like Theseus, but unlike Hippolytus, this paragon of primitive heroism did not yet respect the monogamous limits of pardonable and faithful desire:

122   Craint-on de s'égarer sur les traces d'Hercule?
       [Can one fear to go astray in Hercules' footsteps?]

454   Hercule à désarmer coûtait moins qu'Hippolyte,
       Et vaincu plus souvent, et plus tôt surmonté,
       Préparait moins de gloire aux yeux qui l'ont dompté.
       [Hercules was less difficult to disarm than Hippolytus, and defeated more often, and as he was easier to overcome, brought less glory to whomever conquered him.]

Adultery and the punishment of a monstrously bloodthirsty tyrant are again mingled together in the final deed that occupied Theseus while away from Troezen. It is true that the adulterer was not he but Pirithous, whom Theseus had doubts about helping and who ended up being devoured by monsters while Theseus alone remained to inflict the law of retaliation on the tyrant. This law seems to be Law itself in this tragedy, where Desire, and often speech and prayers, negate themselves and punish their own object:

957   Je n'avais qu'un ami. Son imprudente flamme
       Du tyran de l'Epire allait ravir la femme;
       Je servais à regret ses desseins amoureux...
       [I had but one friend. His imprudent passion led him to abduct the wife of Epirus' king; I regretfully served his amorous goals...]

962   J'ai vu Pirithoüs, triste objet de mes larmes,
       Livré par ce barbare à des monstres cruels
       Qu'il nourrissait du sang des malheureux mortels.
       [I saw Pirithous, the wretched object of my tears, delivered by this barbarian to cruel monsters, whom he fed the blood of unfortunate men.]

969   D'un perfide ennemi j'ai purgé la nature;
       A ses monstres lui-même a servi de pâture...

[I purged the world of a treacherous enemy, who served as food for his own monsters...]

XVII.

Hippolytus' emulation is contrasted with Theseus' heroism, as the son's chaste passion is contrasted with his father's prodigality in love, and his restorative disobedience in favor of Aricia with the tyrannical judgment of the old regime. The tension in the passage from one generation to another has been grasped by the poet with psychological insight so impeccable that it tends to become historical insight. The common characteristic in the son's various attitudes toward his father's image, viewed subjectively, would today be termed an inferiority complex, while from an objective viewpoint, the increase in rationality of these attitudes goes hand in hand with an increase in interiorized repression. The father, for his part, does not understand his son at all; he overlooks both his disobedience and his emulation. On the subject of his chaste passion, Theseus' credulity in accusing Hippolytus of unpardonable desire does not prevent him later on from also accusing him of unfaithful desire (ll. 1422-26). Thus a fourth combination, that of the two transgressions, is chimerically attributed to the one person who knows only pardonable and faithful desire.

XVIII.

Hippolytus' chastity as the absence of desire (an element provided by the classical sources) has already ceased to be a fact six months before the curtain rises. Nevertheless it continues to circulate as a theme on the various characters' lips, usually with a repressive function and always as an *objection*, opposed to some hope or suspicion or realization about love (in this way Racine must also have attempted to reconcile his enamored character with the ascetic of the Greek and Latin originals). Hippolytus holds up his own chastity as an objection to Theramenes who suspects him of being in love (ll. 66-72, 95-96); Aricia opposes it to the optimism of Ismene who wishes for her a requited love (ll. 400-16, 443-62); and Hippolytus almost uses it against his own confession of love (ll. 529-38). Oenone opposes it to Phaedra's hope (ll. 775-80, 787, 789), but Phaedra's hope overturns the objection (ll. 781-86, 788, 790). Hippolytus opposes it to the slander and to his father's accusations (ll. 1092-1113). Phaedra opposes it in vain to the reality of her own jealousy (ll. 1205-10, 1220-24), and again on her lips the objection does not have a repressive function but provokes love to the point of torment. Nothing is taken away from the pardonable nature of the love that is an exception to this chastity in the manner in which Racine presents it in the preface: "J'ai cru lui devoir donner quelque faiblesse qui le rendrait un peu coupable envers son père..." (I felt that I must give him some weakness which would make him slightly guilty toward his father...). But conversely, the fact that he cherishes a much more normal love than Theseus' polygamous fickleness does not spare Hippolytus a repressive feeling of guilt which, faced with the king, almost makes him feel close to Phaedra:

991   Dieux! que dira le Roi? Quel funeste poison
       L'amour a répandu sur toute sa maison!
       Moi-même, plein d'un feu que sa haine réprouve,
       Quel il m'a vu jadis, et quel il me retrouve!
       [God, what will the King say? How fatal a poison has love spread through-
       out his household! I myself, full of a passion of which his hatred
       disapproves, how he knew me then, and how he will find me now!]

       XIX.

While Theseus' superficial love affairs did not seem to diminish his heroic boldness in any way, faithful desire, which takes away from Phaedra the strength to rule, also diverts Hippolytus from the activities through which he normally expressed his emulation. The energy absorbed by love in general is squandered and lost as far as the work of civilization is concerned:

129   On vous voit moins souvent, orgueilleux et sauvage,
       Tantôt fair voler un char sur le rivage,
       Tantôt, savant dans l'art par Neptune inventé,
       Rendre docile au frein un coursier indompté.
       [You are seen less frequently, proud and aloof, racing your chariot along
       the shore, or, skillful in the art which Neptune invented, taming a wild
       horse for the rein.]

549   Mon arc, mes javelots, mon char, tout m'importune;
       Je ne me souviens plus des leçons de Neptune;
       Mes seuls gémissements font retentir les bois,
       Et mes coursiers oisifs ont oublié ma voix.
       [Everything hinders me, my bow, my spears, my chariot; I no longer
       remember what Neptune taught me; the woods echo only with my groans
       and my inactive horses have forgotten my voice.]

If not directly for this reason, it is certainly with the concurrence of this contradiction from which his values are not exempt that Hippolytus will die. It has been observed, on the subject of the great concern for verisimilitude in classical tragedy,[2] that two of the lines just quoted

2. See Jacques Scherer, *La Dramaturgie classique en France* (Paris: Nizet, 1950), pp. 380-81.

justify in advance the behavior of the horses in Theramenes' narration:

1535   La frayeur les emporte, et sourds à cette fois,
        Ils ne connaissent plus ni le frein ni la voix.
        [Carried away by terror and deafened, they no longer recognize his rein
        or his voice.]

Line 132 anticipates the fact that the horses had grown unaccustomed to the rein, line 552 that they had forgotten Hippolytus' voice. Yet Hippolytus had already broken them in and tamed them, for want of monsters already subjugated and monsters to be subjugated still:

99   Qu'aucuns monstres par moi domptés jusqu'aujourd'hui...
        [To this day no monsters have been subjugated by me...]

948   Souffrez, si quelque monstre a pu vous échapper...
        [Permit me, if any monster should have avoided you...]

Hippolytus' emulation is acted out on the stage of a world already expurgated of the most brutal forms of the irrational—monsters; if there are any left in Epirus, Epirus, where the Acheron flows, is at the edge of the civilized world, far from Troezen. At the slightest negligence in the rationalizing force, however, the bestiality that Hippolytus has to tame, the horses, demonstrates the *instability* of a civilization built on *imperfectly tamed* instincts, referred to by Freud (see p. 16). Hippolytus will die because of the horses' uncontrollable, animal fear in the face of the monster. The son's civilizing deeds, less brutal and more advanced, become vain in an instant if the irrational in monstrous form, whose elimination had been his father's task, regressively rises again. The monster is, in fact, literally *indomptable* (l. 1519). The letter of Phaedra's words comes close to that of the last line quoted when she offers herself as a monster to the punitive hand of Hippolytus, worthy son of a hero:

703   Crois-moi, ce monstre affreux ne doit point t'échapper.
        [Believe me, this frightful monster must not escape you.]

Thus the blind irony which the tragic future so often opposes to the spoken word deserves rather to be called pathos when a shaken Hippolytus seems to be asking permission to travel about the world in search of ways of emulation, asking it of his father with whom the contrast is so crushing:

933   Assez dans les forêts mon oisive jeunesse
        Sur de vils ennemis a montré son adresse.
        Ne pourrai-je, en fuyant un indigne repos,
        D'un sang plus glorieux teindre mes javelots?
        Vous n'aviez pas encore atteint l'âge où je touche...
        [In these woods, my inactive youth has revealed its skills to paltry enemies

long enough. Could I not flee this unworthy idleness and stain my spears
in more glorious blood? You had not yet reached my age...]

945   Et moi, fils inconnu d'un si glorieux père...
       [And I, unknown son of a glorious father...]

947   Souffrez que mon courage ose enfin s'occuper.
       [Let my courage at last find some task to occupy it.]

       XX.

The desire to do justice to Aricia, for whom he had declared himself
ready to face even civil war (ll. 735-36), is the unfortunate youth's
interrupted wish that he addresses to his father as he dies:

1566   Dis-lui qu'avec douceur il traite sa captive.
       Qu'il lui rende...
       [Tell him to treat his prisoner kindly, to give her...]

It is the only one of his wishes to be fulfilled. The injustice of the old
order, which survives Hippolytus as well as its own validity, will be
partially and belatedly rectified by it: so partially and belatedly as to
produce the sense of an unchanging, continually recommencing everyday
life that submerges not only the head of the man drowned for having
been chosen as an object of desire by the return of the repressed, but also,
especially, the memory of her who had dared to embody that desire. The
reconciliation of Theseus and*Aricia worthily, desperately, concludes
the tragedy with its melancholy acquiescence. Only the individualistic
interpretations of tradition could have brought about such a custom as
that of frequently omitting Theseus' closing speech in theatrical produc-
tions in order to elevate Phaedra's last lines:

1647   Allons, de mon erreur, hélas, trop éclaircis,
       Mêler nos pleurs au sang de mon malheureux fils.
       [Now that my error has, alas, been cleared, let us go and mingle our tears
       with my wretched son's blood.]

1652   Et pour mieux apaiser ses mânes irrités,
       Que, malgré les complots d'une injuste famille,
       Son amante aujourd'hui me tienne lieu de fille.
       [And the better to appease his angered shades, let his lover, in spite of the
       plotting of a criminal family, be a daughter to me now.]

9

The Ultimate Negation: Two Comparisons with Other Texts

I.

Theseus' appeal for Phaedra to be forgotten just after her death is part of the final speech of the tragedy. Before reconstructing the scattered series of couplets to which it belongs and which recall each other through their exclamatory tone and the common theme of the scandal, an observation must be made that connects the seventh symbolic negation with the third in particular. The negation of the tragedy itself as a mythical repressed is the ultimate appeal for silence, which affects above all a repressed that is not yet mythical and is still within the action of the tragedy. We now know that Hippolytus and Theseus are both afraid to know Phaedra's desire long before they actually learn of it. The former's silence, due, according to Racine's preface, to his noble spirit, makes it possible for the latter to ignore and misinterpret events to the very last minute. In defending this possibility, Theseus approaches moral cowardice when the catastrophe has occurred and the final confession is imminent. He fills up Phaedra's final, terrible silence by virtually imploring her never to break the silence:

1597   Mais, Madame, il est mort, prenez votre victime:
       Jouissez de sa perte, injuste ou légitime.
       Je consens que mes yeux soient toujours abusés.
       Je le crois criminel, puisque vous l'accusez.
       Son trépas à mes pleurs offre assez de matières,
       Sans que j'aille chercher d'odieuses lumières,
       Qui ne pouvant le rendre à ma juste douleur,
       Peut-être ne feraient qu'accroître mon malheur.
       [But, my Lady, he is dead, accept your victim: rejoice in his loss, whether unjust or no. I am willing for my eyes to be deceived always. I believe he is guilty, since you accuse him. His death is reason enough for my tears, without my searching for the hideous truth, which could never restore him to me and might merely increase my grief.]

Silence is considered cowardly by Theseus on only one occasion in the tragedy, and only when the crime it is supposed to cover up is nonexistent:

1081   Traître, tu prétendais qu'en un lâche silence
Phèdre ensevelirait ta brutale insolence.
[Traitor, you hoped that Phaedra would keep a cowardly silence and bury your vile insolence.]

Hippolytus' silence is not due to any obligation to respect a vow, as in Euripides. It is at first an instinctive choice, a reflex of his gentlemanly manners, that Hippolytus would conceal the already compromised Phaedra's retreat, by retreating himself.

667   Madame, pardonnez. J'avoue, en rougissant,
Que j'accusais à tort un discours innocent.
[Forgive me, my Lady. Blushing, I must confess that I wrongly thought your innocent words were guilty.]

The silence implied by good breeding becomes a silence of magnaminity when it is kept up for the sake of that very father whose credulity is wronging Hippolytus:

1087   D'un mensonge si noir justement irrité,
Je devrais faire ici parler la vérité,
Seigneur; mais je supprime un secret qui vous touche.
Approuvez le respect qui me ferme la bouche...
[Rightly angered at such a black lie, my Lord, I should let truth speak out now; but I will hide a secret that concerns you. Approve the silence that seals my lips...]

Hippolytus allows himself to die from a pure sense of the scandalous. In his generous silence there is a certain amount of fear, as at the basis of his father's self-blinding, which inevitably diminishes his nobility to the advantage of her whom the horrified silence conspires against even when it is actually sparing her. To Aricia, who obeys him by keeping the secret, though with difficulty, Hippolytus presents it as something that must be hidden even from themselves, that must be forgotten, if possible, as soon as it is heard:

1345   Je n'ai pu vous cacher, jugez si je vous aime,
Tout ce que je voulais me cacher à moi-même.
Mais songez sous quel sceau je vous l'ai révélé.
Oubliez, s'il se peut, que je vous ai parlé...
[Judge whether I love you, for I could not keep from you all that I wished to keep from myself. But remember under what conditions I have revealed it to you. Forget, if possible, that I spoke to you...]

II.

Thus, Hippolytus' silence, the crux of the tragic action, becomes on the one hand an anticipation, at a nonmythical level, of the refusal to give voice to the repressed that the appeal to forget the myth extends to the entire tragedy. On the other hand, it comes to reflect, through a general fright in the face of the repressed, the lack of authority, which it has made irreparable and which in turn provides the basis for the action and the tragedy itself. The empty semicircle of the third symbolic negation has let something escape which the outer circle of the seventh negation attempts, but too late, to enclose in oblivion. The poet has in fact shown more courage than his characters in the face of the repressed; and the paradox of this tragedy, which is ashamed of itself, is that it exists and is by definition uneffaceable, just as the words that reveal Phaedra's desire are irreversible. The elements that remain to give voice to the repression, directly and periodically, are the appeals to forget, now aimed at unpardonable desire, now at myths concluded long ago, now at potential myths still unfolding, now at myths just concluded. Only the myth of the glory of heroic deeds surely deserves to be remembered eternally; and it is moving that in the text such a wish is reserved for the deeds that Hippolytus has not carried out and never will, rather than for those of Theseus:

950   Ou que d'un beau trépas la mémoire durable,
       Eternisant des jours si noblement finis,
       Prouve à tout l'avenir que j'étais votre fils.
       [Or let the lasting memory of an honorable death render eternal glory to a life so nobly ended, and show future generations that I was your son.]

Shame instead invites eternal oblivion for Theseus' dissolute love affairs, as also for Pasiphaë's monstrous ones and, three times, for Phaedra's perverse love as well, in life and in death. Here, at last, is the whole series of the relevant appeals:

93   Heureux si j'avais pu ravir à la mémoire
      Cette indigne moitié d'une si belle histoire!
      [I would have been happy to conceal the memory of the shameful half of such a beautiful tale!]

251   Oublions-les, Madame. Et qu'à tout l'avenir
      Un silence éternel cache ce souvenir.
      [Let us forget them, my Lady. And may eternal silence keep this memory from future generations.]

719   Phèdre…Mais non, grands Dieux! qu'en un profond oubli
      Cet horrible secret reste enseveli.
      [Phaedra…Oh God, no! Let this awful secret be forgotten and remain buried.]

1349   Madame; et que jamais une bouche si pure
      Ne s'ouvre pour conter cette horrible aventure.
      [My Lady, may such pure lips never open to recount such a hideous tale.]

1645   Elle expire, Seigneur. — D'une action si noire
Que ne peut avec elle expirer la mémoire!
[She is dying, my Lord. — Oh that the memory of such terrible deeds could die with her!]

Having returned to its starting point, with the seventh negation, my analysis of the text of *Phèdre* is complete. If its completion does not immediately coincide with the end of my discussion, it is because I find it useful to add two brief comparisons with other seventeenth-century French dramas. These comparisons are meant to be a means of external verification of historical problems alluded to in my analysis, of that concerning the relationship between the work and its date of composition. From the very first pages, I had made a methodological choice. In order to understand a literary work, I stated, any problem concerning the psychology of creativity or of artistic enjoyment must become a historical problem, and in turn any historical problem must become a semiotic problem, which may be solved by examining the letter of the text. Later I stood by this choice when faced with the problems, absolutely essential to my exposition, that *Phèdre* poses in relation to its date. Indeed, there are some historical notions contributing to singling these out that cannot be derived from the text but precede one's knowledge of it: the relation of some aspects of the history of French drama in the seventeenth century to the problem of incest, of some general cultural aspects of Racine's age to the problem of myth, of some aspects of Jansenist ideology to both of these. Nevertheless, in order to solve these problems that have emerged from the text and then proved to be indispensable in its comprehension, I have consulted practically nothing but the text. If, through the text, history was, so to speak, the first to question, it was the text alone that answered. When a historical problem arises out of a work's mode of existence, is there any less arbitrary way to solve it than by following the path leading into its depths? I am not tempted to deny that there are other ways; but the choice of an outward path leads to greater arbitrariness, since the number of connections of meaning within a text is essentially finite whereas the number of those between the text and the *mare magnum* of history is, of course, infinite.[1]

---

1. Within this infinite number, a lucky chance is sometimes sufficient to single out a pertinent relationship. Such would appear to be (so much so that I cannot refrain from noting it) the relationship that may be established between the importance my interpretation of *Phèdre* gives to such terms as "scandal," "conceal," "oblivion" and the importance that the same concepts had, according to Michel Foucault, in the establishment of generalized internment from 1656 onward. The repressive function of this institution mingled criminals with the insane, the sick, and the unemployed and, through the desire to avoid scandal, pointed to "an important change in the conception of evil": see Michel Foucault, *Histoire de la folie à l'âge classique* (Paris: Gallimard, 1972), pp. 159-61.

By attempting to prove the validity of a particular interpretation of *Phèdre*, all I have done so far is to make evident as many connections of meaning within the text as I could. In the remaining pages, I am not searching for external proof but only for counter-checks of the above interpretation. Moreover, I have attempted to reduce as far as possible the arbitrariness inherent in choosing an external direction by selecting as terms of comparison and verification, in the most restricted chronological space: (a) a work by the same author based on a different myth; (b) a work by a different author based on the same myth. For the first comparison historical circumstances designate Racine's *Iphigénie*, which immediately precedes *Phèdre* (1674) and is his only other tragedy to raise the question of myth as pagan supernatural. For the second comparison I have taken *Phèdre et Hippolyte* by Jacques Pradon (1632-98), which was performed at the same time and in competition with Racine's tragedy and which at first received greater acclaim from the theatergoing public.

(A)

In choosing the mythical theme of *Iphigénie*, Racine was faced with a supernatural element that he had been able to ignore earlier in composing a tragedy like *Andromaque*, also based on pagan mythology. The marvel of the winds being stilled and finally restored to the Greek fleet by the Gods, the archaic religious aspect of the human sacrifice demanded by the oracle, these were elements that could not be eliminated from the myth of Iphigenia in Aulis. Nevertheless, there were at least two versions of the ultimate fate of the victim, or of her identity—whether Iphigenia was actually slain or replaced with a deer by the goddess Diana—from which Racine could choose his denouement. The tragedy's preface provides Racine's explanation for choosing the version he did and then cites Greek authors and sources for justification, according to a literary custom in which respect for verisimilitude was confused with that for the authority of the classical tradition. The vagueness of both of these, however, leaves ample room for a choice that was really an invention: the invention of a human victim, but one who was different from Iphigenia. This is the character of Eriphile, whom, Racine says, "j'ai pu représenter telle qu'il m'a plu" (I was able to represent as I pleased); and without this character, he states again: "je n'aurais jamais osé entreprendre cette tragédie" (I should never have dared to undertake this tragedy). Otherwise there would have been good reason to abandon with repugnance the modern revival of such a myth:

Quelle apparence que j'eusse souillé la scène par le meurtre horrible d'une personne aussi vertueuse et aussi aimable qu'il fallait représenter Iphigénie? Et quelle apparence encore de dénouer ma tragédie par le secours d'une déesse et

d'une machine, et par une métamorphose qui pouvait bien trouver quelque créance du temps d'Euripide, mais qui serait trop absurde et trop incroyable parmi nous.*
[How could I have sullied the stage by the brutal murder of a virtuous and likeable person such as Iphigenia was required to be in this play? And how again could I have ended my play with the aid of a goddess *ex machina* and a metamorphosis that might have seemed believable in Euripides' day but would be too absurd and too unbelievable for us today?][2]

In these two motives for the unacceptability of the authentic versions of the myth, we again find that sense of myth as *scandal,* at whose expense I claimed that *Phèdre* had been conceived and composed. We may also recognize the two different forms of this scandal, which seemed to me to be intimately linked and interchangeable. To stain the stage with the massacre of Iphigenia, innocent, and even virtuous and likeable, would have been a terrible *moral* scandal. For a goddess to intervene *ex machina* for the metamorphosis of a young girl into a deer, which was absurd and unbelievable to an audience more enlightened than that of Euripides' age, would have been a scandal to reason, a *rational* scandal.

At this point one cannot help observing that, in writing *Phèdre,* Racine challenged precisely these two scandals that in the preface to *Iphigénie* he called insurmountable in a modern tragedy. Hippolytus is no less innocent, virtuous, or sympathetic than Iphigenia, yet Racine takes care not to alter the myth to save him from death. The monster spewed up by the sea is no less unbelievable and absurd than the metamorphosis of a girl into a deer, yet Racine ventures to describe it with absolute poetic conviction. Besides, even when compared to the text of *Iphigénie,* the justifications given in the preface for modifying the myth are not persuasive: they denounce the moral or rational scandal of the rejected versions better than they demonstrate that the adopted version is exempt from these. The stilling of the winds remains a marvel and so does their powerful outburst once the human sacrifice is over. That Eriphile might actually *deserve* the death that awaits her, simply because in the last two acts she reveals Iphigenia's flight to Calchas from jealous envy, seems rather untenable if one considers that her condemnation to death derives from an oracle and has been contemplated since the first scene in which the character appears (ll. 427-30, 525-26). Neither a rational nor a moral scandal seems to have been substantially avoided by Racine's solution. What then did he gain from Eriphile?

According to the oracle, Eriphile will die as soon as she knows whose daughter she is. However, we eventually discover that she is a secret daughter of Theseus (a fortuitous point of contact with *Phèdre*) and Helen;

---

2. In the quoted *Œuvres complètes,* the preface of *Iphigénie* is on pp. 687-91 and the text on pp. 693-752 (see p. 12, n. 2, on the numbering of the lines).

that same Helen through whose fault a war is about to be fought, through whose fault the winds are indispensable to the departure of the Greek fleet, through whose fault the sacrifice in turn becomes necessary, through whose fault, in effect, the plot of *Iphigénie* is what it is. Clytemnestra expresses strong feelings to Agamemnon about his brother's wife:

1277   Que dis-je? Cet objet de tant de jalousie,
      Cette Hélène, qui trouble et l'Europe et l'Asie,
      Vous semble-t-elle un prix digne de vos exploits?
      Combien nos fronts pour elle ont-ils rougi de fois!
      Avant qu'un noeud fatal l'unit à votre frère,
      Thésée avait osé l'enlever à son père.
      Vous savez, et Calchas mille fois vous l'a dit,
      Qu'un hymen clandestin mit ce prince en son lit,
      Et qu'il en eut pour gage une jeune princesse,
      Que sa mère a cachée au reste de la Grèce.
      [What am I saying? Does this cause of so much jealousy, this Helen who troubles both Europe and Asia, seem a prize worthy of your exploits? How many times have we blushed for her! Before the fatal knot joined her to your brother, Theseus had dared to abduct her from her father. You know, and Calchas has told you a thousand times, that a secret union put this prince in her bed and the outcome of this was a young princess, whom her mother kept hidden from the rest of Greece.]

Yet Clytemnestra does not know that this secret daughter is close at hand, that she is none other than Eriphile, a prisoner in the camp; and a few lines earlier she demanded the sacrifice of Helen's only known daughter, Hermione, instead of her own daughter:

1267   Le ciel, le juste ciel, par le meurtre honoré,
      Du sang de l'innocence est-il donc altéré?
      Si du crime d'Hélène on punit sa famille,
      Faites chercher à Sparte Hermione sa fille.
      Laissez à Ménélas racheter d'un tel prix
      Sa coupable moitié, dont il est trop épris.
      [Are the heavens, the just heavens, honored by murder; do they thirst for innocent blood? If Helen's family is to be punished for her crime, let them fetch her daughter Hermione from Sparte. Let Menelaus buy back at such a price his guilty half, by whom he is so enraptured.]

The idea was derived from Euripides, but in the context of Racine's work, it is a perfect expression of the inner logic that inspired the addition of another daughter for Helen as a corrective to the myth. The innocence or guilt of the intended victim is much less important than the innocence or guilt of her mother. It is not an unacceptable scandal for an innocent person to be oppressed, because it is not, with the heredity of guilty ancestors weighing upon the victim, a senseless scandal. It would be unacceptable, because meaningless within the dogma of predestination and inherited original sin, for Iphigenia, daughter of an innocent mother, to perish as a victim rather than Hermione or Eriphile, who are innocent like her but daughters of a guilty mother. In this sense, Clytemnestra has the same right, as a spectator to whom Racine dared to present the unattenuated version of the myth, to be shocked that the heavens seem to have a thirst *du sang de l'innocence:* innocence is transmitted or not through one's blood. We already know what relationships are latent in *Phèdre* between the Jansenist ideology, the symbol of the condemned race, and the revival of the myth. In *Iphigénie* another guilty mother, Helen, stands in the same relationship to her daughter, Eriphile, as does Pasiphaë to Phaedra and Eve to the entire human race. The character's own faults are not enough to sanction Eriphile's massacre, just as Hippolytus' death must not be understood as a punishment for having disobeyed his father. The tragic and mythical catastrophe, as a scandal, can in no way be redeemed by a meaning which refers to its point of arrival, but only to its fatal and ancestral point of departure. Representing original sin, this point of departure is the forbidden desire, of which Hippolytus is the object, Phaedra and Eriphile the heirs.

Moreover, Eriphile does not resemble and anticipate Phaedra merely because she is the daughter of a guilty mother or because she loves without hope and suffers and sins through jealousy. The preceding analysis of *Phèdre* authorizes me to refer with the concept symbolic negation of shame (= repressed) to the fact that this character moves entirely within the semantic area of the verb *cacher.* Naturally, the fact that her name and her birth are concealed provides the dramatic opportunity for revealing only at the end the homonymy of the two Iphigenias, in which the oracle, too, concealed its meaning:

241   Et son silence même, accusant sa noblesse,
        Nous dit qu'elle cache une illustre princesse.
        [Her very silence, bearing witness to her nobility, tells us that she is
        keeping an illustrious princess from us.]

432   Un oracle toujours se plaît à se cacher.
        Toujours avec un sens il en présente un autre.
        [An oracle always likes to be mysterious. It always gives one meaning
        together with another.]

1751   Thésée avec Hélène uni secrètement
        Fit succéder l'hymen à son enlèvement.
        Une fille en sortit, que sa mère a celée ...
        [Theseus, secretly joined to Helen, followed her abduction by a union. A
        daughter was the issue, whom her mother kept hidden ...]

This last line recalls one we have already encountered:

1286   Que sa mère a cachée au reste de la Grèce.
        [Whom her mother kept hidden from the rest of Greece.]

But Eriphile must hide her love and, because of her love, herself. The
conflict between silence and speech in the presence of her confidante, to
which may be added her appeal to the hero she loves to be allowed to
leave the camp, which is the site of the action, needs no further comment
for anyone who recalls Phaedra's words:

477   Ah! que me dites vous! — Je me flattais sans cesse
        Qu'un silence éternel cacherait ma faiblesse,
        Mais mon cœur trop pressé m'arrache ce discours,
        Et te parle une fois, pour se taire toujours.
        [Ah, what are you saying! — I continually hoped that an eternal silence
        would conceal my weakness, but my heart, too hasty, tears these words
        from me and speaks to you once, never to speak again.]

512   Et combattre des feux contraints de se cacher?
        [And to fight against a passion forced to remain secret?]

756   Dieux, qui voyez ma honte, où me dois-je cacher?
        [Ye Gods, who see my shame, where must I hide?]

889   Souffrez que loin du camp, et loin de votre vue,
        Toujours infortunée et toujours inconnue,
        J'aille cacher un sort si digne de pitié,
        Et dont mes pleurs encor vous taisent la moitié.
        [Far from the camp, far from your sight, always wretched and unknown,
        allow me to go and hide a fate so worthy of pity, half of which is still
        concealed by my tears.]

The most significant difference between Eriphile and Phaedra must be
sought in the play of emotional identifications. We know with what
irresistible force Phaedra wins over her spectators for herself; and we
know that in *Phèdre* this particular emotional identification is paramount,
and to sustain it the entire tragedy has had to be constructed according to
the logic of symbolic negations. On the contrary, in *Iphigénie* Eriphile is
a marginal character and, moreover, she is placed in a progressive conflict
of interests with the protagonist, who undoubtedly benefits from the
main emotional identification. She would therefore have been destined
to appear totally odious, had not her role as a scapegoat for the mythical
repressed prompted Racine to use her as a modest experiment in
solidarity toward a repressed of the worst kind. We read in the preface
that Eriphile "mérite en quelque façon d'être punie, sans être pourtant
tout à fait indigne de compassion" (deserves to be punished in a way, yet
is not totally unworthy of compassion). Something entirely different may
be derived from such compassion, as Racine was to demonstrate three

years later. But if one were to read *Iphigénie* sympathizing with Eriphile, his reading would be going utterly against the grain. The grandiose joy of the final marvels is in no way diminished—except perhaps by Iphigenia's goodness in mourning her (ll. 1789-90)—by the shedding of her blood. If the winds begin to quiver happily, the Greek fleet can set sail toward Troy and the avenging of Menelaus. The war that because of Eriphile's sacrifice is no longer to be delayed will in fact expiate the shame caused by her mother. In *Iphigénie,* which ends on the threshold of the myth of the Trojan war, the latter is already prophetically celebrated as the triumph of a just and heroic repression. Thus in the wish for eternal remembrance that the tragedy contains, both the themes and the rhymes form a direct contradiction to the appeals to consign the myth to oblivion contained in *Phèdre,* where the repressed is the victor:

381   Voyez tout l'Hellespont blanchissant sous nos rames,
      Et la perfide Troie abandonnée aux flammes,
      . . . .
387   Et ce triomphe heureux qui s'en va devenir
      L'éternel entretien des siècles à venir.
      [Behold the whole Hellespont growing white under our oars and treacherous Troy burning....and this glorious triumph which will be eternally remembered for centuries to come.]

1559   J'espère que du moins un heureux avenir
      A vos faits immortels joindra mon souvenir;
      Et qu'un jour mon trépas, source de votre gloire,
      Ouvrira le récit d'une si belle histoire.
      [I hope at least that a happy future will include my memory in your immortal deeds; and that one day my death, source of your glory, will introduce a splendid history.]

(B)

The mediocre poet who hastily ventured to *doubler* Racine on the myth of Phaedra and Hippolytus (in the theatrical jargon of the period, *doubler* meant to appropriate a subject on which an author was already working, and then to produce the play in competition with him) was not the first in France to expunge the incest from this myth. One Gilbert (*Hypolite ou le Garçon insensible,* 1647), and a certain Bidar (*Hipolyte,* 1675), had already taken steps to insure its compatibility with contemporary *bienséances* by making Phaedra merely Theseus' fiancée and not his wife. Nevertheless, the explicitness, the insistence, and the emphasis with which the protagonist of Pradon's *Phèdre et Hippolyte* denies that the flame consuming her is incestuous are worth noting for two interdependent reasons. First, because it seems likely, on the basis of the points of contact between the two tragedies, that Pradon, who claimed in the preface that the composition of his verses had occupied only three months of his time, had knowledge, before the performance, of Racine's tragedy, which had cost him two years of work. Secondly, because in Pradon the only person to hear the speech in question knows full well, as does the audience, that Phaedra is not yet married to Theseus. The result is thus awkwardly lacking in dramatic function; its function is rather that of a *réclame*, a polemic, or a precept, and cannot be explained without the rivalry with Racine. Here it is neither a Freudian nor a symbolic negation simply because the minimum of necessary depth is lacking:

> Non, non, les derniers noeuds des Lois de l'Hyménée
> Avec Thésée encor ne m'ont point enchaînée,
> Je porte sa couronne, il a reçu ma foi,
> Et ce sont mes serments qui parlent contre moi.
> Les Dieux n'allument point de feux illégitimes,
> Ils seraient criminels en inspirant les crimes;
> Et lorsque leur courroux a versé dans mon sein
> Cette flamme fatale et ce trouble intestin,
> Ils ont sauvé ma gloire, et leur courroux funeste
> Ne sait point aux Mortels inspirer un Inceste,
> Et mon âme est mal propre à soutenir l'horreur
> De ce crime, l'objet de leur juste fureur.
> [No, no, the final knots of the Laws of Marriage have not yet joined me completely to Theseus; I wear his crown, he has accepted my vows, my words speak against me. The Gods do not light illicit fires, they would be criminals to inspire crime; and when their anger filled my breast with this fatal passion and deep agitation, they saved my reputation. Their deadly rage cannot inspire Mortals to Incest, and my soul is not ready to withstand the horror of this crime, a just reason for their anger.][3]

This lesson in theatrical conformism, in respect for the audience, for the rules, for morality, and for the Gods, which is imparted to Racine by his rival through the words of his Phaedra, would be less interesting if it were unique. If, however, Pradon was able to read Racine's masterpiece beforehand, he must have sensed that it did not expose itself to cheap competition merely because of the moral scandal that it contained. He, who had begun his tragedy with the most conventional of prodigious and baneful omens (I, 1), who had introduced into it a no less conventional oracle (III, 2), and who had kept only the indispensable supernatural details in recounting Hippolytus' death (V, 5), also knew that he had managed things more properly than Racine in respecting his contemporaries' rational tolerance of myth. The hesitation, full of profound

---

3. *Le Théâtre de Mr de Pradon* (Paris, 1732), pp. 170-71. I have modernized the spelling.

significance, with which Racine had accepted the tale of the descent into hell in his text, is contrasted in Pradon with a much more "modern" and flatly pre-Enlightenment diffidence, where the genesis of the tale is actually revealed in two stages. It is popular credulity, uncouth and visionary, that provides the basis for mythical rumors; but if enlightened skepticism rejects them on the one hand, on the other the Machiavellism of the great exploits them. Hippolytus replies thus to his confidant, who has taken them seriously:

> Quoi? tu ne rougis pas d'une telle faiblesse?
> Prétends-tu m'éblouir des Fables de la Grèce?
> Peux-tu croire un mensonge? Ah! ces illusions
> Sont d'un Peuple grossier les vaines visions;
> Sans doute que Thésée a voulu faire croire
> Que jusques aux Enfers il peut porter sa gloire,
> Mais jamais aux Mortels de cet affreux séjour
> L'inexorable sort n'a permis le retour.
> Peut-il (enorgueilli d'une Race Divine)
> Dans les bras de Pluton enlever Proserpine?
> Traverser le Cocyte avec Pirythoüs,
> Bien qu'ils soient des Héros, Idas, c'est un abus,
> Quoiqu'au dessus de nous ils sont ce que nous sommes,
> Et comme nous enfin les Héros sont des Hommes.
> [What! are you not ashamed at such weakness? Do you wish to dazzle me with the Fables of Greece? Can you believe a lie? Ah, these illusions are the vain visions of an uncouth People; no doubt Theseus wanted it to be thought that he could bring his glory into the Underworld, but inexorable fate has never allowed Mortals to return from this frightful land. Could he (swollen with the pride of a Divine Race) snatch Proserpine from the arms of Pluto? To cross the Cocys with Pirithous is wrong, Idas, even if they are Heroes; even though they are above us, they are what we are, and like us, Heroes are really Human.][4]

When Theseus reappears, he rewards his son's rationality with an explanation that confirms it, praises it, and takes it for granted. In passing, the recollections of a Senecan or Virgilian Underworld become the very substance of deceit:

> Non pas, comme l'ont cru mille Peuple divers,
> Qui me font aujourd'hui revenir des Enfers,
> Du reste des Humains je distingue Hippolyte,
> A cent autres j'ai peint le Styx et le Cocyte,
> La flamme et les horreurs de ces Fleuves ardents,
> Et la sombre pâleur de leur mânes errants;

4. Ibid., pp. 161-62.

Mais je crois vous devoir un récit plus sincère,
Votre esprit est guéri des erreurs du vulgaire.
J'ai dû par politique en répandre le bruit,
J'ai d'un pareil projet un vain Peuple séduit...
[I am not, as countless different Peoples believe, returning from Hades today; I distinguish Hippolytus from the rest of Mankind; to a hundred others I depicted the Styx and the Cocys, the flames and the horrors of these blazing rivers and the grim pallor of the wandering souls. But I feel I owe you a truer account, your mind is now free from the errors of commoners. I had to spread the rumor for political motives, I overcame a vain People with such a plan...][5]

One need not inquire of a poet of Pradon's stature how such a demystification of myth can coexist in a single text with omens, oracles, and monsters. In the course of many pages I have attempted to demonstrate that an incredibly detailed and profound coherence is one of the results into which analysis may translate the immediate value judgment of a masterpiece. I believe that the result of an equally systematic analysis of the ugly would confirm its incoherence, but this is hardly an attractive task and has perhaps never been rigorously attempted by anyone. A purely negative coherence (in its lack of poetic daring) nevertheless links the two rejections by which Pradon tried to differentiate himself explicitly from Racine, thus offering us a final verification of the link between the two greatest pieces of daring in *Phèdre*. The moralistic rejection of incest conforms to the rationalistic rejection of myth.

5. Ibid., p. 187.

II
Theoretical Part

...une théorie dont les concepts restent obscurs, ou qui n'est que partiellement explicite, n'a pas beaucoup d'intérêt, ne fût-ce que parce qu'il est alors, en général, impossible de démontrer qu'elle est fausse. En revanche, on gagne toujours quelque chose à formuler avec précision une théorie, même absurde.

RUWET, *Introduction à la grammaire générative*

10
Limits of the Field and Aims
of the Method

If the discussion that I am about to undertake in the following pages were to be accompanied by examples on every appropriate occasion that presents itself, I should have had to conceive a much larger volume, so large that in all probability it would never have been written. The reader will therefore suffer from a shortage of summarizing exemplification, at least on those occasions in which he will not be able to provide it himself, for a theoretical discussion may also suggest the examples that it does not furnish. Nevertheless, this discussion derives entirely from the previous detailed examination of a single example. It may be considered as an attempt at developing systematically, in the direction of the general, the same methodological premises that I attempted to develop analytically, in the direction of the specific, in the first part of this book.

The example, however, will not so much consist of a particular literary text, Racine's tragedy, as of particular analytical procedures I conducted on that text. In Part I, the elaboration of the theoretical proposals was reduced to the absolute minimum necessary for the experimental grafting onto them of the analysis of the tragedy. Because of my empirical literary background, I felt a strong need to justify the interest in these propositions with an example that would be as extensively elaborated as possible. In the relatively short opening chapter, I was determined to maintain a discreet balance between the risk of being too vague and that of a premature and false rigor. I might not even have seen any cause later to abandon this discretion, were it not for the fact that, in retrospect, the exhaustive elaboration of one example both favored and called for that of the theoretical proposals. The result is this second part. Perhaps with its swift pace and concentration, it may gain in clarity what it loses through an almost total lack of new examples.

In the preliminary chapter of Part I, I asserted that the literary scholar can and should turn to Freud and derive from his work, not so much a correct psychology of the author, the audience, or the character, but rather models that pertain to the internal coherence of a language having, hypothetically, something in common with the language of the human unconscious. This presumed a reference to the important truth that, in Freud's description, the human unconscious may be known only insofar as it manifests itself as language. But of the forms of language or of manifestations of the unconscious examined by Freud—dreams, parapraxes, neurotic symptoms, jokes—the first three are noncommunicating forms of language, or even have the characteristic of disturbing communication. Only the last one implies conscious, voluntary, and socially institutionalized communication—the joke. Of course, the language of literature also implies this type of communication, and Freud's study *Jokes and their Relation to the Unconscious* (1905) is the work of his that comes closest to the problem of the relationship between literature and the unconscious. Thus, by implication, any more detailed consideration of this problem must reckon with this particular book. Not only will it be a constant point of reference in the following pages, but at a certain point (Chap. 12) I shall have to summarize it in part, comment on it from the perspective that concerns me, and attempt to adapt its terminology to that of much more recent studies on linguistic and literary theory.

The opposition between communicating and noncommunicating language clearly separates Freud's book on the joke from a book like *The Interpretation of Dreams* when one considers their respective objects, and the former is of far greater interest to the literary scholar. Nevertheless, the polemics that the first part of this study directed against the traditional applications of Freudian psychoanalysis to literature did not stress that particular opposition in those places where it indicated the truly fertile points of reference in the master's work. Indeed, I still believe that the literary scholar can learn infinitely more from *The Interpretation of Dreams* than from all that Freud ever wrote about art. The distinction lay rather between, on the one hand, all of Freud's great works of description of the unconscious through its manifestation as language, and on the other, his attempts at interpreting works of art in the light of psychoanalysis, centered not on language and its internal coherence but on the psychology and biography of the author. Having made this observation, I shall define the unique position that the book on jokes holds in Freud's work, so to speak, on two fronts. First of all, as I already noted, it is the only case in which the return of the repressed, or the semiotic manifestation of the unconscious, may be grasped in an act of socially institutionalized verbal communication. As I have no difficulty at all in considering the tales analyzed in the book as literature, and often of a high standard, I can say of this book what would be impossible to say for *The Interpretation of Dreams:* in it, from beginning to end, Freud discusses literature. Fortunately, however, he discusses it without ever shifting his attention from the fact of language, or from the necessary and impersonal psychological premises of its communication, to the individual psychology or biography of the person who produces it. This is what, in the second place, distinguishes the book from those studies that Freud devoted to official works of art and their authors.

Today, perhaps, these last-mentioned studies do not serve as a model for anyone and a polemic directed against them may seem anachronistic and superfluous. Nevertheless, Freudian psychoanalysis (often contaminated by that of Jung) has not ceased to be an extremely important point of reference for every kind of literary discussion in French culture of the past fifteen years. Today, as a consequence, it is also beginning to assume the same position in Italian culture. I have no intention of embarking on a history or a case by case discussion of all the recent incidences of psychoanalysis in literary theory and criticism. The synthesis of my reservations about each of these, and of my convictions about the choice to be made among the alternatives outlined in Freud's work, may better be introduced by a few systematic considerations. Today more than ever before, studies on literature present a babel of different methods, implying that there has always been, and still is, disagreement over the very objects to be studied. The question of *what* is to be studied should logically precede the question of *how* it is to be studied. Nevertheless, since one cannot know exactly what is being studied without at the same time clearly knowing what is *not* being studied, it seems to me that the first question to be asked should concern the whole and the parts of what *can* be studied.

The system of necessary and sufficient factors in every act of linguistic communication has been established by Roman Jakobson in a famous article, precisely with the aim of specifying those instances of linguistic communication in which the poetic function is dominant.[1] I should like to refer to this system of necessary and sufficient factors, though not in order to ask, as the great linguist does, to which dominant function each of these may give rise. I prefer to articulate the issue along the lines of the following two questions. First, in those instances where we take for granted that the poetic function is dominant, and we are speaking of a literary work, what is the specific consistency assumed by the necessary and sufficient factors of the act of communication? Secondly, to which of the categories of existing studies—since there exist a vast number of heterogeneous studies concerning the literary phenomenon—does each of these factors respectively give rise?

Let us distinguish with Jakobson: (1) a verbal MESSAGE; (2) an ADDRESSER

---

1. Roman Jakobson, "Closing Statement: Linguistics and Poetics," in *Style in Language,* ed. Thomas A. Sebeok (Cambridge, Mass.: M.I.T. Press, 1960), pp. 350-77.

who utters it; (3) an ADDRESSEE who receives it; (4) a CONTEXT in reality to which it refers; (5) a linguistic CODE in which it is formulated; (6) a CONTACT, physical in nature, through which it is transmitted. It should be clear that the specific consistency of these six factors will differ according to whether I consider the act of literary communication as such, constantly repeated through time, or, in each instance and above all, as an act of linguistic communication. Let us suppose, for example, that a friend is reading aloud to me in a room a poetic composition of many centuries ago. If I consider the simple and immediate act of linguistic communication, leaving out the literary institution from which it is derived, I shall have this constellation: (1) the MESSAGE will be the composition; (2) the ADDRESSER will be the friend reciting it; (3) the ADDRESSEE myself listening to it; (4) the CONTEXT will be the subject of the composition, insofar as I am informed of it; (5) the CODE will be the language of the composition—French or Italian or English etc.; (6) the CONTACT will be that which is established between my friend's voice and my ears, and which may be disturbed by a noise in the room or outside. Everything, in short, will be as though my friend addressed a sentence or a discussion on some topic to me, improvised at that moment and never to be repeated.

If, instead, I consider the act of literary communication as such, that is, as postulating an enduring social institution and an occasional individual participation in it, I shall necessarily have to modify the consistency of all the factors except (1) the MESSAGE. That is, I shall have to consider: (2) as the ADDRESSER, not someone who happens to be reading, but the author of the composition, long dead; (3) as the ADDRESSEE, not only someone who happens to be listening, but the whole series of listeners and readers, amateurs, and scholars who study the composition in the course of time; (4) as the CONTEXT, not only the amount of information that the composition imparts on its subject, but all the circumstances of reality distant in time that may be implied there; (5) as the CODE, not only the French or Italian or English language, but the set of norms or conventions of the literary genre taken into account by the composition, either by observing them or by violating them; (6) as CONTACT, not the momentary acoustic one, but the transmission, whether oral or written, in manuscript or in print, of the text of the composition over a period of time, including possible alterations.

In fact, the existence of a literary work cannot give rise to studies, nor even be an object of discussions, that do not take into account either one of these factors regarded singly or various combinations of more than one of them. One might discuss (1) the MESSAGE itself according to innumerable criteria. Above all, this first and fundamental factor, in relation to which the constellation of all the others is organized, will demonstrate clearly that my extrapolation from Jakobson can tell us very little about the methods of literary studies, but merely provide a preliminary identification and distinguishing of the objects. One might discuss (2) the ADDRESSER, the person and life of the author, in relation to the work or apart from it, or of the authors if there are more than one, or the authorship of the work if it is uncertain or disputed. The studies in this field range from a problem such as the Homeric one to biographies of the living; and it is unnecessary to add that even among biographies extremely diverse methods will be encountered. One might discuss (3) the ADDRESSEE, the fortunes of the work over a long or short period, in ancient or recent times, through collective or individual testimonials, factual or critical. The studies in this field range from the sociology of the nature and size of the audience, to the history of criticism, which reviews the opinions of readers who are considered authorities. One might discuss (4) the CONTEXT, the historical circumstances in which the work was produced and the author lived, either because they form the object of the work's discourse or because they might have conditioned the work during its genesis. Here the range is from a simple informative commentary on an allusion contained in the text to the relationships suggested by every variety of historicism or modern genetic structuralism. One might discuss (5) the CODE, all the links that exist between the individual work and subsequent and preceding literature, whether systematic links such as its belonging to a literary genre or individual ones such as reminiscence or resemblance. Here, too, the range is from the normative attitude of criticism before Romanticism and from the positivist search for the sources, to every variety of the modern studies on the tradition of the forms, themes, or styles. One might discuss (6) the CONTACT, the transmission of the text by physical means over a period of time, its integrity, authenticity, and fidelity, or, contrariwise, the cuts, interpolations, and corruptions it has suffered. This is the field of textual philological studies, which may be said to have preceded and surpassed all the others in scientific rigor, though they too present a variety of methods. Moreover, unlike all the others, they develop chiefly in pathological situations, though these are more frequent than the outsider might suppose, or when the text of a work is *not* intact or authoritative.

There arises the question of the usefulness of schematically distinguishing these objects of the studies, since the distinction between them tells us so little about the methods. This doubt seems further justified, I hasten to add, in that an individual study of a literary work very rarely takes all six factors into consideration, and it is also fairly unusual for any one of the factors to be examined in isolation from the others. The majority of literary studies, whatever their method, have carried out all the possible combinations of these six objects, each in its turn. Most often, the connection between two or more of these is so close that the problems faced by scholars would not even arise, or would be insoluble, if it were to be ignored. Conversely, it is just the failure to recognize it that on other occasions does not permit the problems to be posed or renders them insoluble.[2] Thus, in all my discussion there should not be any hint of proposing the criterion of a clear separation between the six fields of study as a criterion of the purity, coherence, or rigor of the method. The fact is, however—and it justifies or should justify this discussion—that it is as profitable to recognize the effective connections between the different factors of a phenomenon as it is harmful to confuse them as though they were not distinct at all.

A modest but significant proof of this may be found at a level below, or outside, a familiarity with the literary phenomenon or a professional qualification to discuss it. Anyone with experience in teaching literary history will realize that nothing characterizes the discourse of the un-initiated as much as the continual confusion between the text of a work, the life of its author, its fortune in the course of time, its relationship to its own age, its place in the literary system, and the vicissitudes of its transmittal. At a less elementary but didactically symmetrical level, one need only think of the present crisis of literary histories and of our uneasiness when reading the more outdated handbooks. Nothing charac-terizes their discourse as much as the confused shifting observed above, which can be encountered in one sentence in every three. And if one wishes positive proof at a higher level, the principal lines of modern criticism were laid down at the beginning of this century by overcoming the gross confusion between textual and biographical reality; this calls to mind not only Benedetto Croce, but, for example, a key work that long remained unpublished, Proust's *Contre Sainte-Beuve*. A method does not necessarily gain in purity, coherence, and rigor by imposing a considera-tion of the factors of literary communication in isolation but undoubtedly does so by teaching one to distinguish between them.

It is, then, precisely this constant risk of confusion between the experience of the addresser and the language of the literary message that vitiates Freud's essays on art. This is not a chance occurence. The relative dilettantism of these works does not justify the illusion that merely a little cunning applied to Freud's methodology without a change in approach can transform the risk of confusion into an illuminating connec-tion. Instead one should realize that the risk is inherent in Freud's discovery itself, in the intrinsic relationship between the science he founded and the study of literature. As a revolution in psychology, psychoanalysis was inevitably to alter profoundly a well-defined area of

---

2. See Appendix 5, "On the Intellectual Division of Labor."

literary studies—biography. At the same time, however, as the discovery of a language it was irresistibly tempted to invade the language of the literary work with its own analytical methods, and then to mix these results with those deducible from the other languages spoken by the author's unconscious, including the vicissitudes of his life as symptoms, thus turning the analysis back upon the person himself.

Freud's avowed intention in each show of interest in official art is invariably restricted to formulating psychological and biographical comments at the inviolable periphery of the aesthetic event. This limiting attitude of discretion, stemming from his very solid but traditional nineteenth-century humanistic *Bildung,* always prevents him, as E. H. Gombrich has convincingly demonstrated,[3] from realizing the most important repercussions of his discovery in the field of art. It was, of course, not actually possible for his incursions into this field to stop just at the borders of the aesthetic experience, if the seat of the aesthetic experience is truly language and if there can be no psychoanalytical discourse without the analysis of a language. Nonetheless, a Freudian analysis of dreams, parapraxes, or symptoms, however exemplary it might be as an analysis of language, is inconceivable without the individual history of a man, by which it is elucidated through countless threads and which in turn it helps to elucidate. Indeed, if we may speak here at all of a message in dreams and even in parapraxes and symptoms as a fact of language, we shall be obliged to affirm that this message may neither be interpreted nor considered important except in relation to an addresser. Who would be prepared to make the same statement about a literary message?

It is not enough to repeat that the languages of dreams, parapraxes, and symptoms, as distinct from that of literature, are noncommunicating and even less are socially institutionalized. Indeed, to recognize their nature as languages, unknown or misunderstood before Freud, means to recognize that these languages always speak to someone, even if to someone whom we do not know and who does not know he is being addressed. Yet, it should be added that their internal coherence does not require that minimum of self-sufficiency that would make them comprehensible to another person; for the most part, even the subject who is the addresser ignores their meaning. These are messages whose meaning is so repressed that it cannot be communicated and in fact normally has no addressee. If we consider the neurotic symptom in particular, psychoanalytical therapy consists merely in finding an addressee for this message within the person of its addresser, the patient, through the mediation of

3. E. H. Gombrich, "Freud's Aesthetics," *Encounter,* 26, no. 1 (1966): 30-40. See also the three essays having the collective title "Psychanalyse et littérature" in Jean Starobinsy, *La Relation critique* (Paris: Gallimard, 1970), pp. 255-341.

another addressee, the psychoanalyst, who is impersonal and skilled in deciphering. The extent to which such a situation differs from that of the literary message is quite obvious: in one sense it is the opposite, therefore explaining the misunderstanding and the suspicion that a comparison between the languages of literature and of the unconscious often arouses. The literary message virtually always postulates an addressee, and if it does not find one, either by chance or through incomprehension, it does not exist, it fails in the act of communication. Even the tempting analogies between the indecipherable nature of dreams and some literary phenomena, for example, much of western lyric poetry of the last hundred years, do not affect the diametrical opposition between the absence and the virtual indispensability of an addressee. The indecipherability of these texts is never so complete as to cause the act of communication to fail inoffensively, as would occur, for example, if they were written in an unknown language. Along with the glimmer of meaning that the addressee might perceive, and even if he grasped none at all, he would in any case understand the indecipherability itself as a connotation of meaning, usually esoteric or provocative. In extreme cases the act of communication will end here, but it will nonetheless have taken place and in its own way involved an addressee.

A message that postulates an addressee similarly requires that minimum of self-sufficiency lacked by the semiotic manifestations of the unconscious. I refer to a minimum of self-sufficiency because I do not believe that the comprehension of the literary message is independent of the circumstances of reality in which its addresser created it, nor of those in which its occasional addressee enjoys it, nor of those which may have influenced it during the passage of time between its creation and its enjoyment. The literary message is not torn from history at its birth, and it does not travel through history armed with an unalterable comprehensibility. It possesses a maximum of self-sufficiency for only as long as this can be supported by sufficiently stable historical circumstances, or when favorable ones are recreated. The precariousness and rarity of such optimal conditions render useful such contributions as those of the textual philologist, the literary historian, the historian *tout court,* and the biographer, who, in the systematic terms proposed above, are concerned respectively with the contact, the code, the context, and the addresser. All these contributions are aimed at increasing the understanding of addressees, far removed in time, of the literary message, precisely because in time that maximum of self-sufficiency tends to decrease toward the minimum. The object of the biographer's interest is a set of real situations concerning the addresser, of which the creation of the message was by no means independent. Neither was it independent of other sets of real situations: the collective circumstances of political and economic history that are a part of the context, the equally collective ones preexistent in the literary and cultural history of which the code is a part. The fact is, however, that a literary message is generally comprehensible, to a greater or lesser degree, even *without* a detailed knowledge of all these real circumstances.

The possibility of doing without a detailed knowledge of biographical circumstances seems to be necessarily greater than that of doing without the others. Let us consider the case where a real break in historical continuity has occurred, or where the message comes from a spatially distant cultural tradition. Here, the contributions of all types of philologists and historians might be needed, not only to increase the message's comprehensibility, but even to lay its foundations. Can one really imagine a case in which the biographer's contribution would have a similarly fundamental importance? It would appear not, if literature as an institution has an obviously social aspect, even when one attempts to extend the concept of literature beyond the traditional limits of this institution, as I shall attempt to do later (Chap. 13). A message needing to be retraced to the biography of its addresser in order to be understood would not be a literary message. By treating an actual literary message in this way, one arbitrarily equates its language to that of the human unconscious, which is noncommunicating because it lacks the minimum of self-sufficiency.

It is in this minimum quantity that for now the irreducible difference between the two languages will have to be identified, while it is the modes of their internal coherence, self-sufficient or not, which will constitute the basis I assert for their resemblance. We shall be able to find out more about the difference only after the basis for the resemblance has been stated less hypothetically. Nevertheless, we are beginning to understand why Freud, the marvelously penetrating biographer of Dora, the "Rat-man," and the "Wolf-man," disappoints us when he attempts a penetrating biography of writers and artists. The exercise, which consists in interpreting a literary message as one would interpret a dream, a parapraxis or a symptom, ignoring that aspect of it which is directed toward the addressee and adopting as a means and an end that aspect concerning the addresser, fails to do justice to the message, the addressee, or the addresser. In other words, it easily becomes an unsound critical exercise and is unlikely to be better as a biographical exercise. It is a typical example of the methodological danger of failing to distinguish between the various factors of literary communication. Nearly the whole history of the relationship between psychoanalysis and literary studies is one of voluntary imprisonment in or attempted escapes from this vicious circle: ADDRESSER → MESSAGE → ADDRESSER; the biography refers to the work which in turn refers to the biography. In less prudent hands than

Freud's, the confusion soon became even more serious and apparent, and the bad name acquired by methods inspired by Freud among professional literary scholars was not without justification.

Of a quite different interest is the method introduced later by Charles Mauron, with the name of "psychocriticism."[4] It is based on a special type of comparison, "superimposition," between different passages of works by the same author, and in any case involves an analytical and open-minded dwelling at some length upon linguistic facts in order to elaborate some frequently invaluable interpretations. Nevertheless, the method does not finally result in the total or partial interpretation of this or that work, but rather the identification of constants which may be derived from several passages of one or more works and which, as constants, refer back to something preceding the works, their author's unconscious. Thus at times in Mauron's writings, it may be a straightforward biographical exercise, having its point of departure in the texts, that breaks the vicious circle, reducing it to its second half: MESSAGE → ADDRESSER. On the other hand, it may be an equally correct exercise that attempts to interpret the variants in the light of the constants, to read deeply into the work by means of what is presumably revealed by the author's unconscious: ADDRESSER → MESSAGE. Anything, however, that has no specific part in either the author's experience or the work is irrelevant, and it is only when they leave the object of the discourse undecided between these two alternatives that Mauron's results seem to me to be tenuous.

At the present time, the influence of Freudian psychoanalysis in French culture is stronger than ever, and is filtered mainly through that reinterpretation of the master's writings, which the work of Jacques Lacan claims to be. This is a rereading that lays an extremely strong emphasis on the fact that Freud described the unconscious as a language, which is a fact even more interesting, for all literary scholars, than the effects of the discovery of the unconscious on those who occupy themselves with biographies. For this reason, I shall hereafter frequently refer to the thought of Lacan, who, moreover, with one brilliant and virtually inimitable exception,[5] has never personally put into practice the analysis of literary texts. His thought, however, can be used as the pretext for a nondifferentiating assimilation of the language of the unconscious to that of literature, a tendency encouraged by the crisis of communication in modern literature and by theoretical and polemical rejections of communication. There is, then, a risk that the addressee and his function will be deliberately ignored. The addressee will then figure only as a surviving

4. A theoretical synthesis is to be found in Charles Mauron, *Des Métaphores obsédantes au mythe personnel: Introduction à la Psychocritique* (Paris: Corti, 1964).

5. Jacques Lacan, "Le Séminaire sur 'La Lettre volée,'" in *Ecrits* (Paris: Editions du Seuil, 1966), pp. 11-41; Eng. trans. as "Seminar on 'The Purloined Letter,'" *Yale French Studies*, 48 (1972): 39-72.

witness, excluded from any active part in the meaning, a message-symptom having meaning in itself only because of the addresser's having presumably had an unconscious. The functional elimination of the addressee and even of the message (together with that of the meaning, a move considered to be liberating), leads us to rewrite the vicious circle of the worst of Freudian tradition as follows: ADDRESSER → ADDRESSER. Moreover, the liberation *from* meaning, celebrated as a liberation *of* meaning or as the creative will claimed from the addressee, in practice makes the apparently opposite vicious circle of ADDRESSEE → ADDRESSEE equivalent to the one just mentioned.[6]

Yet, on one occasion, Freud completely avoided this vicious circle and, interestingly enough, in just that case involving the least awe-inspiring of literary messages. I am referring, of course, to the book on jokes, and the paradox is only apparent. The modest nature of the material exempted Freud from the excess of academic respect normally displayed before the majesty of the aesthetic sphere. At the same time, the jokes' anonymity removed the temptation of becoming interested in the person of an author. Thus, a way was cleared for the semiotic analysis with which Freud had already successfully experimented on dreams, parapraxes, and symptoms. This time, however, not only did the self-sufficiency of the message correspond to the substantially reduced importance of the addresser, but its dialectic dependence on a literary code and its much richer and more unpredictable references also corresponded to a historical context. One cannot really say that the move from a noncommunicating to a communicating language has hindered Freud's analytical genius in confronting the formal features and semantic contents of the texts. The strongest proof of this lies in a seemingly obvious fact, whose very obviousness contains the methodological example directly opposed to that of Freud's works on art: the semantic contents that emerge from the analysis are much more varied, relative to the historical context, than those normally deducible from the noncommunicating languages of the unconscious.

Even in dreams, parapraxes, and symptoms, of course, Freud never immediately postulates the elementary oppositions of meaning that are dominant in the unconscious, but rather he identifies them by means of semiotic analyses that take into account a historical context. This is the essential (and sometimes overlooked) difference from Jung and his archetypes. The history in question, in the case of noncommunicating languages, can be for the most part only a history of the individual, and

6. See Appendix 2, "Constants, Variants, and Misreadings," and, on the *nouvelle critique* in general, Cesare Segre's comments in *I segni e la critica* (Turin: Einaudi, 1969), pp. 67-72; Eng. trans. as *Semiotics and Literary Criticism*, trans. John Meddemmen (The Hague and Paris: Mouton, 1973), pp. 54-58, and Michael Riffaterre, "Le Formalisme français," in *Essais de stylistique structurale* (Paris: Flammarion, 1971), pp. 261-85.

the area of the basic meanings accessible to analysis is inevitably circum-scribed by the same elementary oppositions that define it. Thus, in the literary studies inspired by Freud, naive attempts at biography and psychology go hand in hand with an exercise that has attracted no less discredit, nor deserved less: the perpetual deciphering of the same few symbols that involve the oppositions of phallus and castration, father and mother, the prenatal state and birth, life and death, food and excrement. It is an exercise in which Freudian eyes ought to recognize the features of tautology, of never erring yet never imparting any information except for a series of cases that may be listed quickly and abstractly, though they produce various textual results.

First there is the case—Freud was legitimately interested in examining it whenever possible—in which the poetic imagination anticipated by decades, centuries, or millenia, truths that would have to wait to be formulated until psychoanalysis touched upon them, fully grasped them, or, at least, questioned them. Then, there is the chronologically opposite and complementary case, in which the poetic imagination, after Freud, took pleasure in dealing with themes that derived from truths formulated by psychoanalysis. I am postulating, in both cases, contents that are as precise as they are limited, as pertinent as they are in them-selves abstract. Without detracting in any way from the importance of the problem of this reciprocal privilege that Freud recognized in the poets and then the poets, so to speak, recognized in Freud, one may maintain that similarly, in other cases, the variety of the contents of literature makes necessary a knowledge of dynastic history or political economy rather than of psychoanalysis. Very different and far more important is a third case, in which a pre- or post-Freudian literary work has taken up a psychic reality, which psychoanalysis has singled out as one of its principal and not merely occasional contents, and has insistently elabo-rated it and necessarily also formally organized itself around it. Using examples in which this psychic reality, for example, the Oedipus complex, was pointed out by Freud himself, I very much doubt whether it would not be prejudicial to any anlysis to ignore the insistence on it in *Hamlet* or *The Brothers Karamazov.* There it seems all the more obvious because it surfaces in historically well-defined forms, even though it is presumably a psychic reality of very broad historical import.

We now come to what is perhaps the most interesting case: that in which the insistence on a psychic reality singled out by psychoanalysis is instead "concealed," in which it is plausible that some referent of real, natural, or primary experience is hidden in the unreality of the mysterious and even overtly supernatural referents that alone are mentioned by the letter of the text. For example, from the mystics to the Romantics, from St. John of the Cross to Wagner's *Tristan,* I should not know how to interpret the metaphysical and erotic Night of which some texts speak if I did not associate it with the boundless, regressive longing for a physical state—the prenatal state. This physical state is still more universal than the Oedipus complex; the nostalgia it inspires is no less historically determined. There is often a relation between the impenetrability of the forms and the regressiveness of the contents, which certainly increases the "chances" of the interpretative symbolism of Freudian tradition. This is not surprising, for contents that are markedly "irrational" or enveloped in particularly "obscure" forms move the language of literature closer to that of dreams. For instance, the obsessive and frenzied nature of Poe's fantasy adds an undeniable interest to the identification of latent necrophilic constants in his tales.[7] It is the proverbial hermetism of Mallarmé's poetry that makes the semantic constants, all linked originally to the trauma of the death of a female love-object, invaluable in its interpretation.[8] Yet the interpretative symbolism of Freudian tradition is still threatened internally by the risk of its reducing and impairing that which it interprets, and it is limited externally by the quantitative and qualitiative importance of the texts to which it would be inapplicable without some degree of arbitration.

In his book on jokes, however, and without realizing it, Freud provided an example of semantic analysis which is applicable to literature in a quite different way because it follows the literal thread of the text much more closely. For once, there are no fixed meanings in his analyses, not even the most elementary or most profound ones articulated in the unconscious. It is as though Freud had guessed here that the area circumscribed and the level preestablished for such meanings can indeed still be arrived at from a concrete text, but only through an act of abstraction that eliminates the concreteness and ends up by giving predictably uniform results in every case. Is it therefore irrelevant, my readers might ask, that the author of analyses of jokes, carried out with such a marvelous feeling for the text, should also be the discoverer of the human unconscious? It is anything but irrelevant, yet if I were to anticipate the reasons for this, I should have to shift the discussion from semantic contents to the formal characteristics identified by Freud in the texts. For the present, I shall merely observe that, even with respect to these characteristics, the book is unique among his works.

Freud, while claiming energetically that in dreams the form is an

---

7. I am referring to the famous monograph, for which Freud wrote a very brief preface, by Marie Bonaparte, *Edgar Poe: Sa vie—son œuvre* (Paris: Denoël & Steele, 1933; reprint ed. Paris: PUF, 1958).

8. This is an exegetical tendency in which are linked, despite enormous methodological differences, Mauron, *Introduction à la psychanalyse de Mallarmé* (Neuchâtel: La Baconnière, 1950); Adyle Ayda, *Le Drame intérieure de Mallarmé* (Istanbul: La Turquie Moderne, 1955); Francesco Orlando, "Le due facce dei simboli in un poema in prosa di Mallarmé," *Strumenti critici*, 7 (1968): 378-412; Giampiero Posani, *Mallarmé: il tramonto di Dio e il mezzogiorno del capitale* (Naples: Guida, 1975).

irremovable part of signification, or even that one may call only the manifest form a dream and not its latent contents,[9] obstinately limited himself, in discussing official literature, to assigning to form the function of "softening," "toning down," "altering," "disguising" any major scandal in the contents.[10] In his writings on official literature, far from adding anything to the signification, the form seems rather to remove something that is socially and, therefore, aesthetically unacceptable to communication. In the book on jokes, the precision of his formal analyses, as well as the penetrating faithfulness and often beauty of his semantic analyses, are all the more inspired, because Freud had only the instruments of an age-old rhetorical tradition to rely on. The foundations of modern linguistics, laid out at almost the same time by Ferdinand de Saussure, would have remained unknown to him, not because of being chronologically out of phase, but as a result of the intellectual division of labor. In the preliminary chapter of the present volume (p. 7) I referred to this lost historical coincidence as a limitation and no doubt it is a limitation; yet the argument may also be reversed, giving us further cause to admire the least renowned of Freud's great books.

9. Sigmund Freud, *Introductory Lectures on Psycho-Analysis, Standard Edition,* 15: 177, 183.
10. Freud, *Creative Writers and Day-Dreaming, Standard Edition,* 9: 153; idem, "A Special Type of Choice Made by Men," *Contributions to the Psychology of Love,* I, *Standard Edition,* 11: 165; idem, "Some Character Types Met with in Psycho-analytic Work," *Standard Edition,* ibid., 14: 329; idem, *Introductory Lectures on Psycho-Analysis,* pt. 1, *Standard Edition,* 15: 99; idem, *Introductory Lectures on Psycho-Analysis,* pt. 3, *Standard Edition,* 16: 376; idem, "Dostoevsky and Parricide," *Standard Edition,* 21: 188.

11
Toward a Definition of the Return of the Repressed in Literature

It was relatively easy to demonstrate the ways in which the language of literature cannot be compared to that of the unconscious, and how one setting out to study literary problems may go astray, through either lack or excess, if he does not perceive this difference clearly enough. The discussion intended to point out what the two languages have in common will be incalculably more difficult than this *pars destruens.* Even despite the shortcomings in their preparation or subjective attitudes, at least three sciences would have to be appealed to, and they do not seem objectively ready to answer the call. Indeed the most "exact" of the three, linguistics, would be involved particularly in its least developed branch, semantics. In psychoanalysis it is precisely the semantic, not to mention the rhetorical, implications that have never been investigated and ordered in the manner or to the extent necessary. From the field of literary studies, whose objects it is essential but not sufficient to distinguish in order to find one's bearings amid a babel of methods, only a relatively small number of recent works can be of help. Thus, I must now restate the conviction, already expressed and put in practice in Part I: every precise hypothesis concerning a text and every exhaustive experiment carried out on the basis of it, though exposed to all the drawbacks which may derive from the imperfections of the theory, is at present more useful than any kind of more abstract exercise. Even now, of course, I shall not pretend to arrive at any definite conclusions as I reexamine the *pars construens* of the theoretical proposal which, in Part I, came before experiment and hypothesis. It is a question rather of establishing a certain number of firm concepts, of indicating the most serious doubts, and of defining the major problems.

One sentence in Part I, though not italicized in context as a definition, may be assigned the responsibility of a true definition of the artistic, and in particular the literary, phenomenon, according to the Freudian perspective in question. "A return of the repressed made accessible to a

ommunity of men but rendered harmless by sublimation and fiction. . ."
p. 19). It was no accident, however, that this sentence appeared at the
point at which the problem of the relationship between literature and
established order, raised in connection with *Phèdre*, was briefly extended
to include the succeeding evolution up to the present day. A number of
historical examples, and no longer an individual one, momentarily
justified the range of the definition. Yet can the expression "return of the
repressed"[1] really be extended to include the "contents not conforming
to the established order" mentioned at that point, or rather to the new
ideological and political contents, not necessarily related to sex, that
literature has taken up from the Enlightenment onward? Did there not
seem occasionally in my discussion to be a rather free-and-easy fluctuation
between the individual, unconscious, and sexual meanings of Freudian
origin, now in current usage ("that person is repressed"), and the no less
current politico-ideological meaning of the noun and verb ("the movement
was repressed," "police repression")? What proportion should be established between the two meanings, if the sentence quoted above is to be
taken as a serious definition?

What may seem even more questionable is that the hesitation that I
have just challenged was between the reference to certain possible
contents of a literary work and the reference to certaiñ others. Whatever
meaning one might wish to give the expression "return of the repressed"
in that sentence, it came at the climax of a discussion arising out of the
presence of a content that did not conform to the established order in a
tragedy of Racine—Phaedra's desire. In the theoretical premise occupying
that early chapter (exactly like the preceding pages of this second part),
the relationship between the unconscious and literature was not postulated according to the presence of contents, whatever their nature, in the
literary work. Rather there were properties presumed common in the
respective languages, which led to the setting up of a relationship. Indeed,
if dreams, parapraxes, symptoms, and jokes are semiotic manifestations
of the unconscious, and as such present certain constant characteristics, it
will then be possible to refer to the return of the repressed in relation to
the characteristics just as it is possible to do so in relation to the manifestations. Thus, it is of little importance that the expression was not actually
used yet in that introductory chapter. The preliminary theoretical
proposal contained there could easily have been formulated as follows:
literature or poetry is the seat of a socially institutionalized return of the
repressed, if, hypothetically "the language of poetry, like that of jokes

1. The following comments, on the use of the expression "return of the repressed" in the
first part of this book, serve the aims of a discourse in progress; nevertheless, the theoretical
questions arising out of its usage are exposed in as much detail as I am at present able to give
only in Appendix 1, "The Compromise-Formation as a Freudian Model."

has something in common with the inner logic of the unconscious" (p. 7).[2]

"Logic," "internal coherence," "characteristics," "properties" of a language: my terminology remains hesitant, and justifiably so. Nevertheless, it seems clear that we are now dealing with something different from the contents of the language itself: with a set of its qualities that I can call generically formal. If such qualities are sufficient to make a language the seat of a return of the repressed, the expression, when used in relation to that language, begins to acquire a third possible meaning. This is a unitary, if rather vague, meaning, which is contrasted with the two meanings I indicated when referring to the contents of literary works. As an outcome of this we now discover a second and broader hesitation, which may be described approximately in traditional terms as a fluctuation between a reference to form and a reference to content.

To sum up, then: in the proposition according to which literature is the seat of a socially institutionalized return of the repressed (the theoretical proposition developed throughout Part I), the expression "return of the repressed" actually or potentially took on in succession the following meanings:

(1) return of the repressed as the presence of formal qualities which may be assimilated to those of the language of the unconscious, according to Freud's description (pp. 4-7);

(2) or (2a) return of the repressed as the presence of contents censured by the social repression associated with sex (pp. 11-18);

(3) or (2b) return of the repressed as the presence of contents censured by ideological or political repression (pp. 18-20).

All of these terminological and conceptual comments concern the discussion preceding the actual analysis of the text of *Phèdre*. What happens, however, in the course of the analysis? Which of the three meanings or what combination of them turns out to be operative in the phase conceived as an experimental verification of the hypotheses concerning the poetic text? It is in this phase, I believe, that the absence of any real, fundamental contradictions in the fluctuations noted previously is implicitly assured, justifying the impression of unity that the essay, in spite of everything, may convey. Indeed, there is a return of the

2. As the dates of publication of the two books translated here reveal, I was unable to avail myself of the great work by Ignacio Matte-Blanco, *The Unconscious as Infinite Sets: An Essay in Bi-Logic* (London: Duckworth, 1975). For the moment I am pleased to observe that my insistence on a "logic" of the so-called Freudian unconscious, an experimental insistence, limited to literary theory and analysis, is supported by the authority of a work of much greater exactitude and of far wider import.

repressed in the very fact of the spectator's emotional identification with a character who embodies perverse desire and is completely guilty according to the social repression associated with sex. This is the second of the meanings that I differentiated, and it is, in the abstract, a meaning that refers to the content of the text. But in the concreteness of the text this content never emerges—my analysis is intended to prove this very point, first in general terms (pp. 21-39), then in detail (pp. 40-109)—without subjecting itself to a model like that of Freudian negation. Although this model dominates the whole of the text, it is never occupied by any other content. But the model of Freudian negation is a formal one, which in and of itself may be occupied by various contents; and it bears the characteristics of the language of the unconscious in being a semiotic compromise-formation which allows one to say yes or no to anything simultaneously.

Not only, then, is the first of the meanings of "return of the repressed" that I distinguished revealed to be as operative in my analysis as the second, because it is always present in the text of *Phèdre*, but, in the case of Racine's tragedy, it may even be said that the second tends to coincide exactly with the first. In other words, perverse desire could not have been acceptable as content in the literary work without the latter's also accepting the formal model capable of filtering it. The third meaning of "return of the repressed" is only indirectly pertinent to *Phèdre;* in fact it was considered before the analysis of the tragedy chiefly because a later literary evolution was being discussed. The themes of the failure of the father figure, the setback to established order caused by perverse desire, and of the proposal of an alternative order are not developed as ideological-political dissension. They are strictly motivated by the return of the repressed in a sexual sense and are wholly involved in its symbolic negation. Thus, "return of the repressed" always has in effect a single meaning in my analysis of *Phèdre.*

This conclusion may seem particularly comforting because the decisive unifying point has been identified in a formal aspect. Until now we have had no reason to lose sight of the fact that the traditional risk of methodologies inspired by Freud in the study of literature is a rough description of contents. However, it should be noted that the model of Freudian negation is far from exhausting all aspects of the text of *Phèdre* that may be termed formal. My analysis of *Phèdre* is almost exclusively semantic. This does not mean that within it the letter of the signifiers used by the poet is not frequently taken into account, or that the signifiers are not observed and compared; but this is only because they fall into groups and issue a specific signified in every case and never, or almost never, because they form stylistic, metric, or phonetic structures. My analysis concerns the side of the signified; it continually touches on that of the signifiers, because the two fit indissolubly together; but it nearly always treats the latter as a means in the exercise that concerns the former, and not as an end in itself.

I am well aware of the price of this provisional but necessary analytical abstraction and in particular of the dissatisfaction that may be caused by the fact that an essay on *Phèdre* has apparently been conceived as though the tragedy were not written in alexandrines, when, indeed, these are probably the most extraordinary group of alexandrines in French literature. But it is very difficult for an analysis to do without such necessary, even if provisional, abstractions. What matters is that the existence of the aspects of the work that are excluded is not at odds with any affirmations made about those aspects taken into consideration.[3] In these terms, it would still be possible to find, or at least imagine, an analysis proceeding from opposite and complementary strategic choices, into which ours could potentially be integrated. The same might be said of another strategic choice to which my analysis conforms and which sets it apart from the many (perhaps too many) recent studies that isolate and favor the narrative dimension of the texts studied. Mine is the direct opposite of an *analyse du récit.* It breaks down the text's own syntagmatic order into a series of quotations, generally overlooking the factors that depend on this, such as the actual succession of the verses and the course of the dramatic narration, in order to favor the reconstruction of a latent paradigmatic order in the text (p. 40); that which was identified for *Phèdre* in the system of symbolic negations. Nevertheless, to have pointed out that the analysis which refers back to this system is one that is concerned with the side of the signified raises a considerable new doubt.

In the introductory chapter, I mentioned that an essential point of contact between the respective languages of poetry and of the unconscious lay in what I termed the "predominance of the letter," or the "dominance of the verbal signifier" over the signified (pp. 6-7). On the one hand, Freud's analyses of dreams, parapraxes, symptoms, and jokes reveal that the unconscious engages in all kinds of mixing or shifting from one meaning to another, if the signifiers offer even the most casual coincidence, the vaguest resemblance, the most absurd possibility of being broken down. The unconscious, Freud states explicitly, tends to treat words as things. This is a point stressed by Lacan, in his ingeniously suggestive but, unfortunately, ostentatious and asystematic way, to the extent that he defines the unconscious as that which takes everything literally, as the domain of the signifier. In Lacan's thought, the dominance of the signifier goes so far as to question the very conception of meaning established by Saussure on an equilibrium or a symmetry between the two sides of the sign.

On the other hand, all modern reflection on poetry, whether concerned

3. See Appendix 5, "On the Intellectual Division of Labor."

with the writers' self-consciousness or the science of linguists, the specula-
tion of philosophers or the observations of critics, has insisted unduly on
the decisive importance of something that may essentially be grouped
under the name of signifier—to the greater or lesser detriment of the
importance accorded to the signified. From Mallarmé's famous objection
that verses are made of words rather than thoughts, one may range as far
as the theories of the Slavic formalists, for whom the poetic function of
language is that which stresses the signs themselves and reveals, in
Jakobson's terms, their "palpability."[4] Even the idealistic Italian aesthetic
tradition, with its emphasis on the identity of content and form, would
not seem so far removed from this trend if Croce's critical methods had
not so upset the balance in the direction of content. More recently, in two
studies on Dante by Gianfranco Contini, which certainly were not written
under Lacan's influence, one reads expressions that would nevertheless
appear to have been borrowed from him: "attention given the signifier
which is not impaired by that given the signified";[5] and even: "borderline
cases from which the dominance of the signifier over the signified clearly
emerges".[6]

Thus, the respect for the letter that is called for when dealing with the
language of the unconscious is equaled, though for reasons at first sight
quite different, by the respect for the letter demanded when dealing with
the language of poetry. This potential or partial convergence is most
interesting, and leads one to fantasize with a sense of regret about the
abortive hypothesis of an aesthetics derived from Freud, which might
have moved from the outset in the direction of specific formal tensions
rather than moving toward a more or less questionable study of contents,
symbols, psychology, and biography, which is what in fact occurred. But
was the allusion to the dominance of the signifier in my introductory
chapter later taken up and developed in the course of the analysis? And,
if so, how can this be reconciled with the statement that my analysis
concerns the aspect of the signified and shows relatively little interest in
that of the signifiers?

Let us have some examples. The verbal signs to which my analysis
attributes a central importance in the text of *Phèdre* are undoubtedly
monstre and *cacher*. Regarding their signifier, can one really speak of
dominance, preponderance, or prevalence with regard to the signified?
As far as *monstre* is concerned this is not only certain but obvious: the
poet plays almost openly on the shift between the moral-metaphorical

---

4. Roman Jakobson, "Closing Statement: Linguistics and Poetics," in *Style and Language,*
ed. Thomas A. Sebeok (Cambridge, Mass.: M.I.T. Press, 1960), p. 356.

5. Gianfranco Contini, "Un esempio di poesia dantesca (il canto XXVIII del Paradiso),"
in *Varianti e altra linguistica: Una raccolta di saggi (1938-68)* (Turin: Einaudi, 1970), p. 477.

6. Contini, "Un'interpretazione di Dante," in *Varianti e altra linguistica,* p. 385.

and the physical-literal sense of the word. The reality of mythical monsters in the discourse causes the monstrousness of perverse desire to be taken literally; in turn the monstrousness of perverse desire causes the reality of the mythical monsters to be taken seriously (pp. 26-28, 29-31, 54-56, 69-78, 99-104, and passim). A single signifier commands two objectively different meanings and, in assimilating them, transforms them into a more profound unity. The arbitrary verbal act that imposes such unification would be inconceivable in scientific or practical discourse and can occur only in poetic discourse—or in that of dreams, parapraxes, symptoms, and jokes. Anyone who thinks that a comparison with these latter phenomena is too bold because the double meaning of *monstre* is codified by the language need only observe, as I did, that the entire tragedy is built around that double meaning: it forms a bridge between the mythical elements of Hippolytus' death, Theseus' heroic deeds, Phaedra's line of descent, and the Jansenist sense of predestination.

We shall have even stronger grounds for speaking of an affinity with the language of the unconscious if the semantic process in question is considerably less obvious and therefore still more arbitrary. This is the case of *cacher,* which, as I have tried to demonstrate, unifies elements of objectively different content in *Phèdre:* the indications of the return of the repressed and the apparent eclipse of the repression, the prostration of Phaedra and Theseus' disappearance (pp. 77-79, 81, 92-94, and passim). The coincidence of these two situations, from the very beginning of the tragedy, is transformed by the unity of the signifier into a profound relationship of meaning, conditional or causal. Here no double meaning is codified by language, but only a bipolarity of references created obscurely within the text. To derive other, less central examples of these two from my analysis would be easy, were the solution to the problem not already in sight. The new unity outlined by the multivalent signifier as it repeats itself on the side of the signifiers, is then by definition (Saussure's), outlined on the side of the signified, thus giving rise to a new unity of meaning. This is why my analysis was able to make use of the principle of the dominance of the signifier while hardly ever abandoning the side of the signified. We must simply realize that, in the language of poetry or literature, the dominance of the signifier may take on two different aspects.

One implies dominance over the things signified, the shifting from one to another or mixing of more than one: it gives rise to an essentially semantic process and, thus, every time I have encountered it in the text of *Phèdre,* it has fallen within the competence of my analysis, formulated in the terms which are familiar to us. It should be added that this process is not necessarily linked to the permanent multivalence of individual verbal signifiers. If this were so, it would be impossible to identify in it a

dominant principle of the noncommunicating languages of the unconscious. Dreams, parapraxes, and symptoms express themselves through
verbal signifiers only in a very limited number of cases. In dreams it is
mostly images, in many types of parapraxes and of symptoms it is gestures
and modes of behavior that act as nonverbal signifiers and assert that
principle in their relation to the signified. Furthermore, the added
difficulty presented to the analysis by these nonverbal signifiers compared
to verbal ones — because they are less easily divisible into single units — is
also encountered in the nonverbal signifiers of the languages of other
arts than literature: the figurative arts, the cinema, music. The same
difficulty also arises for the language of literature if one tries to take into
consideration units made up of verbal signifiers but larger than the
individual word. Here, however, one is dealing with a theoretical
difference which, in literary interpretative practice, is frequently overcome
without much danger. Anyone who studies a literary text knows full well
what he means when speaking of an "image" or a recurring "theme";
elements like these may act collectively as signifiers, in relation to
particular meanings, just as well as the individual word. Thus, the
dominance of the signifier *cacher* in *Phèdre* gives rise to a theme which, as
I have pointed out, involves verbs that are synonyms of *cacher;* and this
should not seem contradictory, even though by definition synonyms
have a common signified and different signifiers. Thus, *monstre* also
gives rise to larger units, and there is also a dominance of the signifier
for the image or theme of the monster, for the complementary one of the
labyrinth, and for some of their components.

The other aspect assumed by the dominance of the signifier in poetry
or literature is that which emphasizes its acoustic effect, its phonic
consistency. Even from this viewpoint, the signifier is anything but
independent from the meanings it circumscribes, rather, in this instance,
its dominance coincides exactly with the poet's ability to derive additional
meanings from a purely acoustic effect, the mere phonic consistency of
the signifier. Thus arise the phonic, metric, or stylistic structures which,
as I observed earlier, are consciously avoided by the process of abstraction
that controls my type of analysis. To give but one example, when in
Part I (pp. 31 and 91), I quoted lines 965-66 of *Phèdre:*

> Moi-même, il m'enferma dans des cavernes sombres,
> Lieux profonds, et voisins de l'empire des ombres.
> [He imprisoned me in dark, deep caves, close to the realm of the dead.]

I commented on them by inserting them into a set of independent
meanings, some of them linked by the dominance of the signifier *cacher.*
The actual proximity to the kingdom of the dead of these dark and deep
caves that served as a prison for Theseus in Epirus derives its signified in

this complex; or, rather the signifiers making up the two lines quoted take on their signified in it. But those meanings I termed supplementary, which nonetheless emerge from the sensual dominance of the signifiers, are here due to the unique acoustic effect of the latter, particularly to the juxtaposition of at least seven nasal phonemes that create an echo (*en*ferma, *dans, som*bres, pro*fonds*, voi*sins*, *em*pire, *om*bres), and whose frequency might pass unnoticed or might seem annoying if these lines did not refer to dark and deep caves. Now, regarding this aspect of the dominance of the signifier, not only did I not remark on it in this instance, but in the whole of my analysis there is not a single remark referring to it. Perhaps there is just one, which takes into consideration the most famous enjambment in French poetry, in line 1446 of *Phèdre*, a metrical effect (p. 78). It would be superfluous to reiterate that this particular strategic choice is in no sense an underestimation of this aspect of the poetic phenomenon, nor of its special kinship to the semiotic behavior of the unconscious, which tends to treat words as things.

12

Freud's Approach and the Formal Return of the Repressed

If the analysis attempted in the first part of this book is both formal and semantic in nature, as seems by now established, the generic use of the terms "content" and "form" would henceforth appear to be insufficient for the purposes of my discussion. The "content" indeed belongs to the side of the signified, of which I began to speak in Saussurian terms; but one cannot speak of form with reference only to the signifiers. The signified are also organized into formal structures in the text of *Phèdre* and, as we have seen, it is these that occupy my analysis. Therefore, instead of continuing to contrast those two traditional terms, I shall need to link them and refer to a "content-form." The reader with some acquaintance with structural linguistics will be thinking at this point of Louis Hjelmslev's *Prolegomena to a Theory of Language*, which refers to "content-form," and in which Saussure's bipartition of the sign into signifier and signified gives way to a division into four, implying in turn not four concepts but six. Hjelmslev calls the side of the signifier *expression plane* and that of the signified *content plane*. Both these planes postulate a *purport* which has no individual linguistic existence or which "exists provisionally as an amorphous mass, an unanalyzed entity."[1] On the one side, there is the inarticulate phonetic *continuum,* expression-purport; on the other, equally undivided, is the real or conceptual *continuum,* content-purport. On both planes it is only when the purport is demarcated by a linguistic *form* (in ways that differ from one language to another) that it becomes linguistic *substance* of the form itself.

No doubt it is both useful and possible for a literary text or discourse, as it is for any other discourse, to distinguish the "expression-form" from the "content-form," and the former and the latter respectively from the "expression-substance" and the "content-substance," and the linguistic combination of all four from the nonlinguistic "expression-purport" and

1. Louis Hjelmslev, *Prolegomena to a Theory of Language* (Madison, Milwaukee, and London: University of Wisconsin Press, 1961), p. 50.

"content-purport." However, Hjelmslev's distinctions have more than once inspired analyses of literary texts in which they were not applied, as they could or should have been, to discourse of any kind, but rather as an attempt to grasp the specific organization of the sound and/or the meaning in literary texts as such.[2] I myself made such an an attempt in studying a prose poem by Mallarmé.[3] Thus even now, if I state that my analysis of *Phèdre* concerns the "content-form" rather than the content or meaning in general, clearly two different things may be understood by "content-form": that which, according to Hjelmslev, may be identified in any discourse, or a complex of structures of meaning, relationships of oppositions and similarities, which characterize *Phèdre* as a literary text.

It is also clear that the statement would be inexact in the first sense and is justified only in the second, because my analysis is concerned with that very complex of structures of meaning. Thus, the same need arises to specify the applications of the division of the sign according to Hjelmslev, as it did with Jakobson's system of the factors of communication, once I have attempted (Chap. 10) to transfer it from linguistic communication in general to the particular form of communication which we call literature. Though we still lack any real definition of the latter, we should not be surprised by this need. We must obviously conceive the relationship of literature to language as that of a part to a whole, but as a part having its own characteristics with which all general concepts must reckon; and, furthermore, presumably as if language were not the only semiological whole of which literature is a part. It is both the existence and the nonexclusive nature of this relationship of part to whole that frequently contributes to linguists' diffidence when faced with the literary applications and specifications of their general concepts.

Equally evident is the need to extrapolate the terminology that may be derived from Hjelmslev if, as well as discussing "content-form" as distinct from "content-substance" and "expression-form," I can also speak of "content-purport" as distinct from all of these. I recalled that, according to Hjelmslev, the "content-purport" has no linguistic existence, and thus in a certain sense, and by definition, is that about which one cannot speak. But only in a certain sense. When Hjelmslev observes that the French words *je ne sais pas* and the English words *I do not know* and words from other languages "despite all their differences have a factor in common, namely the purport, the thought itself,"[4] it is indeed true that one cannot speak of this purport unless it has become the substance of a

2. See Cesare Segre, *I segni e la critica* (Turin: Einaudi, 1969), p. 81, n.; Eng. trans. (The Hague and Paris: Mouton, 1973), p. 67, n. 40.

3. Francesco Orlando, "Le due facce dei simboli in un poema in prosa di Mallarmé," *Strumenti critici,* 7 (1968): 378-412.

4. Hjelmslev, *Prolegomena,* p. 50.

form that circumscribes it, using words of French or English or another language. Nevertheless, it is also true that in the sentence quoted above, in his linguistic metalanguage, Hjelmslev himself effects the act of abstraction which identifies that purport as the factor common to formulations in various languages. In order to carry out this act of abstraction, to identify a conceptual "content-purport" as the common factor in two different formulations (and by definition, if the form is different, so is the substance), there is no need, in my view, for the two formulations to belong to two different languages. The French words *je ne sais pas* not only have the same "content-purport" as the English words *I do not know,* quoted by Hjelmslev, but also as the French words *je l'ignore.*

What in all of this may be of interest to the scholar of literature? Above all, the fact that to be able to speak of "content-purport" with reference to a specific work, as with reference to any individual discourse, is a process of abstraction infinitely easier than speaking of it with reference to a language or, even more so to languages as a group. One might argue as to whether something that has not been endowed with linguistic formulation is knowable by man, and an idealist will say that anything having no linguistic existence has no existence whatsoever. But it seems less debatable to me that many other discourses, literary or not, can speak of the "content-purport" of *one* individual discourse, which is considered as literary, whether they do it spontaneously, as for example a historical witness, or artificially, as for example an explanatory paraphrase. The metalanguage of the scholar is only one of many and obviously one of the most artificial. The idealist might then object that the "content-purport" of a literary work is interesting only because it has become the substance of a form. He might even argue that only this form is of interest. In extreme cases he may declare it ineffable, thus preventing any kind of analysis, and then the scholar's metalanguage will contradict itself or be reduced coherently to silence. I share none of these attitudes, however, even if the result at which I arrived above (Chap. 11) located the decisive point of unification of my analysis of *Phèdre* in a formal aspect—thus avoiding, as I mentioned, a rough description of contents. This might seem surprising as the result of a discussion inspired by Freud, if it were to leave us exposed in return to what I shall term the formalistic temptation.

The meaning of my words will be clear because this is a temptation that has exerted its influence over most of modern aesthetic thought, whose general currents I have mentioned, beginning with the claims of the first great writers of the bourgeois crisis in the nineteenth century. The effective results have been and continue to be innumerable and often increasingly pretentious, and they will probably continue to be so for at least as long as the crisis of the bourgeoisie itself remains unresolved. From its outset, many artists, critics, philosophers, and linguists have clearly seen, confirmed, and closely examined, often irrefutably, the rigid conceptual distinction between what is or is not yet a part of literature, between the potential "content-purport" and the substance already formed from it, to use terminology extrapolated from Hjelmslev, which should by now be clear. This distinction is indispensable to understanding the specific function of the literary phenomenon among all the other phenomena of human reality, but it easily becomes an idealistic alibi if it creates the illusion that the connections between literature and reality are nonexistent or of secondary importance. It would seem no mere accident that an awareness of this distinction has continued to grow since the culmination of the bourgeois era, both with respect to its indispensability and to the abuses to which it may lead. I suppose that those who have become aware of it, especially artists, have benefited, even without realizing, from an increasingly peremptory social conditioning, that of the modern intellectual division of labor, and have both suffered its harm and been taken in by its mirage. A strongly specialistic attitude may inadvertently lead one from having clear ideas about a particular occupation to the illusion of its autonomy or supremacy. A note by the young Marx observes that: "The occupation assumes an independent existence owing to a division of labor. Everyone believes his craft to be the true one. Illusions regarding the connection between their craft and reality are the more likely to be cherished by them because of the very nature of the craft."[5]

If, however, an awareness of this dependence does not abolish the conditioning, it can, in theory at least, eliminate the need to create illusions. There is no reason to fear a priori that the conceptual distinction in question must inevitably generate the idealistic illusion, or that the identification of form as constituting the literary phenomenon must cause one to yield to the formalistic temptation. A Marxist outlook, which links the "content-purport" of a work of art to the political and economic situation preceding its genesis, may effectively condition one who analyzes how in a work this purport has become the substance of a form; and it may in turn benefit from the results of such an analysis. I can say the same of a Freudian view of that "content-purport," which is every possible return of the repressed inherent at a given point in history in the social repression involving sex. My analysis of *Phèdre*, insofar as it can be regarded as valid, is a proof of this.

Whereas I spoke at first in general terms of "content" and of a relative sexual or ideological-political return of the repressed, I shall, henceforth, speak much more restrictively of "content-purport." Nevertheless, I will

5. Karl Marx and Friedrich Engels, *Collected Works* (New York: International Publishers, 1976), 5: 92. See also Appendix 5, "On the Intellectual Division of Labor."

not discuss it in order to claim generically the existence, in relation to literature, of an actual or conceptual raw purport, which precedes any literary or even linguistic viewpoint and is susceptible of being considered outside both of these. The usefulness of this terminological specification will immediately become more obvious, if I now undertake to refer point by point to Freud's book on jokes.[6] It was just these particular problems that led me to realize that the lesson to be learned from the only text in which Freud characterized the return of the repressed in a communicating language is of a more general importance than was apparent at first glance. Anyone who agrees that I may accept as good literature the tales in which Freud analyzed jokes will not be surprised if I believe that some of the broad outlines of his examination of this limited textual category can be extended to literature in general.

Freud immediately poses the problem of deciding what it is that makes the first example a joke. He adopts the procedure of "reduction," attempting to express the same "thought" in other words. He observes that the character of the joke is then inevitably lost and concludes that it is linked to the "form," to the "wording in which it is expressed" (16-17). This obviously pertains to the entire category of jokes, that play upon the true verbal signifier (*Wortwitze*). For another category, however, Freud has to admit that changes in wording are feasible without destroying the joke; but even in this case, beyond a certain point one reaches the point of reduction that causes the joke's elimination, and this is when the "train of thought" is altered (51-52). These are the jokes that play upon the latter (*Gedankenwitze*). Freud terms "techniques" of the joke and analyzes with great detail and insight the complex of its characteristics which may be suppressed, along with the very essence of the joke, through the procedure of reduction. The quality of being a joke depends on the techniques, or, in other words, on the indissoluble "expression-form" and "content-form," with a greater degree of specific dependence on the former in the case of verbal jokes compared to those that play with thoughts.

The reduction that destroys the joke as such by altering the wording or the train of thought is still carried out on the basis of the joke, however, and still retains something that is a remnant of it. I tend to conceive of this something as a conceptual "content-purport," preceding and external to the formation of the joke and, obviously, understandable only in that it takes on a new form in the reduction. Let us consider the first example in Freud, borrowed from Heine: "he treated me quite *famillionairely*." Here the proposed reduction is, "he treated me...quite familiarly, that is, so far as a millionaire can." The sentence Freud adds just following

6. All quotations are taken from Sigmund Freud, *Jokes and their Relation to the Unconscious, Standard Edition*, vol. 8. Page references are given in parentheses in the text.

this, however, is merely a second, more abstract, proposal of reduction: "a rich man's condescension...always involves something not quite pleasant for whoever experiences it" (17). These three statements, of which only the first is a joke and to which, I believe, could be added as many more following the same criteria, obviously have a different "content-form" and thus "content-substance" in each case. Nevertheless, they have in common a conceptual "content-purport," just as *I do not know, je ne sais pas,* and *je l'ignore* have, and as formulations of quite unequal length can have, for example, a brief passage of literary language and a long passage of interpretative metalanguage that "reduces" it in stages.

It would seem, therefore, that one cannot really speak of "content-purport" unless at least three discourses are involved: the two that supposedly have a common "content-purport" and a third that abstracts it as something shared by the other two, a formulation, a reformulation, and a confirmation, if only implicit, of their relationship. I could say that in Freud's book the examples of jokes constitute the first discourse, the proposed reductions the second, and the comments that precede and follow the comparison, which take advantage of the abstraction of a "content-purport," the third. I believe that any interpretative work aiming at objectivity proceeds in essentially the same manner when dealing with any kind of literary text, as long as its main concern is the message and not the addresser, the context, the code, the contact, or the addressee. Once again, I have merely demonstrated the application to the metalanguage of literary interpretation of a principle recognized by linguists on a more general basis, one which has been termed "the metalinguistic function of discourse."[7]

The process of reduction and the possibility it offers of abstracting a "content-purport" by comparing an uncharacterized form to a characterized form, provides the basis for an important distinction effected by Freud, the distinction between jokes "lacking in substance" (*gehaltlos*) and those "of great substance" (*gehaltvoll*). The "substance" or value in question is naturally that which we ascribe to the "thought" within the joke after having exposed it via the process of reduction (92-95), and which must not be confused, therefore, with the value of the joke itself, or rather, in

---

7. See A. J. Greimas, *Sémantique structurale* (Paris: Larousse, 1966), pp. 72-73, in particular: "This principle of the equivalence of unequal units...; when applied to the facts inside a language, emphasizes the metalinguistic aspect of the functioning of discourse, which from that moment appears as important as its linguistic aspect proper. To put it simply, this principle merely means that something may be presented just as easily in a simple manner as in a complicated one, that a single word may be explained by a longer sequence and, inversely, a single word may often be found to refer to what had previously been conceived in a developed form." See, too, Roman Jakobson, "Boas' View of Grammatical Meaning," in *The Anthropology of Franz Boas,* Memoirs of the American Anthropological Association, no. 89, *American Anthropologist,* 61, no. 5, pt. 2 (1959): 143-44.

the final analysis, with that of its technique. The distinction is between a case in which the form is self-sufficient and another in which its value is present alongside a preceding and external value, attributed to the conceptual "content-purport." But another, more important distinction is made in the book, again between the case of a self-sufficient form and one whose resources serve the purposes of something else, by which they, the resources, are in turn strengthened beyond measure. I am referring to the distinction between "innocent" (*harmlos*) and "tendentious" (*tendenziös;* 90) jokes, which, as Freud points out, does not coincide at all with the preceding one (92). How should we deal with these two distinctions, if we read or summarize Freud's text at this point, in the hope that it will be possible to extend its thesis to literature in general?

The distinction between jokes that lack or do not lack valid substance opposes the form to any type of "content-purport." If we were to extend this distinction to literature in general, we should experience some difficulty, particularly because it would be much more problematic to determine the limits within which we might still speak of literature than it was for Freud to establish which texts should be analyzed as jokes. Thus, while we might not always doubt the formal qualification of texts that seem to be lacking in a conceptual "content-purport" of great substance or value, we might hesitate to refer as literature to other cases of indisputable value for fear that the formal qualification was insufficient. The former could occur with commonplaces being expressed through sublime verses, the latter with great texts of a scientific, political, historical, journalistic, moral, philosophical, or religious nature. And yet there might be some instances where the indisputable value of the "content-purport" would demand singling out for its own sake, despite the presence of an equally indisputable and valid formal qualification. Freud has nothing new to tell us about the manner of such a case of coexistence within the confines of the joke. The distinction in question remains as impossible to reject as it is to apply, as long as the limits of literature continue to be entirely undefined.

Fortunately, where the distinction between tendentious and innocent jokes is concerned, Freud has many new things to say about the coexistence of something that may be considered as "content-purport" with that which is articulated at the level of "content-form" and "expression-form." "Tendentiousness" is, of course, a particular kind of "content-purport" and is in fact the return of the repressed considered at that level. "The repressive activity of civilization brings it about that primary possibilities of enjoyment, which have now, however, been repudiated by the censorship in us, are lost to us. But to the human psyche all renunciation is exceedingly difficult, and so we find that tendentious jokes provide a means of undoing the renunciation and retrieving what was lost" (101). What kinds of tendentiousness are possible within the joke? In the first place Freud divides these into "hostile" and "obscene," according to whether the return of the repressed is inherent in the social repression which restrains sexuality or that which restrains aggressivity (97). Aggressivity, however, does not necessarily pick on individuals as its direct target.

In a series of pages that are among the most admirable he ever wrote, Freud demonstrates first of all that the tendentious joke is inclined to attack people in positions of authority, and therefore is apt to become critical or rebellious toward authority itself (104-5). He then discovers a category of aggressive jokes with false targets, which "are in a position to conceal not only what they have to say but also the fact that they have something—forbidden—to say" (106). Here, behind the superficial derision of an inappropriate or undeserving victim, is concealed a penetrating attack on a social condition through the people who most directly benefit from it or are most directly responsible for it (105-9). The attack may, however, also be aimed at "institutions, people in their capacity as vehicles of institutions, dogmas of morality or religion, views of life which enjoy so much respect that objections to them can only be made under the mask of a joke and indeed of a joke concealed by its façade" (108-9). Thus, there arises the category of "cynical" jokes, whose protagonists' most secret thought "would like to say seriously 'the man is right,' but, owing to an opposing contradiction, does not venture to declare the man right except on a single point, on which it can easily be shown that he is *wrong*" (109). Finally, with a single, excellent example, Freud illustrates the possibility of "skeptical" jokes, which question the conditions of truth and the certainty of knowledge (115).

It is all the more evident that in these jokes the "wit" lies in a linguistic compromise-formation, because Freud often reexamines them from the viewpoint of their tendentiousness after having examined them in the preceding chapter from that of their technique. Tendentiousness is no ordinary "content-purport." To recognize in it the return of the repressed considered as "content-purport" means also to postulate something particular in the corresponding "content-form," if by definition the return of the repressed is a semiotic manifestation of the unconscious. This would immediately lead us back to form or technique as being that on which the existence of the joke depends; it should, in fact, be able to exist even without tendentiousness in the contrasting category of "innocent" jokes. Before considering Freud's final conclusions on the subject, I must dwell a bit longer on the problem of tendentiousness as "content-purport." I should observe that, according to Freud's division, it corresponds more or less exactly to the meanings (2) and (3) of the expression "return of the repressed" spelled out above (Chap. 11) in reference to my analysis of

Phèdre. Respectively, "obscene" tendentiousness and meaning (2) involve contents that are censured by the social repression surrounding sex, and "hostile" tendentiousness and meaning (3) involve contents censured by ideological and political repression.

It may seem rather an exaggeration to speak of the latter contents with respect to jokes that are aggressive on a purely individual level, but even these are made at the expense of the social pact of nonaggression in its historically determined forms. But anyone who has read the pages in which Freud interprets on the basis of their tendentiousness those that are "aggressive toward a false target," "cynical," and "skeptical," will agree that the interpretation in each case involves the foundations of an established order, or of fixed current beliefs. I shall relate only one convincing example. Here is the more amusing of two anecdotes that are commented upon together:

> An impoverished individual borrowed 25 florins from a prosperous acquaintance, with many asseverations of his necessitous circumstances. The very same day his benefactor met him again in a restaurant with a plate of salmon mayonnaise in front of him. The benefactor reproached him: "What? You borrow money from me then order yourself salmon mayonnaise? Is *that* what you've used my money for?" "I don't understand you," replied the object of the attack; "if I haven't any money I *can't* eat salmon mayonnaise, and if I have some money I *mustn't* eat salmon mayonnaise. Well, then, when *am* I to eat salmon mayonnaise?" (49-50).

Freud already examined this anecdote from the standpoint of its technique (50-53), but his commentary in the chapter on tendentious jokes is quite astonishing, if one remembers that many conservatives have seen in him (and many progressives have reproached him for being) an advocate of repression:

The two anecdotes are simply epicurean. They say: "Yes. The man is right. There is nothing higher than enjoyment and it is more or less a matter of indifference how one obtains it." This sounds shockingly immoral and is no doubt not much better. But at bottom it is nothing other than the poet's *"Carpe diem,"* which appeals to the uncertainty of life and the unfruitfulness of virtuous renunciation. If the idea that the man in the "salmon mayonnaise" joke was right has such a repellent effect on us, this is only because the truth is illustrated by an enjoyment of the lowest kind, which it seems to us we could easily do without. In reality each of us has had hours and times at which he has admitted the rightness of this philosophy of life and has reproached moral doctrine with only understanding how to demand without offering any compensation. Since we have ceased any longer to believe in the promise of a next world in which every renunciation will be rewarded by a satisfaction — there are, incidentally, very few pious people if we take renunciation as the sign of faith — *"Carpe diem"* has become a serious warning. I will gladly put off satisfaction: but do I know whether I shall still be here tomorrow? *"Di doman non c'è certezza."*

I will gladly renounce all the methods of satisfaction proscribed by society, but am I certain that society will reward this renunciation by offering me one of the permitted methods—even after a certain amount of postponement? What these jokes whisper may be said aloud: that the wishes and desires of men have a right to make themselves acceptable alongside of exacting and ruthless morality. And in our days it has been said in forceful and stirring sentences that this morality is only a selfish regulation laid down by the few who are rich and powerful and who can satisfy their wishes at any time without any postponement. So long as the art of healing has not gone further in making our life safe and so long as social arrangements do no more to make it more enjoyable, so long will it be impossible to stifle the voice within us that rebels against the demands of morality. Every honest man will end by making this admission, at least to himself. The decision in this conflict can only be reached by the roundabout path of fresh insight. One must bind one's own life to that of others so closely and be able to identify oneself with others so intimately that the brevity of one's own life can be overcome; and one must not fulfil the demands of one's own needs illegitimately, but must leave them unfulfilled, because only the continuance of so many unfulfilled demands can develop the power to change the order of society. But not every personal need can be postponed in this way and transferred to other people, and there is no general and final solution of the conflict. (109-10)

The almost imperceptible step from repressed in a sexual sense to repressed in an ideological-political sense that occurs in the first part of this book is neither new nor arbitrary in a genuinely Freudian perspective. I do not believe one should be surprised at this, despite widespread prejudice and misunderstanding. Both systematic descriptions of the psychic apparatus successively proposed by Freud postulate the individual's interiorization (censure, super-ego) of a repression that transcends him in that it precedes him and is collective. Thus, in the discourse of psychoanalysis, which is preeminently a historical science concerned with the individual, an irreducible space is left open to the occurences of a wider sense of history. For this reason, with even the most trivially individual example of a repressed, the sin of gluttony, the repression in whose spite it asserts itself is still a social fact. The language in which the former asserts itself may well be that of a mere joke, but it can secretly go so far as to negate the latter. If the joke is very good, and it is Freud who develops its reduction, out of it will emerge the most important social problems of the height of the bourgeois era: from the ideological void following the decline of religion to the masking of the advantage of a privileged minority as a moral precept. Perhaps the hypothesis of a return of the repressed in a communicating language, whether it is restricted to jokes, as Freud did, or taken further, leads inevitably to the same threefold result with its double bifurcation, between reference to form and reference to content, and then between reference to sexual contents or ideological-political contents. It would seem to be no random occurrence that the three most important aspects of Freud's thought are reflected in this threefold result: (1) the knowability of the unconscious through its manifestations as language and their characteristics; (2) the underlying primacy of sex, or more correctly of the "pleasure principle" compared to the "reality principle," in the psyche; (3) the conception of civilization as the perpetual evolution of a constant dialectic between repression and repressed.

We have seen that tendentiousness in jokes corresponds as "content-purport" to the last two cases. But the time has come to examine what particular elements in the corresponding "content-form" must be postulated on the basis of "content-purports" of this kind. Tendentiousness may or may not be present, said Freud, and thus there are "innocent" jokes. Nevertheless, if we return to the broader instances just identified behind the two types of tendentiousness we find something in both of them that may be generalized, something whose indispensability to a communicating language, though it be a language dependent on the unconscious, we can no longer deny. From example (2) derives the need for such a language to produce pleasure, within its addressee if not its addresser. Otherwise what would be its point? From example (3) derives the need for such a language to be filtered through compromise-formations. How else could it find a place within a social institution? But if every joke shares these needs, the latter will also be extendable to those formal or technical features whose elimination disperses the joke and in whose absence it cannot exist. Not surprisingly, then, in the initial analysis dedicated to them, the techniques themselves seemed to Freud to be necessary but not sufficient for the existence of a joke (28, 42, 73, 80). Neither is it surprising that at a much more advanced stage of the discussion than that in which he established the difference between innocent and tendentious jokes, Freud ends up by criticizing this distinction, recognizing that the joke is never quite free from tendentiousness (132-33).

The technique, in fact, generates pleasure in itself (94-5), but it does so by protecting the access to certain sources of pleasure from a repressive prohibition that would otherwise preclude it by effecting a typical compromise (130). Thus, the return of the repressed that takes place in the "content-form" still implies some satisfaction of both these instances that can also assert themselves separately as "content-purports," and which as such I have so far always termed "tendentiousness." I am certainly not maintaining that in this way the three meanings of "return of the repressed" postulated in the first part of this book merge together, and I still believe that their differentiation is useful. But it does seem to me that only at this point, by means that completely avoid every formalistic temptation, is it obvious why meaning (1) concerning "content-form" may either include meanings (2) and (3), concerning the purport, or do without them. A communicating language, though dependent on the unconscious — jokes or literature as a whole — may or may not be tendentious in its purport, but it cannot help but be tendentious in its form.

If this form (forgive the unavoidable pun) forms pleasure and is formed as a compromise, with what pleasure and what compromise are we dealing? The question is crucial, of course. By asking it and seeking an answer in Freud's text I shall have ceased avoiding the crux of this question, around which my discussion has so far been revolving at a distance: what is it that hypothetically assimilates the language of literature to that of the unconscious? The strictly psychological solution to the problem is that both the pleasure and the compromise are to be brought back to an "economy . . . in psychical expenditure," as is also the accommodation of tendentiousness as purport within the joke (118-19). However important it may be, there is no need to sum up Freud's discussion of the issue here, for we are concerned with the strictly semiotic causes and effects of this "economy." The techniques of the joke could accomplish this by introducing into a communicating adult language modes of treating words and thoughts that are familiar in early childhood and preserved in the unconscious, but rejected by the adult and conscious use of words and thoughts.

Let us take verbal jokes as an example. As we have seen, their manipulation of the signifiers involves the "expression-form" even before that of the "content-form," and this brings us closer to the phonic aspect of the dominance of the signifier so essential to poetry. Freud observes, "We notice, too, that children, who, as we know, are in the habit of still treating words as things, tend to expect words that are the same or similar to have the same meaning behind them" (120); and so "the connecting paths which start out from *words* are in the unconscious treated in the same way as connections between *things*" (177). Thus, the force of a "tendentiousness," in order to attract a thought downward to its unconscious elaboration and turn it into a joke, may be exerted by selecting "from among the possible forms of expression the precise one which brings along with it a yield of verbal pleasure" (177). The coincidence between the infantile inclination and the treatment of language by the unconscious does not constitute a problem: "For the infantile is the source of the unconscious, and the unconscious thought-processes are none other than those — the one and only ones — produced in early childhood" (170).

On the other hand, the dominance of the signifier implies a mingling of meanings, that shifting from one meaning to another with which we are familiar. "The pleasure in a joke arising from a 'short-circuit' like this seems to be the greater the more alien the two circles of ideas that are brought together by the same word — the further apart they are" (120). How could one fail to recall that quite similar observations could be and have been made not only about word-play but about all kinds of rhetorical figures which, in literary language, link ideas that are unconnected and distant from each other? We might immediately think of the principal instance of metaphor, and particularly of its use by Baroque, symbolist and surrealist poets. Yet, the boldness of the connections surely cannot be regarded as directly proportionate to the pleasure stimulated. I also believe that the criteria proposed by Freud in a note to rationalize the immediacy of the value-judgment are extendable from puns to include all other figures. "If, by means of a word with two meanings or a word that is only slightly modified, I take a short cut from one circle of ideas to another, and if there is not at the same time a link between those circles of ideas which has a significant sense, then I shall have made a 'bad' joke. In a bad joke like this the only existing link between the two disparate ideas is the one word—the 'point' of the joke.... A 'good' joke, on the other hand, comes about when what children expect proves correct and the similarity between the words is shown to be really accompanied by another, important similarity in their sense" (120-21). It seems highly probable to me that some extraordinary poetic metaphors linking entirely unconnected ideas in a profoundly relevant way on the basis of similarities with no more rational a pretext than verbal homophony merely succeed in confirming an "infantile expectation," which continues to linger in the unconscious.

Now let us consider the example of jokes that play upon thoughts. If the pleasure and the compromise in question are again considered at a genetic level, the very fact that I use the term *play* suggests that, at this level, the distinction from the class of verbal jokes practically disappears. "During the period in which a child is learning how to handle the vocabulary of his mother-tongue, it gives him obvious pleasure to 'experiment with it in play,' to use Groos's words. And he puts words together without regard to the condition that they should make sense, in order to obtain from them the pleasurable effect of rhythm or rhyme. Little by little he is forbidden this enjoyment, till all that remains permitted to him are significant combinations of words" (125). Freud had, in passing, already mentioned as sources of pleasure the affinity between particular techniques of the joke and techniques characterizing a completely different kind of literature, that composed in verse: "It is also generally acknowledged that rhymes, alliterations, refrains, and other forms of repeating similar verbal sounds which occur in verse, make use of the same source of pleasure—the rediscovery of something familiar" (122). Freud had, in fact, introduced a third class of jokes between those in which the technique plays on words and those in which it plays on thoughts. These are jokes in whose technique "we can single out as their common characteristic the fact that in each of them something familiar is rediscovered, where we might instead have expected something new" (120). With the references to rhymes and so on, we come very close to the boundary, emphasized earlier (Chap. 11), between a dominance of the signifier that stresses its phonic consistency (and only literary language is capable of doing this systematically) and a dominance of the signifier whose effect passes through the signified, thus making it typical of all the languages of the unconscious, including the noncommunicating ones. Naturally, one may speak of techniques only with reference to communicating languages, but it should by now be obvious that similar techniques are themselves vehicles for the return of the repressed.

What is most pertinent to my discussion is not the psychogenesis, the primary, nonsensical, but undisturbed pleasure that a child derives from words and its subsequent gradual repression. It is rather the compromise by virtue of which this pleasure returns in the form of a repressed that could not otherwise return. As I move toward a Freudian theory of literature, the unconscious must necessarily concern me more than the infantile, the compromise with pleasure more than pleasure without compromise, the point of arrival of the verbal and logical apprenticeship more than its point of departure or its development. Literature is, in fact, a social institution which presumes that this apprenticeship has been completed (or, if we consider literature for children, and why should we not, that it is at least at a very advanced stage). Moreover, Freud himself does not seem to distinguish clearly between the entirely undisturbed pleaure of nonsensical word-play itself and the pleasure it can generate because it is prohibited play. *"Whatever the motive* (italics mine) may have been which led the child to begin these games, I believe that in his later development he gives himself up to them with the consciousness that they are nonsensical, and he finds enjoyment in the attraction of what is forbidden by reason. He now uses games in order to withdraw from the pressure of critical reason. But there is far more potency in the restrictions which must establish themselves in the course of a child's education in logical thinking and in distinguishing between what is true and false in reality; and for this reason the rebellion against the compulsion of logic and reality is deep-going and long-lasting. Even the phenomena of imaginative activity must be included in this (rebellious) category" (125-26).

This last statement could again lead us toward "content-purports" which alone, in this perspective, definitely represent a return of the repressed, not against sexual or ideological-political repression, but against that which I may term rational repression. For an example of this we need search no farther than the monsters in *Phèdre*, because of their unreality. The same applies to every possible example of "content-purports" considered unlikely and illogical, from ancient myth to modern surreality.

It is among similar "content-purports" that we find those which concerned Freud when, in the most important essay after the book on jokes from the viewpoint of literary theory—the essay entitled *The Uncanny*—he used an almost analogical expression like "return of the surmounted."[8] Nevertheless, if rational repression, understood merely as a respect for logic and reality in the use of language, involves a repressed, then the seat of that repressed must be within language itself: language on both of the indivisible sides of the form that constitutes it, "content-form" and "expression-form." And with this conclusion the central question of my discussion has finally been answered. The "formal return of the repressed" (let us so name it) is that in which may be pointed out a constant common to the language of literature and that of the unconscious.

8. See Appendix 1, "The Compromise-Formation as a Freudian Model," pp. 250-51.

13

Literature between an Excess
and a Lack of Rhetoric

Far from deceiving myself into the belief that I have solved a problem at this point, I should be happy merely to have posed it correctly. The infantile, unconscious manipulation of words and thoughts, whether it may or may not be led back to a "dominance of the signifier," nevertheless modifies something in the relationship between signifier and signified, or between sign and meaning (the terminological hesitation corresponds to problems that are still open). It disturbs the transparency of the relationship, which one might (incorrectly) believe to be normal or prevalent, when it is actually ideal or, at least, exemplary, in an adult and conscious use of language. The seat of the "formal return of the repressed," along with its pleasure and its compromise, comes entirely within this modification, and the latter is perhaps the only original contribution of my discussion. This modification, in fact, in many of its varieties, constitutes one of the principal objects of a science which is more than two thousand years older than psychoanalysis or structural linguistics—rhetoric. For the same reasons that one may claim that ancient rhetoric was something of a precursor of structural linguistics, because, under the name of tropes and figures, its object was modifications in that ideal relationship of transparency between signifier and signified, one should also claim that, in this newly acquired perspective, it was a precursor of Freudian psychoanalysis and thus one should speak of a rhetoric of unconscious language as one has always spoken of a rhetoric of literary language.

In an article published in 1955 Lacan wrote: "...in the elaboration of the most original phenomena of the unconscious, dreams and symptoms, one may recognize, in the most unexpected ways, the very figures of obsolete rhetoric, which appear in their usage to give it the most subtle of specifications."[1] And a year later: "And its modes are difficult to conceive

---

1. Jacques Lacan, "Variantes de la cure-type," in *Ecrits* (Paris: Editions du Seuil, 1966), p. 361.

without recourse to tropes and figures, those of sentences and words (*sententiarum aut verborum*, in a note) just as in Quintilian, and which go from accismus and metonymy to catachresis, antiphrasis, hypallage, and even litotes. . ."[2] In the same year, 1956, a linguist like Emile Benveniste observed: "One is struck by the analogies which suggest themselves here. The unconscious uses a veritable 'rhetoric' which, like style, has its 'figures,' and the old catalogue of tropes would supply an inventory appropriate to the two types of expression. One finds in both all the devices of substitution engendered by taboo: euphemism, allusion, preterition, litotes. The nature of the content makes all the varieties of metaphor appear, for symbols of the unconscious take both their meaning and their difficulty from metaphoric conversion. They also employ what traditional rhetoric calls metonymy (the container for the contents) and synecdoche (the part for the whole), and if the 'syntax' of the symbolic sequences calls forth one device of style more than any other, it is ellipsis."[3] I myself will add another comparison to these conscious ones, which may be even more striking because the intellectual division of labor, not having prevented a convergence of ideas, emphasizes its spontaneity: the infantile (and unconscious) tendency "to expect words that are the same or similar to have the same meaning behind them," which is mentioned in a sentence from Freud quoted above (Chap. 12), seems like a rebellion a priori against the rational, adult truth of Saussure's *arbitraire du signe*. I do not believe that a linguist of Jakobson's great interdisciplinary broad-mindedness had in mind Freud, or his book, or that sentence, when he summed up the following frequently quoted opinion of his with a partly identical expression: "This propensity to infer a connection in meaning from similarity in sound illustrates the poetic function of language."[4]

No sooner has the discussion of the similarities between the two languages reached a conclusion and a confirmation, however, than one of their differences returns, if not to compromise the discussion, at least to complicate it—now less worryingly than before only because our vision of things has become more particularized. If the joke can be grouped with literature as a communicating language, the languages of dreams, parapraxes, and symptoms stand apart because they are noncommunicating. Thus, the respective function or condition of the two rhetorics will be to communicate or not to communicate. Let us take dreams as an

2. Lacan, "Situation de la psychanalyse et formation du psychanalyste," in *Ecrits*, p. 466.

3. Emile Benveniste, *Problèmes de linguistique générale* (Paris: Gallimard, 1966), pp. 86-87; Eng. trans. as *Problems in General Linguistics*, trans. Mary Elizabeth Meek, Miami Linguistics Series, no. 8 (Coral Gables, Fla.: University of Miami Press, 1971), p. 75.

4. Roman Jakobson, "Language in Operation," in *Mélanges Alexandre Koyré* (Paris: Hermant, 1964), vol. 2, "L'Aventure de l'esprit," p. 280; see also his "Closing Statement," in *Style and Language*, pp. 368, 371.

example. I can safely term "signifiers" (generally nonverbal, of course) those aspects that comprise the "manifest content" (*Trauminhalt*), according to *The Interpretation of Dreams,* and "signified" those that comprise the "latent content" (*Traumgedanken*). I may also say that in the dream the former never have a transparent correspondence, free from modifications, with the latter: the hypothetical signifiers, which might have seemed transparent in relation to the actual signified, are regularly supplanted by others. This is exactly what occurs in the most simple of poetic metaphors, but the result of the rhetoric of the dream is that the dream does not transmit anything comprehensible even to the consciousness of the person who has dreamed it.

If, by definition, there is something expressed and something concealed wherever a signifier is supplanted by another, the reciprocal implication does not always tend toward the same sense. To what extent can one compare a rhetoric whose aim is to express, even while concealing (literature, including jokes), to a rhetoric whose aim is to conceal while nevertheless expressing (dreams etc.)? The authority of the quotations from Lacan and Benveniste confirms the basis of the legitimacy of this comparison; but it is Freud himself who provides the necessary indications as to the limits of this legitimacy. In carrying out a more restricted comparison between "joke-work" (*Witzarbeit*) and "dream-work" (*Traumarbeit*), Freud observed that the processes common to both—"condensation," "displacement," "indirect representation," "nonsense"—may, in the dream, be exaggerated "beyond all bounds" (179), "to the point of a distortion which can no longer be set straight" (179). There is, in fact, no need for comprehensibility to act as a limit at all, quite the contrary. For the joke, however, "The condition of intelligibility is binding on it; it may only make use of a possible distortion in the unconscious through condensation and displacement up to the point at which it can be set straight by the third person's understanding" (179).

I shall attempt to translate this into rhetorical terms (not of ancient, but of a more recent, rhetoric) as follows.[5] A language characterized by *figures,* or alterations in the ideal relationship of transparency between signifier and signified, or between sign and meaning, or by *deviations* with respect to a *degree zero* of signification (difficult to define but necessary to

5. Henceforth my main point of reference will be the volume, by six different authors, *Rhétorique générale* (Paris: Larousse, 1970). See also Jean Cohen, *Structure du langage poétique* (Paris: Flammarion, 1966); Gérard Genette, *Figures* (Paris: Editions du Seuil, 1966), pp. 205-21; idem, *Figures II* (Paris: Editions du Seuil, 1969) and *Figures III* (Paris: Editions du Seuil, 1972); Tzvetan Todorov, *Littérature et signification* (Paris: Larousse, 1967), pp. 91-118; Juri M. Lotman, *La struttura del testo poetico* (Milan: Mursia, 1972); Michael Riffaterre, *Essais de stylistique structurale* (Paris: Flammarion, 1971); Cesare Segre, *I segni e la critica* (Turin: Einaudi, 1969), pp. 61-92; Eng. trans. (The Hague and Paris: Mouton, 1973), pp. 48-77. (I have not attempted to update this essential bibliography for the period between 1973 and 1978.)

postulate), or sometimes by a plurality of meanings[6] which is not hierarchical but neither is it accidental or faulty, should allow for the *reduction* of the figures by the addressee, otherwise communication will not be possible. I hasten to add that only in exceptional cases does the addressee's ability to carry out the reduction coincide with the ability to replace the figural formulation with an explicitly nonfigural reformulation (a proposal of degree zero), having the same conceptual "content-purport" as the former. This was the meaning that I previously gave to the term "reduction" (Chap. 12) in commenting on Freud's use of the same term; but this was a narrow or restrictive meaning, less suitable for the immediate process of the addressee's understanding than for the metalinguistic activity of the scholar. All that is normally necessary for the addressee, in order to ensure communication, is that an automatic and implicit correction take place, thus virtually reestablishing degree zero (or, more prudently speaking, some sort of degree zero).

This is a risk, as I have already mentioned (Chap. 10), which literature, and especially poetry, has frequently faced in the last hundred years for historical reasons that we shall not investigate here. It is not a risk, however, in the case of dreams, parapraxes, and symptoms, because its opposite, the establishment of communication, may well be one. If, by availing myself of the concept of figure, I may use a quantitative concept such as *figurality rate* in an abstract sense,[7] the problem of the opposition between communicating and noncommunicating languages, which I have periodically encountered from the start, will at last be explained in its respective terms. In fact, I called noncommunicating languages of the unconscious those whose figurality rate cannot go below a certain minimum level, because the function of figurality is that of concealing even when expressing. For literature as a whole, however, as Freud realized in the case of jokes, the figurality rate cannot go above a certain maximum level, because the function of figurality there is to express even when concealing. A dream, a parapraxis, or a symptom is revealed at the end of every Freudian interpretation as a conglomeration of figures, sometimes incredibly dense, and, in any case, conceding only minimal space to a nonfigural expression of its latent contents. To claim with Lacan that the unconscious is the realm of the signifier is really to say that in the languages of the unconscious there are never any trans-

6. On the figure as a polysemy, see Appendix 2, "Constants, Variants, and Misreadings."
7. Can one really consider something abstractly as quantifiable when obviously not in a concrete sense? I believe that one can, not least because it would appear that Freud, having no alternative, often accepted this procedure with the concept of psychic energy. See also in Matte-Blanco, *The Unconscious as Infinite Sets* (London, 1975), the audacious treatment of a question like the "measurability" of unconscious processes, using the fascinating example (p. 203) of the Egyptians, who never succeeded in conceiving a measurement of temperature in numbers, but only in words.

parent signifiers because no signified is ever disclosed; thus the signified is always invisible and only the signifier is visible. To claim with modern rhetoric that a verbal language is *opaque* when it attracts attention to itself by clothing itself in figures, instead of remaining imperceptible and allowing its meaning to be immediately apparent, is to point out a similarity to the languages of the unconscious, whose opacity is so extreme as to be literally obscurity.

Strictly speaking, only these noncommunicating languages are truly languages of the unconscious, if the unconscious is founded by the phenomenon of repression, which by definition prevents particular latent contents from being brought into consciousness and still more from being communicated to others. The need that nevertheless induces one to express them, through the compromise-formations of the relative return of the repressed, would not be pertinent to the problem of the connection between the unconscious and literature unless one agrees here as well to generalize, for all languages, whether noncommunicating or communicating, Freud's observations on comparing dreams to jokes, in which we know what the compromise protects: "Dreams serve predominantly for the avoidance of unpleasure, jokes for the attainment of pleasure" (180). Whatever the case may be, the communicating language of literature does not differ from those that truly belong to the unconscious solely because its figures must be reducible. There is a further and no less important difference — my failure to mention it must no doubt have led to some hesitation about the discussion so far — which is that literary language does not have to be completely figural.

Some readers will reasonably have found my statements about the similarities between the two types of language tenable as long as literature is not conceived as the complex of what this term generally refers to in current usage, but rather as comprising the greater part of lyric poetry, perhaps a certain amount of the fiction and drama of this century, and just a few texts from earlier periods. Again I allude to texts whose figurality rate is so high as to vie with the hermetism and apparent nonsense of dreams and to defy the need for intelligibility, presumably with the author's wish or consent. But how, these readers will have wondered, can one justify proposing comparisons with the language of the unconscious for the countless other examples of lyric poetry, fiction, or drama, whose figurality is much less dense, or, more reasonably still, for those texts that are considered as literature by the empirical aesthetic consciousness and qualified as such by current usage, even though their aims are scientific, political, historical, journalistic, moral, philosophical, or religious.

This doubt is, at first glance, entirely justified and therefore productive. I do it justice by admitting that in literary language figurality encounters limits not only on its possible density, but on its very presence; but on the other hand, I maintain that it encounters them more remotely and rarely than is traditionally believed. It was only to facilitate the exposition that previously I discussed figures only as local alternatives, easily circumscribed in their context, in the relationship of transparency between signifier and signified, or between sign and meaning. Indeed, the object of ancient rhetoric was no broader in scope than this. Nevertheless, the rhetoric conceivable at present—and in fact, revived, as was predictable, on the basis of the premise coherent with structural linguistics that we have examined—can take into consideration figures of all dimensions and kinds: figures of the signifier, figures of the signified, figures of meter and of rhyme, figures of grammar, figures of syntax, figures of logic, figures of the relationship to real facts, figures of narrative, figures of the succession of various sections of the text, figures of the addressee and addresser as internal functions of the text, figures of the physical support of the language, figures of departure from already established conventional figures, and so on. In some cases the figure will be contained in the space of a couple of lines of text, in others its space will be the thousands of pages constituting an entire immense work.

Since I can refer only to other books already written and books waiting to be written for detailed examples, I shall limit myself here to a single hypothesis, which no one will have difficulty in documenting. A non-realistic novel of any age, though I am thinking of the so-called "magic realism" of the twentieth century, could be written with the strictest avoidance of figures of style such as metaphors, yet could contain an undeniably high figural density, though one which would be analyzable only on the basis of units in the text that are larger than those by which figures of style are usually examined. I should add that my analysis of *Phèdre* could undoubtedly be transcribed entirely into the terms of figures based on larger units, and then the figurality of Racine's text would turn out to be extremely dense. Nevertheless, Racine, the "classical" poet, employs figures of style only with sobriety and muted effects, which have been the subject of one of Leo Spitzer's most subtle and thorough analyses.[8]

8. Leo Spitzer, "Die klassische Dämpfung in Racines Stil," in *Romanische Stil- und Literaturstudien* (Marburg: Lahn, 1931), 1: 135-265; Fr. trans. as "L'effet de sourdine dans le style classique: Racine," in *Etudes de style* (Paris: Gallimard, 1970), pp. 208-335. This "classical mute" which acts as a common denominator for all kinds of style, seems related by nature to Freudian negation, and in some passages Spitzer comes close to stating this in terms of linguistic repression and repressed (e.g., pp. 136-37).

It should be pointed out here that, in my opinion, the neorhetorical viewpoint in no way supersedes the work of the three great German scholars, in each of whom and in his own way the sense of the relationship between message and code is so strong: Ernst Robert Curtius, Leo Spitzer, and especially Erich Auerbach. It rather points to a much more attentive rereading, and to a consideration of every possible transcription that might be experimented with mentally.

If my analysis of *Phèdre* was not already formulated with an explicit articulation of the model of Freudian negation in terms of figures, neither timidity nor incoherence should be blamed. Nor is it due merely to the failure to mature of my present hypotheses. My work was, and is, conditioned by a shortage of precise conceptual and terminological instruments, which derives from the particular interdisciplinary position of its premises. The possibility of greatly extending the concept of figure beyond its traditional sense, and of tracing many different features of literary language back to this least common denominator, has been proposed by recent studies that have not the slightest link with the Freudian perspective. Some time ago, Lacan and Benveniste drew attention to the analogies between the rhetorics of the unconscious and literature. Implicit in the quotations from them was a long and difficult program of concretely comparative work, holding Quintilian in one hand and Freud in the other, which, to my knowledge, has never been attempted in an exhaustive manner by any scholar or group of scholars.

The rebirth of and even the interdisciplinary fashion for rhetorical studies, supported by structural linguistics in its maturity, or renewed by generative linguistics in no longer premature incidences, might now justify the hope for a rigorous and exhaustive execution of that program, in spite of the fact that French interdisciplinary fashions are making us pay for a few objective results with a lot of discussion which, to put it euphemistically, is itself figural. If I may allow myself to indulge in a figure at this point, it would seem that one cannot often cross the frontier of the intellectual division of labor without paying an exorbitant toll. In other cases in which these frontiers are not crossed at all and instead run the risk of being reified, the opposite effect of the same cause is somewhat preferable, all things considered.[9] In the most admirable contributions of neorhetoric to date, the formalistic temptation is unmistakably present. But one should ask oneself whether this does not serve as a temporary guarantee of the greatest possible rigor, from a linguistic point of view, while waiting for the eventual verification of a broader viewpoint. In any case, it is a comforting thought that, if the analogies between the two rhetorics do indeed exist, any more detailed study of literary rhetoric, even if it totally ignores the relationship with that of the unconscious, can only ameliorate the problem.[10] The neorhetorical extension of the concept of figure incalculably strengthens the theoretical premise on which my

9. See Appendix 5, "On the Intellectual Division of Labor."

10. An exemplary methodological approach would instead seem to be that which, starting out from figures of the order of the narrative signifiers and availing itself of the excellent "Discours du récit" in Genette, *Figures III*, pp. 65-273, arrives at an interpretation of them by bringing them back into the logic of Freudian negation: a case in point is the article by Francesco Fiorentino, "Le figure di stornamento in un racconto di Balzac," *Strumenti critici*, 26 (1975): 31-49.

entire discussion is based and, above all, allows its formulation to be specified once more.

My hypothesis, then, is that the figure as an alteration of the relationship of transparency between the signifier and signified has its origin in the asocial and functionally noncommunicating languages of the unconscious. There it is free to become denser, and it dominates to the point of concealing itself as it conceals the meaning that it nevertheless expresses by a compromise. In a communicating language, under the surveillance of the conscious ego, the figure could only occur as a disturbance or error, if, speaking absurdly, man were an animal totally lacking an unconscious and having as an inborn prerogative an absolutely transparent use of words and a strictly logical use of thoughts. The former and the latter are, on the contrary, a conquest and a restriction for man; to take pleasure in figures against this restriction acquires the value of a "formal return of the repressed." In other words, the figure assumes a new, socially institutionalized function, which is a compromise turned in the opposite direction and a pleasure that may be transmitted to others.

If we continue to consider things quantitatively, the tolerable figurality rate of a communicating language may vary greatly below a given maximum level that coincides with the limit of comprehensibility, unless the latter is voluntarily crossed. Within the space thus delimited, however, there is another fluctuating limit, which I do not believe can be defined on a qualitative basis and below which the empirical aesthetic consciousness will react to a text by saying that it is not literature; only above this limit will it say that a text is literature. Indeed, if we were to rely solely on the empirical aesthetic consciousness as a criterion we should often be led astray, since it has other preestablished designations at its disposal and thus, in other cases, will react to the figurality rate by saying of a text that it is a joke, a speech, a *réclame,* a beautiful letter, or a fine private discussion. Yet, I doubt whether it is possible to define literature on a qualitative basis, because the pertinent criterion must be the (analyzable) figurality rate and not, for example, the text's destination, which is purely literary or perhaps totally heterogenous. If this were not the case, no one would ever have mentioned literature in referring to works whose aims are scientific, political, historical, journalistic, moral, philosophical, or religious, yet it is a fact that people have always done so. At most, what might happen is that a shift in historical circumstances would render the original heterogenous destination useless or less effective, leaving a greater emphasis on the figurality objectively inherent in the text. Thus, the text, which a few centuries earlier was presumably valued primarily as a work of science or philosophy, will survive only as literature.

Needless to say, I would not select any judgment of aesthetic value as a pertinent criterion or confuse it with the judgment on the figurality rate. I will avoid this extremely delicate problem for the moment and merely remark that a text may seem at once densely figural and in very bad taste, but in that case what fluctuates, or ought to fluctuate, is not its qualification as literature. Moreover, the opposite may occur as well: to qualify or not as literature is one thing, to qualify as good or bad literature is another. But the quantitative concept of the figurality rate and the dependence upon it of the phenomenon of literature cannot be accepted even provisionally unless there emerges a further choice conditioned by it and having no place in conventional terminology. If there is no solution of continuity in the ideal corpus of all possible texts between the position of a symbolist or Baroque poem and that of a scientific treatise other than that declared by the empirical aesthetic consciousness in reacting to the figurality rate, then neither is there any solution of continuity in literature between the language of the unconscious and that of the conscious ego.

The above-mentioned Baroque or symbolist poem will consist of an orgy of figures, which to the rational eyes of the conscious ego will appear as one continuous delirium. The scientific treatise will be written, as usually happens, in what is perhaps the most neutral and least figural of languages of those we know, under the closest control of the rational consciousness. These may well be two opposite and exceptionally well-defined cases; but in how many intermediate cases, within the ideal corpus of all possible texts, do neutral language and figural language alternate with each other and overlap and contaminate each other? Moreover, is it really possible to distinguish them as clearly as I have done except at the cost of a forcible and conscious abstraction? In this world there is no "content-purport" which a literary-figural form cannot, if necessary, adopt and transform; but neither is there any which cannot exist alongside it, maintaining a form that is much closer to the degree zero. Should the limits, within a single text, not be sufficiently vague or fluctuating to remain unnoticed, the empirical aesthetic consciousness will, at worst, react by speaking of "digressions."

These literary experiences are justified in Freudian terms, if one admits that any object may be considered, both successively and simultaneously, according to the "pleasure principle" as well as according to the "reality principle." Thus, after all, it would be somewhat arbitrary to attempt to decide whether to call literature a language of the unconscious or a language of the conscious ego. The minimum level of the figurality rate would incline one toward the former solution, its maximum level and its variability, toward the latter; and the same applies to the requirement of intelligibility, or, at least, to the indispensability of the addressee. I would say that the figure is the perpetual tribute paid—and how willingly it is paid—by the language of the conscious ego to the unconscious. Thus, according to an open definition, so to speak, literature is any verbal language of the conscious ego (written or oral) which pays to the unconscious, in large or very large measure, the tribute represented by the figure.[11] Naturally, the temptation to speak resolutely of language of the unconscious will be greater when the figural density is at a maximum. This explains why Freud considered the joke as a language of the unconscious, in spite of his own undoubtedly restrictive, official concept of literature.

The "brevity" that is included among the sufficient, but not necessary, characteristics of the joke, though within limits which the dream does not respect, seemed to him to be comparable to the oneiric process of "condensation" (28-29). In more general terms, the rate of figurality or of "deformation" effected by the techniques is always so high in the joke that Freud was led to maintain that the very fact of its having some meaning inevitably suspended rational repression "to protect that pleasure from being done away with by criticism" (131). Moreover, according to Freud, this great intensity of the formal return of the repressed neutralizes the distinction between jokes that have and those that lack great substance or value, for the person laughing cannot distinguish how much of his satisfaction depends on the witty expression and how much on the value of the "thought" disguised by it (132). I shall attempt, once again, to extend the discussion of Freud's great book to literature as a whole and say, therefore, that the maximum figural density possible in a literary text cannot prevent the conscious ego from passing judgment on the actual values of the conceptual "content-purport," which may be defined as such only by the judgment. In literary languages that are progressively less dependent on the unconscious, these values progressively increase in importance, even if conscious rationality, by definition, never forgoes the expressive aid of the figure. But only in the far fewer cases of that which is collectively called literature does this rationality totally abandon its own logic in favor of the logic that reconnects the figure to the unconscious.

What is the purpose of the figure in all the other cases? Undoubtedly we are again faced with a problem as old as the conception we must now accept or reject: the conception of the figure as mere "ornament" of a discourse, which interests us for other, more rational, reasons. I believe that it is impossible to avoid this problem, but that our Freudian perspective can at least help to overcome the distressing hedonism of this traditional conception. Indeed, even and especially from our point of view, the so-called figural ornament introduced into the discourse lavishes pleasure on the addressee, and thus serves to convince and seduce him. But a pleasure whose sensuality lies entirely in the verbal signifiers, and whose game always reveals accessory meanings for them, originates too

11. See Appendix 3, "Definition of Literature and Literature as an Institution."

deeply within the process of signification to be truly added to it without causing some modification. The presumed "addition" of pleasure is actually the interference of another discourse, which stimulates pleasure on the borders of the discourse of reason. On the means and the functions of the interpenetration which may be established on each occasion between these two I have nothing to say generally, even when the discourse of reason is the guide and does not allow itself to be led by the other. The tendentiousness of the formal return of the repressed will enter, in each instance, into a different relationship with all the possible "content-purports," whether these are or are not tendentious in themselves, and whether they have or lack great substance or value.

Nevertheless, by proposing these two alternatives, I am again moving closer than it might appear to the question of judging aesthetic value. Although this is a problem that in the most modern studies seems to be scorned, almost feared, and in any event avoided when possible, I cannot ignore it at this point. In the first part of the book, I referred to an "inexhaustable wealth and perfect coherence" of "relationships of meaning, of oppositions, and similarities" inherent in the text as being the true object of the value judgment that we give to Racine's tragedy (pp. 40, 120). I am not rejecting this criterion now, but I realize that it will have convinced few readers, chiefly because, as we have seen (Chap. 11), my analysis of that coherence and wealth centered around the "content-form" and neglected, or touched only instrumentally upon, the "expression-form." Moreover, we observed that it favored a latent paradigmatic order over the actual syntagmatic order. The difficulty is not simply that this involved definite analytical abstractions for vaulting over the levels of greatest tangibility in the poetic text. It should be heeded generally that a criterion of analysis cannot become a criterion for aesthetic value if the analysis that applies it makes an abstraction of any of the objective aspects of the text, if it is not absolutely complete.[12]

Perhaps the greatest difficulty in objectively establishing a judgment of aesthetic value is that of achieving an integral analysis of a text in its objectivity, of even setting out on an analysis with no abstractions whatsoever. It would be superfluous, after my specific complaints about rhetoric and the unconscious, to stress how far we are from the possibility of approximating this ideal of total analysis. Yet anyone who believes in the objective consistency of texts[13] will prefer to content himself with provisional, partial, and statistical observations, depending on the *consensus gentium,* rather than ignore in a theoretical discussion the question of the aesthetic value judgment, though this obviously can be no more than a factual judgment and extremely difficult to justify. My comments

12. See Appendix 5, "On the Intellectual Division of Labor."
13. See Appendix 2, "Constants, Variants, and Misreadings."

on this matter, prompted by the two different Freudian distinctions that qualify "content-purport" by opposing it to the self-sufficiency of the form, seek only to circumscribe the problem and not to solve it. I chose to study, in *Phèdre*, a masterpiece in which the formal return of the repressed makes common cause with a formidable return of the repressed on the level of "content-purport." The two establish one another, become fused, and in their interpenetration clearly heighten their effectiveness beyond all measure. There can be little doubt that the importance and beauty attributed to the work by an age-old *consensus gentium* depends precisely on this. Thus, the distinction between innocent and tendentious "content-purports," which is valid for literature as it is for jokes even after tendentiousness has been recognized in the form, must be presumed important for a judgment of aesthetic value.

As for the other distinction between "content-purports" with or without great substance or value, even if it were irrelevant to a judgment of aesthetic value it would still create an urgent need to clarify the confusion in danger of arising over the word "value." When I refer to value with regard to the conceptual "content-purport," it can only mean a value according to the extraliterary judgment of the conscious ego. It must be admitted that the content of any literary discourse may be subjected to such a value judgment, once it has been admitted that any figure or figural contexture, however dense, must allow the addressee to carry out a reduction and re-establishment of some kind of degree zero. If we were to conceive in this way not the immediate process of the addressee's understanding, but a reduction in the narrow sense, the substitution of a nonfigural reformulation for the figural formulation, the operation would then, as we know, eliminate the literary discourse as such. Yet, the judgment of aesthetic value, however one considers it, will obviously be centered around the literary discourse as such, that is, around the figural formulation. Consequently, according to the definition of literature that I have proposed, it will be possible to pass value judgments on literature both as a discourse of the conscious ego and as a discourse dependent on the unconscious.

If we term the former a judgment of ideological value and the latter a judgment of aesthetic value, we shall be faced with a presumably permanent dualism, impossible to reconcile. The conscious ego will never give up its legitimate claims, will never convert by virtue of the figural expression to ideological values that are not its own. On the other hand, if it is the figural tribute paid to the unconscious that defines a particular discourse as literature, the claim to evaluate it exclusively on the basis of that which defines it will never come to seem any less legitimate and will not yield to the former. Thus when the two claims enter into conflict, the outcome is very often a partaker in literature with a bad conscience:

with either a bad ideological conscience or a bad aesthetic conscience. In truth, the sharpness of the conflict depends largely on the degree of historical topicality in a work, and this is always toned down by the phenomenon of its long diachronic survival. The fact that an addressee today might not share the Jansenist ideology will not be an obstacle to his aesthetic enjoyment of *Phèdre*. But how can one pass, in the case of *Phèdre*, from a "content-purport" like the Jansenist ideology to the poetic discourse? Is it perhaps that the reduction of the figures of the poetic discourse leads directly to the ideological premises? To account for the fact that things are more complicated than this will mean to criticize readings of a work of art that have a unilateral ideological foundation; in the case of *Phèdre*, for example, that of Lucien Goldmann in *Le Dieu caché*.[14]

If my analysis of the tragedy is correct, the Jansenist ideology as "content-purport" has undergone a singular overturning in the form whose substance it has become. The perverse desire, provided for in the ideology and even an integral part of it, though condemned unremittingly, has become a repressed able to appeal for emotional identification, and yet whose repression remains assured in compliance with the ideology itself. It is precisely to *this* dialectical relationship between repressed and repression, or, in other words, to the overturning of the ideology, that the figures of the poetic discourse refer. We need, however, only think of as many other texts as we wish to know that the return of the repressed in literature does not always consist of the overturning of an ideology and that, instead, it often coincides with it: the ideology itself in some cases *is* a return of the repressed. If we consider them both, in relation to a literary discourse, as possible "content-purports" which become the substance of its form, then in addition to being overturned or coinciding, they might also cut into each other, or remain separate, or each exist without the other. The individual cases are always infinite and difficult to define when the literary fortunes of the discourse of the conscious ego or of the ideology are taken into examination, because these are played out along the slope on which literature gradually descends toward that which can no longer be termed literature; and I have already discussed the precarious nature of this boundary.

Yet one hypothesis tempts me by its high degree of probability: the ideology can enter into a literary discourse with full aesthetic validity only in the form of a return of the repressed, whether intact or over-

14. Lucien Goldmann, *Le Dieu caché* (Paris: Gallimard, 1955), pp. 416-40; Eng. trans. as *The Hidden God* (London: Routledge and Kegan Paul, 1964), pp. 371-91. My reservations do not in any way concern the greater part of the book that is dedicated to Jansenism and the texts of Pascal, in which the figurality rate is so much lower and the ideological discourse so much more complete and exclusive than in Racine's texts.

turned. The more general, though no less probable, hypothesis would go as follows: there exists a priori a homogeneity, sympathy, and solidarity between the return of the repressed as "content-purport" and the formal return of the repressed. This is a hypothesis that favors examples of literature in which purport and form unify their return of the repressed, and it contrasts them with the examples in which we may consider either an ideological purport, which does not give rise to a return of the repressed, or a return of the repressed which is purely and superficially formal. On this point a final extrapolation from Freud's work would seem to be called for, if only for the sake of coherence on the part of one who has already ventured to put forward all the previous extrapolations. According to Freud, innocent jokes usually produce an effect of moderate pleasure and have only a limited success, even when they owe it in part to a valid intellectual content. With equal technique tendentious jokes have at their disposal "by virtue of their purpose" powerful sources of pleasure inaccessible to the former and are generally irresistible, as revealed by bursts of laughter (96).

The success of a literary work is far less ephemeral than the success in degree of hilarity of a joke and, not only on this account, is incalculably more difficult to measure. Nevertheless, judging from the works that the human societies with which I am familiar have consecrated as master-pieces, less by immediate acceptance than by a lasting appreciation, it would appear that neither an unstable ideological validity in the purport nor a gratuitous figural density in the form is sufficient to characterize them. Like the most powerful jokes, great literature is probably always doubly tendentious, though, undoubtedly not everything doubly tenden-tious is great literature. It seems to me that the ultimate and most persistent mystery to which the judgement of aesthetic value refers, that for which only the ideal total analysis could account, is the knot of complicity in masterpieces that is tightened by the two tendentious aspects: a purport which by supposition always constitutes a return of the repressed and the figural return of the repressed onto all facets of the form. In reality, the force of this semiotic combination does not usually coincide with a power to modify the world in practice. This truth must be vigorously reiterated in order to avoid illusions about the literary art, or the constraints imposed on it, and in spite of the risk of disappointing those who might claim that much of literature, past, present, and future would leave its mark on society in a manner that is the opposite of compromise, and that it is able to overcome the contradictions in its own fictitious space, which is a contribution to overcoming them in real life. The theoretical viewpoint, however, even if it does not prevent one from vigorously reiterating a truth, cannot, by definition, be partial or preceptive or optative. The fact that the model that can be extrapolated from the Freudian model of jokes may also account for the phenomena of "committed" literature, while no generalization proceeding from the latter may account for all other literary phenomena, is an insufficient excuse for the lie of art as disinterested contemplation.

14

The Return of the Repressed
in the Series of Contents

My hypothesis regarding the aesthetic privileges of the return of the repressed as "content-purport" will surely meet with the objection that it is an arbitrary generalization, the same objection to which I laid myself open in stating that the formal return of the repressed, under the name of figure, characterizes the literary phenomenon. By referring to recent studies based on linguistics, I had no trouble rendering plausible that it makes sense to speak of figures much more frequently than is generally done. In this new case there is no previous study of which I may avail myself and yet the hypothesis can only be confirmed by the analogous claim that it makes sense to refer systematically with the expression "return of the repressed" to more things than has seemed possible before. By saying "more things," however, I should immediately specify in what sense and at what level.

Earlier on (Chap. 12), the content censured by the repression surrounding sex and by an ideological-political repression seemed to me to correspond respectively to the obscene and hostile tendencies distinguished by Freud. Shortly thereafter, however, I mentioned the broader instances recognizable behind these two kinds of tendentiousness; in the one case, I recalled the Freudian opposition between the pleasure and reality principles, in the other, the Freudian concept of civilization as a dialectic between repression and repressed. By deriving from these in one case the individual instance of pleasure and in the other the social instance of compromise, I did no more than stress the dialectical pole of the repressed in the former case and that of repression in the latter. When the sexual is generalized as pleasure and the ideological-political as compromise, they cease to appear as separate occasions of the return of the repressed against their relative repressions; they themselves become respectively a least common denominator of every repressed and every repression. Consequently, far from increasing the initial number of kinds of tendentiousness or censured contents from two to more than two, I actually reduced it to just one. Certainly, it will not be an augmented list of different "purports" which will enable me to extend the range of the expression "return of the repressed" with reference to the contents of literary works.

The example of *Phèdre* already studied will serve once again to point out the right direction of any further discussion. If I were briefly to summarize the plot of the tragedy, adhering to the level of abstraction of the "content-purport," it would still be clear that the social repression against which Phaedra's desire sins can represent only an ideological repression. It must be assumed that the action takes place in a society whose moral ideology forbids incest, adultery, uncontrolled passion; otherwise the action itself would be incomprehensible. At this level of abstraction, the distinction between censured sexual and ideological contents seems to fade entirely and for the same reason that induced me earlier reduce it to a unity: the repression interiorized within the individual, according to Freud, is always of a social nature. Is then the return of the repressed constituted by Phaedra's perverse desire an ideological return of the repressed? This formulation is surely unacceptable, but for reasons which someone narrating the plot in a broad outline might easily overlook. Let us first of all consider the internal attitude of the character of Phaedra in the face of her own desire; not only is the desire not claimed as legitimate in opposition to the ideology, but it is accepted into the consciousness only with extreme resistance.

Furthermore, my analysis attempted to demonstrate that the same internal contradiction by which the character appears divided marks the entire text, imposing itself on it in the "content-form" according to the model of Freudian negation. It is at this level, not at that of the purport, that the text qualifies itself as literature. My analysis is of this "content-form," which I maintained (Chap. 13) could be transcribed in terms of figures. We realize, therefore, that the character's refusal to accept her own desire on moral grounds, as a psychological situation attributed to her, is not enough to prevent the ideological repression from being challenged by the return of the repressed inscribed in the text. The character could be presented as a submissive victim of ideological repression, and still the author, or rather the actual discourse of the text (the form that the content adopts there) could quite easily challenge the repression. We should then not hesitate to speak of an ideological return of the repressed. In fact, in *Phèdre,* the return of the repressed does not become ideological (and even less ideological-political), not because it has a particular, sexual, nature, but because it stands in a particular relationship, that of the nonacceptance of itself, with respect to the relative repression. This is not for extraliterary reasons which precede the text, but for the very reasons that qualify the text as literary.

If one aims to enrich or to state specifically the various cases of the return of the repressed as content in literature, it would appear that there is no advantage in considering it at the level of an abstract purport. The distinction between sexual and ideological-political, already questionable at this level, does not suffice to comprehend the specific relationship between repressed and repression that takes shape in the text of *Phèdre*—*within* the text; and this applies to every other text as well. The relationship will vary according to a list of cases to be enriched or specified, and the expression "return of the repressed" will acquire additional meanings to those so far identified, as long as a purport, which has already become "content-substance," already been articulated by a form, is taken into consideration. If it is true, as was stated in my hypothesis (Chap. 13), that there exists an attraction a priori between the return of the repressed as "content-purport" and the formal return of the repressed, the former will be susceptible a priori to enter into certain structures determined by the latter. Naturally, this is something I would hesitate to claim for any nontendentious "content-purport." But what does a priori mean in our case? And what element can I abstract at the level of the substance articulated by a form that does not belong necessarily and exclusively to each individual work? Only one answer seems plausible: that which is a priori as regards each individual work at the moment of its genesis will be a posteriori as regards the corpus of already existing works, to literature as an institution and to its code.

As the formalists have already noted, each new work always takes the rules of this code into account but always violates them and thus always leaves them altered, by the very definition of aesthetic originality.[1] Yet, throughout history this code unquestionably maintains a certain number of constants, without which it would be impossible for us to grasp the traditional diachronic unity of the literature of Greco-Roman and Judeo-Christian origin. Thus, if there are also constants for the specific way in which the return of the repressed takes shape in relation to the repression, in the texts where it enters as "content-substance," these must be a part of the literary code, just as the constants of the formal return of the repressed, the codified figures, are notoriously a part of it. It has obviously never occurred to anyone to infer the constants in question from his own experience as an author, reader, or scholar of literature, according to the specific perspective that I am proposing. It may be noted, however, that on the whole these did not escape from the individual

---

1. See Jan Mukařovský, *La funzione, la norma e il valore estetico come fatti sociali* (Turin: Einaudi, 1971), pp. 59-94; Tzvetan Todorov, *Introduction à la littérature fantastique* (Paris: Editions du Seuil, 1970), pp. 7-12; Eng. trans. as *The Fantastic: A Structural Approach to a Literary Genre* (Cleveland and London: Press of Case Western Reserve University, 1973), pp. 5-10.

and collective consciousness of which the literary code has over the centuries been the object. They are often easily recognizable in the outlines of those complexes of norms in which the code specifies itself and which we usually call literary genres.

The level of abstraction that must be selected in order to discuss these constants cannot be the excessively high one of "content-purport," where they evade our grasp because they are as yet unformed. But neither can it be the excessively low level, which I should have to fix if I were to abstract them inductively from the "content-substance" of a plurality of concrete works. I should not know where to begin or where to end an appropriate scrutiny of concrete works: in our case induction is a useless criterion because it is inexhaustible. We must therefore ask ourselves how many and which are the possible situations, still at a fairly high level of abstraction, in which it makes sense to speak of a return of the repressed with regard to the "content-substance" of a text. I would opt for the level of abstraction at which I already found myself when characterizing in *Phèdre* the manner of the return of the repressed imposed on the "content-substance" by the form as a contradiction within the consciousness. This is, of course, not merely within the consciousness of the protagonist and, in any case, not as a psychological state of the character. I have already observed that the dynamics of the return of the repressed, the specific relationship between repressed and repression, imposes itself as an internal contradiction in the discourse of the entire text. The contradiction therefore will thus necessarily occur within the consciousness *of the person to whom the discourse is addressed.*

At this point, the concept of addressee is clearly called into play, but not yet as empirical, historical, real addressee. The empirical addressee can abstain from or refuse to receive this contradiction into his own consciousness, and this means that he has not understood the text or, at least, that he did not like it. Furthermore, the empirical addressee — and this is the most illuminating observation — can confine himself to receiving that contradiction into his consciousness during the reading of the text and only as a function of reading the text. This is what might happen to an austere moralist or to an advocate of complete sexual freedom, who both appreciate *Phèdre* although, for opposite reasons, their views leave no room at all for this contradiction. Their case has already been considered (Chap. 13); it is that in which a judgment of aesthetic value clashes with one of ideological value. The discourse of the text in its objectivity, however, remains unchanged in the presence of these many variations in the empirical addressee. Its "content-substance" is articulated by the form, the form is characterized by figures, the figures may be reduced; and the only function of the addressee that concerns us here is his ability to reduce the figures or, more simply, to understand. This function of the addressee is as unchangeable as the text; that is, it may be compromised or modified only by the same historical circumstances that compromise or modify the intelligibility of the text. I shall, therefore, refer to an addressee-function contained in the text, which may be adopted more or less completely by any empirical addressee; it is to this that the discourse is addressed.[2] I shall also refer to a contradiction within the consciousness, in the case of *Phèdre,* with respect to the addressee-function rather than to the character of Phaedra.

We have thus, for the addressee-function, a case of a return of the repressed which is CONSCIOUS BUT NOT ACCEPTED. This situation (textual, not psychological) is abstract enough that it may be presumed to be found in cases other than that of *Phèdre,* yet it is not abstract enough that it may be presumed to be found in all existing cases. Proceeding from this situation, I shall now attempt to examine, at the same level of abstraction, all the possible situations that differ from this. Since the level is the same, the number of these should not be infinite. I am assuming chiefly that the repression gains ground at the expense of the repressed and covers the entire area of consciousness that I had earlier supposed to be divided by a contradiction. The return of the repressed will now be imaginable only as UNCONSCIOUS. The term "repressed" will have again taken on its narrowest sense and the contradiction will have shifted between the consciousness as a whole and that which lies beneath it. At this point, the reader might ask whether there actually exist literary texts in which a return of the repressed can remain unconscious to the addressee-function. This is not my present concern. I admit, however, that with the hypothesis of an unconscious return of the repressed, we would appear to have touched the lowest limit of the various possible cases; a return of the repressed which is less than unconscious cannot be conceived because of its lack of consistency. I shall therefore continue with the series of hypotheses in the opposite direction. I am assuming that it is the repressed that gains ground at the expense of the repression and that it covers the entire area of consciousness, eliminating the contradiction. It will then not be possible to continue speaking of return of the repressed unless a contradiction survives which is no longer within the individual, into whose consciousness the repressed has now been accepted. This contradiction would involve other individuals, no matter how many, who represent or constitute the society against whose repression the individual repressed asserts itself. I obtain, therefore, a return of the repressed which is ACCEPTED BUT NOT SUPPORTED. In this hypothesis I in fact exclude the possibility of the individual asserting his repressed with a claim that is extended to others, able to proselytize, and aimed at

2. On this point in particular, see Appendix 2, "Constants, Variants, and Misreadings."

changing the world. A purely individual repressed could set itself up as an example, yet still be inimitable or imitable only by exceptional individuals; and it could imply a total, even if tragic, resignation to the fact that the world, historically and metaphysically, stays the same. By tracing these distinctions I have hinted at the following hypothesis in the series or, rather, I have already defined it: a return of the repressed that is SUPPORTED BUT NOT AUTHORIZED. If the following hypothesis is to be obtained, like all the others, by asserting the term that was negated previously, the dialectical contradiction threatens to become a contradiction in terms. An authorization from the established order would seem to put an end to the possibility of referring to a repressed. Let us not forget, however, that more than one code of behavior may be in force within an established order and may come into conflict with each other: juridical, political, military, religious, moral, chivalresque . . . I can conceive of a repressed that would be repressed with respect to one of these codes but not so with respect to another, by which it is authorized. Then I may refer to a return of the repressed which is AUTHORIZED, with the understanding that this means authorized by one or more codes of behavior but not by all of those in force within an established order. Only that which would be authorized by all the codes of behavior could no longer be called repressed; and the number of possible cases, which reached its lowest limit through a lack of consistency, reaches its upper limit through a contradiction in terms.

To sum up, then, at a particular level of abstraction the specific relationship between repressed and repression, in the "content-substance" of a literary work, takes on different forms with respect to the addressee-function, according to whether "return of the repressed" refers to something:

(A) unconscious
(B) conscious but not accepted
(C) accepted but not supported
(D) supported but not authorized
(E) authorized (but not by all codes of behavior).

This series acts, above all, as a starting point for purely logical abstractions, predictable on the basis of the criterion by which it has been obtained. Any negation of a term that occurs at a particular level is also valid for all the terms that occur at the lower levels, and is not valid for any of the terms occurring at higher levels. Any assertion of a term that occurs at a particular level is also valid for all the terms that occur at the higher levels, and is not valid for any of the terms occurring at the lower levels. When the return of the repressed is unconscious, it is, for obvious reasons, neither accepted nor supported nor authorized; when it is authorized, it is, for even more obvious reasons, also supported and accepted and conscious. This applies not only when starting out from the terms at the two extremities, but also from any of the intermediate terms. In fact, still assuming that repression, even when interiorized in the individual, is always social in nature, the series goes from a maximum to a minimum range of repression and from a minimum to a maximum range of repressed, crossing through contradictions that divide an ever widening human space. As long as the repressed is confined to the unconscious, the contradiction is between unconscious and consciousness (situation A); once it penetrates the consciousness, it is within the divided consciousness of an individual (situation B); once it overcomes the individual, it is between the individual and society (situation C); once society is involved, it is between a minority, in a broadly political sense, and established order (situation D); once it has found a place within an established order, it is between one or more codes of behavior and another one or more codes (situation E).

To avoid any misunderstanding, I would insist on the fact that I do not attribute any psychological, sociological, or anthropological value to this series, that is, no value which is directly related to extraliterary reality, even if this were considered as the "content-purport" of literary works. I would instead maintain that all the contradictions in question, just like the one considered so far in concrete form, may impose themselves in the form and in the "content-substance" of a text and must be assumed by the empirical addressee, when he assumes the addressee-function contained in the text.

Three examples: Emma Bovary's desire, unlike Phaedra's, is accepted into the consciousness of the addressee-function before being accepted into that of the character; but it is not supported, nor does it give rise to any claim directed at changing sexual mores or the social order, the condition of women or the mentality of the petite bourgeoisie. It is an example of situation C. As an empirical addressee, I might condemn adultery and despise provincial snobbery, or I might be a feminist and a progressive. If, however, I assume the addressee-function, I shall not be able to *read* Emma Bovary's desire as something that is not accepted (situation B) or as something supported (situation D) without being in danger of not understanding the novel or of not deriving pleasure from it. —A sense of indignation at the ignoble morality of the casuistic and slandering Jesuits is supported in the *Provinciales,* in which there is not a single sentence that is not directed both passionately and practically at putting an end to the abuses in the sacrament of confession and at championing the cause of the innocent and persecuted Jansenists. It is not something authorized, however, because the author is on the side of the party that is worse off as regards the established ecclesiatical order. This is an example of situation D. As an empirical reader, I might be indifferent to the religious scandal of this casuistry and to the practical aims of pillorying the Jesuits and rehabilitating their victims, or I might consider that these practical goals had been fairly achieved three centuries ago. If, however, I assume the addressee-function, I shall not be able to *read* the controversy in the *Provinciales* as if it were something not supported (situation C) or something authorized (situation E); otherwise I might not understand or derive any pleasure from the letters. — Roland's arrogance in refusing to blow his horn and call for help from the emperor's army against the pagans is something that is authorized by the code of honor, because it exalts the Christian knight's courage and has him risking martyrdom for his faith. It is not, however, authorized by the military code, if it indeed exposes the entire Christian rearguard as well as the hero himself to disaster and thus clashes immediately, but in vain, with Oliver's more prudent point of view. This is an example of situation E. An empirical addressee of the Middle Ages might have approved of Oliver's reasoning and of military prudence without a shadow of doubt, or he might have thought that only Roland's foolhardy behavior was praiseworthy and right and proper in every sense. In assuming the addressee-function, however, he could not have *read* Roland's refusal as something that was not authorized (situation D) or authorized by all possible codes (a situation in which one can no longer refer to a return of the repressed); otherwise, he might not have understood or derived pleasure from the poem.

What could be an example of situation A? The very qualification that the return of the repressed be unconscious to the addressee-function seems to make a summary exemplification much more difficult. And it is superfluous to add that the three examples briefly put forward for situations C, D, and E could demonstrate their own aptness and at the same time demonstrate some usefulness in the typology only after an analysis like the one I carried out on an example of situation B — *Phèdre*. Nevertheless, if it was possible to apply the model of Freudian negation to situation B on the condition of postulating the acceptance of the repressed into the consciousness where it nevertheless continues to be negated, an action that drives it back into the unconscious, even if only periodically, will give rise to situation A, to the original model of Freudian negation. In Chapter 3 (p. 19), I formulated the hypothesis that comicality in Molière frequently takes on the role of Freudian negation. When the reasoning of those great comic maniacs, more than one of Molière's protagonists, conceals a return of the repressed, the emotional identification with the character and his comicality seem to become inversely proportional, entering into a relationship of negated and negating element respectively. It might be thought, however, that that which decreases as the character becomes more comical — and increases as he becomes less so — is not so much the emotional identification itself as the *degree of consciousness* of that identification. Naturally, here, the problem is not interesting as a psychological problem referring to the empirical addressee, but as a semiotic problem referring to the addressee-function.

This fluctuation or intermittence of the emotional identification is most notably stimulated in the addressee-function by the protagonist of *Le Misanthrope*. Alceste is destined inexorably to make us laugh frequently, though certainly not always, if, as a female admirer of his observes in the comedy, his mania "has something noble and heroic about it." In this case, we have an alternation between situation A and situation B, and indeed there is no reason to expect that the tendentious contents of a work of literature should all fit into just one of the situations in the series. Since Alceste must have seemed comical more frequently and more obviously to seventeenth-century spectators than to a modern, post-Romantic audience, one might say that to define precisely the limits between situations A and B in the text of the *Misanthrope* is to recreate a historically correct reading of it.[3] And this is not the only case in which the misinterpretation of a text in the course of time may be understood as an arbitrary shifting of the reading from one of these situations to another. The typology should therefore also be helpful in defining certain diachronic vicissitudes in the interpretation of texts.

I would select instead another of Molière's comedies as a purely summary example of situation A: *L'Avare*. Harpagon's mania, unlike Alceste's, is too regressive and degrading to be admitted even for a moment to identification with the ego without being inexorably driven from consciousness into the unconscious by the comic sanction.[4] Thus, while the example I have chosen for the highest level in the series, the *Chanson de Roland*, makes one hesitate in continuing to refer to a return of the repressed because the protagonist is so noble and exemplary, the example which I have chosen for the lowest level makes one hesitate in continuing to speak of emotional identification because the protagonist is so repulsive. In any case, the problem of unconscious emotional identification seems to be linked to that of comicality, whose resources are institutionalized in one or more literary genres: in these, examples of situation A must chiefly be sought. Moreover, Freud's book on jokes surely presents and analyzes more than one example of such a return of the repressed destined—or condemned—to remain unconscious to the addressee-function.

Every reader to whom the typology, now fully exemplified, does not seem entirely meaningless, can amuse himself by finding his own examples of the various textual situations. Since we are dealing with textual

3. See my "Preambulo a una lettura freudiana del *Misanthrope*," *Strumenti critici*, 31 (1976): 384-403 and "Lettura freudiana del *Misanthrope*," *Micromégas*, 6-7 (1976): 19-55.
4. The example of *L'Avare* as well as the theoretical problem of situation A have been reexamined, though briefly, in my "Preambolo a una letture freudiana del *Misanthrope*."

situations and not with the psychology of the characters, it should be unnecessary to advise the reader that one may legitimately speak of emotional identification or, at any rate, of identification proposed to the addressee-function even when there are no characters. A partial example of this was Pascal's *Provinciales,* in which the only characters to take shape are ridiculous and negative like the two Reverend Fathers. The importance of an example like this is reserved for the hypothesis of an inverted identification, one occurring in the values that oppose the disvalues from which the text actually alienates us.[5] To better understand each other, we shall speak of an addresser-function, which is also contained in the text and is not to be confused with the empirical addresser, the historical person of the author. I repeatedly postulated this function earlier on when referring to the discourse of the text, to the form that imposes itself there on the "content-substance," and so on; and, because I spoke of a consciousness to whom the discourse is directed, I should now speak of a consciousness which *directs the discourse.* The identification proposed as the addressee-function is always essentially an identification with the addresser-function and is no different from the capacity exercised by an empirical addressee, to understand a literary text by reducing its figures and enjoy it.[6]

I should like to mention in passing that an identification thus conceived opens up extremely interesting psychological perspectives concerning the ego of the empirical addressee, if one thinks of a theory of the ego such as Lacan's, deduced from Freudian premises: "the *ego* as constituted in its nucleus by a series of alienating identifications."[7] When the so-called characters are delineated in a text, privileged cases of "alienating" literary identification may be created for the empirical addressee, who assumes the addressee-function (one who knows something about this is that empirical addressee of chivalresque romance conceived as a character — Don Quixote).[8] But if the real identification, going beyond the character, is always with an addresser-function, it is clear why earlier I found that the characters were not sufficient to determine the specific situations of the return of the repressed. It is clear, too, why the constants in every specific situation of the return of the repressed seemed to me to be a necessary part of the literary code and often identifiable in the particular rules of the genres. The awareness of the code and of the literary genres

5. The fact that the effect of alienation should nevertheless be the equivalent of an overturned identification was observed by Brecht: "The alienation effect intervenes, not in the form of absence of emotion, but in the form of emotions which need not correspond to those of the character portrayed." "Alienation effects in Chinese Acting," in *Brecht on Theatre: The Development of an Aesthetic,* ed. and trans. John Willet (New York: Hill and Wang, 1964), p. 94.

6. See Appendix 2, "Constants, Variants, and Misreadings," last paragraph.

7. Jacques Lacan, "La chose freudienne ou sens du retour à Freud en psychanalyse," in *Ecrits* (Paris: Editions du Seuil, 1966), p. 417.

8. See Appendix 4, "Literary Identification and Established Order."

by an empirical addresser or author, insofar as it gives rise to options, is that which is currently termed his "poetics." And in this poetics stage the specific situations of the return of the repressed may already be decisively selected by an author, even before they are formed and substantiated in the content of a text by the addresser-function.

For example, the poetics of so-called Romanticism often seem to involve the individualistic choice of a return of the repressed which is accepted but not supported (situation C). And the same thing can be observed even more frequently in the poetics of "art for art's sake," as well as generally, for historical and social reasons not difficult to surmise, in great literature from the rise of the bourgeoisie to the present, by writers who could not help challenging the class to which they nevertheless continued to belong. — The choice of a return of the repressed that is conscious but not accepted (situation B), by which the consciousness is divided and at times even torn apart by laughter, seems to have been preferred by the poetics of the so-called Baroque era, from the late Renaissance onward, and also by the so-called Classical period in France, for historical reasons that are far less clear to me. — A return of the repressed which is authorized, even if by one code of behavior only (situation E), and, for instance, by the chivalresque code, seems to characterize literary genres favored by static social conditions, in which even the most serious conflict cannot become problematic; this is the case of the Spanish theater of honor, in which revenge and murder are celebrated as the fulfillment of duty, with relatively little tension. — I have already remarked that an unconscious return of the repressed (situation A) seems to be identifiable in any comic literary genre, from jokes to comedy. The interpretations that can often be suggested to us in this regard by the theater of Molière ought to take as a point of departure such features as the centering of the comedy around a maniacal protagonist, which have become characteristic of the genre, in effect modifications of the literary code. — Finally, a return of the repressed which is supported but not authorized (situation D) seems necessarily not only to be typical of certain genres in which a practical or, in the broad sense, political aim is provided for by the literary code, but generally also to be typical of the literature of every age in which an active minority has attempted to change, if not revolutionize, the reality of the world, from all the crucial periods in the history of Christianity, to the battle for enlightenment of the progressive period of the European bourgeoisie, to the worldwide struggle of the proletariat against the bourgeoisie, which is still in progress today:

Anyone who struggles and labors to change the world must necessarily be more concerned with the reality principle than the pleasure principle, more with consciousness than the unconscious and more with the correctness of ideologies than the fascination of the figures. This explains why in only one of the five situations that I have abstractly defined is it assumed that the figures use their fascination in the service of a return of the repressed that wishes to change the reality of the world. In all the others, even when there is no Freudian negation of the return of the repressed to divide the individual or the consciousness, it is in effect neutralized by the fictitious importance of the literary institution, which already acts as a Freudian negation as such.[9] Here is a theoretical justification of all the practical intolerance that the acquiescence or idleness of literature can stimulate from time to time, healthy intolerance, obviously, not only when literature yields to its own repressive moment and the two together yield to the established order, but also when it exhibits contents and forms of protest as exhausted as is so often the case today. The political consciousness then protests against the unsuccessful or false or useless protest of literature: words, words, words! But words serve some purpose every time their communicating language, endowed with figures, serves at once to vindicate and recognize that the pleasure principle and the logic of the unconscious have their own profound rights.

No one can permit himself to ignore these rights, especially not anyone who struggles and labors to change the world, not even when the aim of the struggle and the labor is the freedom from need for himself and others; for the voice of desire within man does not readily allow itself to be muffled by the voice of need, and it makes itself heard that much louder as soon as the latter is appeased and silenced. Unlike the voice of need, the voice of desire is never allowed to remain silent. And if the circumstances of reality stifle it, and the illusions of the hereafter no longer satisfy it, it then makes itself heard unintelligibly in the false notes of neurosis, which cruelly avenges the betrayal of the rights of the pleasure principle and the logic of the unconscious upon the individual and upon society. To determine both the political causes and effects of neurosis is a task that goes beyond the subject of this book, as well as beyond the competence of its author. On this point, however, I do believe that the avoidance of a confrontation between Marxism and Freudianism, or an erroneous one, would have very serious consequences for the progress of mankind. This is a danger that will exist as long as psychoanalysis remains a privilege or an instrument of advanced capitalist societies on the one hand and the object of obscurantist exclusion in communist societies or milieux on the other. Thus, satisfying the demand for a less superficial confrontation so that the first of these two situations does not remain an excuse for the other is, in my opinion, the responsibility of *all* Marxist intellectuals.

The problem that I have tackled in this book in attempting to define literature as a phenomenon of which neurosis is the negative side, as the

9. See Part I, pp. 18-19.

positive social side of the human unconscious, is a limited problem but neither extraneous nor secondary to that confrontation. My position may also be considered, if one likes, as an antirepressive apologia of any literature that might deserve it. In the long poem transmitted as a classic over thousands of years, or in a sentence uttered but once in private and registered by no one, we are indebted to the same type of discourse: that which bears institutionally within itself not only a gleam of truth but also a glimpse of rejoicing, even when it springs from the most stifling conditions of reality. This can be a great boon to man and therefore, in Freud's words which I happily quote a second time: "One must bind one's own life to that of others so closely and be able to identify oneself with others so intimately that the brevity of one's own life can be overcome." If this in particular is true, the pleasure derived from literature offers a much more enduring benefit to mankind than the untrustworthy subterfuges of parapraxes, the painful defenses of symptoms, or the hallucinatory gratification of dreams.

TABLE OF EQUIVALENTS BETWEEN THE TERMINOLOGY EMPLOYED

Terminology derived from Jakobson	Terminology derived from Hjelmslev	Terminology of neo-rhetorical origin	Freud's terminology in "Jokes"	New terminology of Freudian origin	
Message, addresser-function, addressee-function	Expression-form and expression-substance content-form	Figures	Techniques	Formal return of the repressed	Judgment of aesthetic value
	Content-substance		Tendentious-ness or innocence	Return of the repressed, or not, in the content-substance: Situations A, B, C, D, E	
	Content-purport	Reduction, degree zero	Reduction, contents having or lacking great substance (value)	Return of the repressed, or not, in the content-purport	Judgment of ideological value
Empirical addresser, empirical addressee					

Appendixes

The Compromise-Formation
as a Freudian Model

Can my discourse still rightly claim to be called Freudian after the terminological and conceptual leap that extends the meaning of "repression" and "return of the repressed" from unconscious to conscious, from individual to social, and from sexual to ideological-political contents, or rather to "nonconformist" contents of every kind? Freud himself once warned against using terms too freely: "one gives way first in words, and then little by little in substance too."[1] I am, in fact, about to make a claim of coherence and not of orthodoxy; there is no reason why I should prefer this to the opposite claim, which is that of originality. That is, unless one does not attribute to the term orthodoxy its only valid meaning by arguing that it is more orthodox to refer to certain parts of the vast production of a master which are less pertinent to a specific subject but more determinative for the coherence of his work as a whole than to refer to other parts of that work which are directly pertinent to the subject but marginal compared to the work as a whole, coherent only on the surface, mechanically deduced or applied. Thus I believe, for example, that anyone maintaining he can start out from Marx, instead of Freud, to establish the foundations of a materialist theory of art will find much more of interest in the first chapter of *Das Kapital*, where the subject is merchandise and there is not a word about art, than in the entire anthology of passages in which Marx and Engels expressed literary or artistic views.

All things considered, the practice of such an "unfaithful" orthodoxy, as compared to the well-known misdeeds of faithful orthodoxy, is the only way of attempting to break free retroactively of the bonds that the intellectual division of labor has always imposed (how could it do otherwise?) on man's genius. If Marx or Freud has modified our entire outlook on human reality, the task of modifying our outlook on a single phenomenon, such as literature, should *also* be based on their thought. Nevertheless, who can assure us that the formidable application of their intellectual energies on a quite different field left them the attitude, the time, and so on, to see personally *also* to that task in the most correct manner?

I believe that in order to decide whether my extended use of the terms in question may or may not be called coherent, or "unfaithfully" orthodox, one must first of all have decided on the answer to a question of much greater import.

1. Sigmund Freud, "Group Psychology and the Analysis of the Ego," *Standard Edition*, 18: 91.

Which of the following two concepts in Freud's thought precedes and determines, which follows and is determined: that of unconscious and that of psychic conflict, with the relative tendency toward compromise in their tendentiousness? Not even with all due respect for the dating of Freud's thought through a work that took such a long time to evolve, can there be any doubt about this abstract primacy. It is Freud's deeply and intimately conflictive conception of human civilization and of the individual psyche within it which opens up space for the unconscious in the psyche or, even better, closes up space within it, and not the other way round. The repression that constitutes the unconscious is merely the result, even though it is for the new science the most radical, the most exemplary, and the most important result, of a chronic conflict: that which begins again for each individual from the moment he *enters* human civilization as a child, and which is a conflict that is chronically identical to civilization. It is not by chance that in Chapter 3, just one page after the terminological definition in question, I was obliged to quote the whole of the famous passage from the first lecture of the *Introductory Lectures on Psycho-Analysis,* in which Freud expounds such a conception of civilization.

I quote now from another of the earliest and thus again from one of the most "introductory" of the *Introductory Lectures:* "It is important to begin in good time to reckon with the fact that mental life is the arena and battle-ground for mutually opposing purposes or, to put it non-dynamically, that it consists of contradictions and pairs of contraries." He does not, for example, say *contains,* but *consists of,* and does not say the unconscious, but mental life, not the larger part but the whole. Freud then continues: "Proof of the existence of a particular purpose is no argument against the existence of an opposite one; there is room for both. It is only a question of the attitude of these contraries to each other, and of what effects are produced by the one and by the other."[2] The latter statement could have been used as an epigraph for the typology of conflictive situations, of structures of the contradiction within the literary work, that is outlined in the final chapter of the present volume. Furthermore, in this same lecture, dedicated to parapraxes, Freud seems to give the example of a typology of *degrees of repression* of an intention, proportional, naturally, to the degrees of its incompatability with another that acts as an obstacle and places it in a repressed position. These degrees of repression are in fact equivalent to degrees of distance from the consciousness and as such are also proportional to different separations from it in time.[3] Repression within the unconscious may well be the ultimate result of psychic conflict, but it is still a subspecies of it. I would hazard the claim that everywhere in Freud, as an ultimate result and as a subspecies, it may be conceived as the starting point or point of arrival of any set of psychic conflicts, which may range from the most unconscious of repressed instincts to the full knowledge of the consciousness.

At this point, I can foresee further objections. Would my proposal, thus, be Freudian only on the condition that it also allows us to go beyond the actual area of the unconscious, moving upward, toward a less extreme or even more generic

2. Freud, *Introductory Lectures on Psycho-Analysis,* pt. 1, *Standard Edition,* 15: 76-77.
3. Ibid., pp. 65-66.

confliction than that which gathers in the phenomenon of repression in the narrow sense? What right does my discourse have to start out from the presumption that the language of literature and that of the unconscious have "something in common," and to pretend to confirm this common characteristic at its point of arrival? A minimum and preliminary reply to such objections must lead us back to the concept of a "formal return of the repressed," which is proposed in chapters 12 and 13 of this book. According to the Freudian model of the joke, which is a joke only because of specific techniques or formal characteristics, and excluding the presence of any kind of content, whether "of great substance (or value)" or "tendentious," I assumed that only the presence of phenomena of the "formal return of the repressed" in a sufficient amount, or, in other words, of a fairly high "figurality rate," can actually define the literariness of a text. That Freudian model, however, did indeed have something in common with the unconscious and it was something essential: it made of the joke a compromise-formation, between respect for sense and pleasure taken in transgressing it, between playing with the signifiers and rearrangement of the signified. By extending this model to the entire area of "figures" in a neorhetorical sense and at the same time pointing out the very principle of the identification of literary language in the "quantity" of figures, I have attempted to provide hypothetically for literary language, on the basis of the transitive property and apart from all the distinctions elaborated in those two chapters, nothing less than a Freudian principle of identification.

"Unfaithful" orthodoxy, certainly, could dare no more. Yet, this first reply is still as I said, minimal, and it would be evasive to pretend that the problem is solved by going back to a hypothetical principle of identification. Indeed, though I have caused the principle of identification of literary language to coincide with formal characteristics, I have nonetheless reserved for "tendentious" contents such a probable role in the qualification of great literature, and such a relatively broad abstract treatment, that the element of doubt contained in the initial question is also justified with reference to the contents alone, and requires a reply that is not minimal and deals with these as well.

In the attempt to establish a homogeneous and progressive series of structures of contradictions in the last chapter of the book, I gradually passed from conflicts which, at the level of reality, we can conceive only in Freudian terms — that conflict between the unconscious and consciousness, or even that within the consciousness — to conflicts which, still at the level of reality, we can conceive without referring to Freud at all — that between a minority in a broadly political sense and established order, that between several accepted codes within an established order. Nevertheless, I warned, even explicitly (p. 182), that this did not mean considering any of these contradictions *at the level of reality,* at which, obviously, even those of the latter type can project themselves in some way within the individuality of one person only, but cannot avoid distributing themselves among a great number of people. In both cases, and particularly in the second, they can also fail to produce any compromise: some people will only remain on one side of the fence and others only on the other. At the level of the literary discourse, the only one to which I wished to refer, no conflict can come into play without involving both factions at the same time, whether situated on this or that side of the fence. And however violent and irreconcilable this imaginary conflict is, the discourse that takes it on in its entirety must act as the discourse of one voice or one single person, directed at each addressee in an undivided way.

A theory that wishes to give a privileged position to this tendentious confliction in the contents of the literary work is not only Freudian because it makes the work *consist of contradictions and pairs of contraries* and attempts to determine *the attitude of these contraries to each other, and what effects are produced by the one and by the other.* As regards the reciprocal position and respective effects of the contents in conflict, this theory will also be able to avail itself of the same model that it had utilized for the tensions that in turn comprised the form, and which is the model of maximum confliction, or, better still, of the strictest, closest confliction discussed by Freud: that which qualifies all manifestations of the unconscious as *compromise-formations.* One after the other Freud thus qualified jokes, as we have seen, and dreams, parapraxes, which are "the outcome of a compromise: they constitute a half-success and a half-failure for each of the two intentions"[4]—and symptoms, which are "the product of a compromise and arise from the mutual interference between two opposing currents; they represent not only the repressed but also the repressing force which had a share in their origin."[5] And elsewhere: "The two forces which have fallen out meet once again in the symptom and are reconciled, as it were, by the compromise of the symptom that has been constructed."[6] We must not allow ourselves to be distracted by an expression like *are reconciled,* because no conciliation was ever more forced, more dynamic, or more dramatic than those of the majority of Freudian descriptions of compromise-formations in the language of the unconscious. Usually, within the silence of this compromise, the voices of the opposing parties are reconciled only in that they both cry out as being unreconciled. Then, a little later, by allowing us to benefit from attention now given to the semantic rather than the energetic contrast, Freud defines the symptom as "an ingeniously chosen piece of ambiguity with two meanings in complete mutual contradiction."[7]

At this point, I would perceive the following difference between a literary work, even the most decisively committed in ideological terms, and one of pure and simple ideology. The latter alone can limit itself to a rational, resolute, and exclusive choice between *two intentions* or *two opposing currents* or *two forces* or, especially, *two meanings.* Here it may be both right and obvious that the error, the enemy, and so on, has no say in the letter of the text. But the characteristic of the great literary work, just as that of linguistic negation, according to Benveniste who compares it to Freudian negation, "is that it can annul only what has been uttered, which it has set up for the express purpose of suppressing."[8] Thus, it is difficult for the literary work not to allow the enemy to speak, even if in only a

4. Ibid., p. 66.
5. Freud, *Introductory Lectures on Psycho-Analysis,* pt. 3, *Standard Edition,* 16: 301.
6. Ibid., pp. 358-59.
7. Ibid., p. 360.
8. Emile Benveniste, *Problèmes de linguistique générale* (Paris: Gallimard, 1966), p. 84; Eng. trans. (Coral Gables, Fla., 1971), p. 73.

temporary, tendentious, indirect, and ambiguous manner; and since the discourse will still be a single one, it will have to become entirely ambiguous in one way or another. This does not necessarily mean that the reader will have any doubts about which of the two contradictory meanings is the right one, but rather that in order to identify himself, accept himself, and select himself as the ego of the work's discourse, he will be unable to avoid comparing himself to every rejected subject other than the ego. In this sense, while it is important for us to remember that Racine and Molière do not have us listen only to the voice of the guilty Phaedra or the ridiculous maniacs, but also to that of innocence, reason, or authority from the other characters, we should not, however, forget about comprehending why Pascal allows the Jesuits to speak at great length, Voltaire, the fanatics, and Brecht, the capitalists.

In the latter cases, it is clear at the end or even from the beginning who is right and who is wrong. Nevertheless, when the intention that is in the wrong is given enough space to achieve *half a success,* and thus to have inflicted on it only *half a failure,* there can logically be no doubt about the diminished character of the success and failure of the opposite intention, the one that is in the right. Moreover, in the literary presentation of a conflict, success and failure can mean different things according to whether one refers to the order of the values proposed for identification or to that of the events imagined in the narration. A not infrequent compromise is, in fact, that which merely inverts the positive and negative signs between values and events: he who is in the wrong must win; he who is in the right must lose. This is an example of one of the many narrative possibilities belonging to the literary work and not to the ideological one, for only in the former can an imaginary, fictitious space be opened up, in which the hallucination becomes social while remaining favorable to contradictions, just as in an individual's dream. To me, nothing seems more faithful to Freud in spirit than to maintain the inevitability of the projection, in this space, of the confliction of all that is human, according to its most intense model, that which includes any manifestation of the unconscious, but which is nevertheless not applicable to the unconscious alone.

Given all this, I am willing to admit that my extensive use of "repression" and "return of the repressed" is not unrelated to the success of Marcuse's work *Eros and Civilization* in the years preceding the 1970s. This is a book which meant much to me and in whose pages one can read the warning that these terms "are used in the non-technical sense to designate both conscious and unconscious, external and internal processes of restraint, constraint and suppression."[9] In Marcuse, however, the extension of the concept is concerned both with art and with the whole of reality and the way one views it, while in my book it concerns a model which not only is applicable to literature alone, but, in effect, to specific literary situations described in detail as such. Any insistence on the influence of Marcuse, in this case, merely serves to prove how far the interdisciplinary inventiveness that surrounds Freudian psychoanalysis is lagging behind on the semiotic, linguistic, rhetorical, and logical front compared to the front involving anthropology, sociology, or politics. This would be a way of ignoring the fact that my

9. Herbert Marcuse, *Eros and Civilization* (New York: Vintage Books, 1961), p. 7.

book implies, and to some extent develops, a reading of Freud according to which the discovery of the Oedipus complex, for instance, with all its immense import, is nevertheless not as momentous as the continued valorization of one or more unattested logical models, or rather illogical or antilogical (questioning a logic) models,[10] which are empty a priori, that is, capable of being filled by the most varied and innumerable historico-individual contents.

The highest example of these models, the principal seat of their dynamics, the origin of their being extendable to every region of human thought, even the completely conscious, is the presence within man's psyche of that region or field of energy or that type of thought that Freud—whether he attempted to define it in topical, energetic, or logical terms—always called the unconscious. The compromise-formation par excellence is the return of the repressed in the narrow sense, which presupposes repression in the same sense, which presupposes the unconscious. No Aristotelian or scientific logic, however, and indeed no logic other than that attributed by Freud to the manifestations of the unconscious either provides for or admits a model like that of the compromise-formation. Within it the dynamic postulate of a clash of psychic energies produces a semiotic result in the languages of the dream, the parapraxis, and the symptom, or a strictly linguistic result in the only case of verbal, communicating language that Freud related to the unconscious—the joke.

Let us return, in the relevant text, to those irreplaceable pages on hostile, cynical, and skeptical jokes. It is only later on that Freud explains that there is always a return of the repressed in the narrow sense in the relationship between the "techniques" that constitute the joke formally and the unconscious. Moreover, how could one fail to observe that "tendentiousness," which is clearly present even if not a constituent, frequently asserts itself as a return of repressed contents without being unconscious in any way? How, too, could one pretend that the one "return" should remain unrelated to the other, instead of postulating a concept and a term inclusive of both? I believe that in using the expression "return of the repressed," I did not so much follow Marcuse's influence at the time, but rather the need for such a concept and such a term. If the expression thus takes on the meaning; *a compromise-formation as the semiotic result of a clash of energies, even beyond a literally unconscious area,* then it is Freud himself who pointed the way to the extrapolation; and in any case, what abstract model cannot be extrapolated, when it serves some specific purpose? Freud gave two examples of this in his work and, not surprisingly, these are the only occasions in which he was really able to discuss the merits of unconscious interferences in a literary language without dwelling on the exploitation of literary texts for psychological and biographical ends as he did in other essays. One instance is in *Jokes;* the other occurs in the essay entitled "The Uncanny" ("Das Unheimliche").

The sensation or emotion of the "uncanny" refers, in this essay with its exceptional wealth of fully developed ideas as well as ingenious suggestions, to "that class of the frightening which leads back to what is known of old and long familiar,"[11] but which has ceased to be known and familiar for an equally long

---

10. Ignacio Matte-Blanco, *The Unconscious as Infinite Sets* (London: Duckworth, 1975); see also Part II, p. 139, n. 2.

11. Freud, "The Uncanny," *Standard Edition*, 17: 220.

time, since it "can be shown to be something repressed which *recurs.*"[12] At the point in the text where this definition is given in terms of a return of the repressed, Freud has not yet set up any distinctions between the various examples of the uncanny which he examines, either according to their belonging to real experience or literary fiction, or according to other criteria. Nevertheless, after recognizing, in a large portion of the examples, the persistence of archaic or infantile beliefs, related to the oppositions between the animate and inanimate, mortality and life after death, and the like, he reconsiders whether that specific definition may be applied in this case. This "no doubt extends the term 'repression' beyond its legitimate meaning,"[13] since these primitive beliefs have never been forgotten and even less been repressed in the narrow sense, either throughout the long individual evolution from child to adult, or the long social evolution from magic to scientific civilization; they have rather been *surmounted* (*über-wunden*).

Thus, even if he does not actually coin it here, Freud virtually and conceptually authorizes an analogical expression such as "return of the surmounted," which means that he treats as variants contents that are or are not typical of the unconscious, compared to a formal model which is definitely typical of the unconscious and which he treats as a constant. Earlier, when asking himself "what has become of the repression" in the case of fear of the dead and of death, he actually identified it in the fact that "all supposedly educated people have ceased to believe officially that the dead can become visible as spirits" and in other analogous cultural conditions,[14] which obviously do not involve a repression in the narrow sense, but only a rational suppression of something. Of what? Whether one calls it a repressed in the narrow and erroneous sense, or in the broad and correct sense, or whether one calls it specifically a "surmounted," what I am really stressing is simply the constancy of a model that is empty a priori. No doubt Freud created it in order regularly to fill a part of it with unconscious contents. But it is clear that he was able to transfer it almost inadvertently from cases of psychic conflict, which have been translated into a repression in the narrow sense, to cases that have only the model in common with such a repression. And when he finally introduces the distinction between examples drawn either from experience or from literature, it is to combine it almost immediately with that earlier distinction between the "return of the surmounted" and the true return of the repressed, which occurs when the uncanny is linked to infantile complexes (and not beliefs).

It is, in fact, literary fiction that seems to him to contain prevalently the return of surmounted and magic beliefs.[15] He admirably conjectures that the uncanny effect of some texts and passages is (one might say) inversely proportional to the degree to which these beliefs have been taken up by the code of the literary genre,[16] and is dependent on the narrative viewpoint or the identification that favors or excludes a particular character, and on the greater or lesser degree of

12. Ibid., p. 241.
13. Ibid., p. 249.
14. Ibid., p. 242.
15. Ibid., p. 247.
16. Ibid., pp. 249-51.

knowledge of the spectator or reader, as well as on the seriousness of the tone selected.[17] Such clear attention to the formal characteristics of the literary discourse is anything but common in Freud. It is thus no coincidence that here, as in *Jokes*, it is accompanied by the extrapolation of the model of the return of the repressed beyond the "legitimate meaning" of the term repression. Both procedures, in both cases, seem to depend merely on the recognition of the communicating, as well as the signifying, nature of the language in question. Like anyone else after him, Freud could not show interest in literature and at the same time treat the model of the return of the repressed in the true and restrictive sense without running the risk of dealing with the language of literature as one deals correctly with the noncommunicating languages of dreams, parapraxes, and symptoms; that is, the risk of dealing with it incorrectly. I have written against the old prejudice that there is no escaping such a distortion if one attempts to study literature on a Freudian basis, and also against the new prejudice that there is no distortion because the difference between communicating and noncommunicating languages is negligible or nonexistent.

I propose to call the compromise-formation, as defined above, the "Freudian model" *tout court*. It will then be obvious that I have spoken of repression and return of the repressed only to describe its two components, or, as I prefer to call them, *opponents*, both when the viewpoint was fixed at the level of literary theory, where the model is empty a priori, and when it was fixed at the level of a literary analysis, which involved the contents by which it had been filled a posteriori. Naturally, an opposition between empty and full variants of the model can have only a relative sense and an empirical use. Even the most abstract variant is "filled" with a minimum of tangible content, conflict, compromise, without which the model that we are formulating would be neither identifiable nor consistent. On the other hand, even the most tangible variant is obtained by "emptying" real fact (in our case, textual, literary fact) by a process of abstraction, without which no model, but only the text, would be identifiable and consistent. Thus, the strictest sense in which it will be useful to speak of empty and full variants is a sense which causes this opposition to coincide either with that between extra-literary and literary area, or with that between undetermined and determined textual areas within literary phenomena, or, in practice, with the distinction between theory and analysis.

In the first part of this book, the use of the fraction $\frac{\text{REPRESSION}}{\text{REPRESSED}}$ answered the need for a formulation of the model at its level of greatest extraliterary generality, while that in which I had symbolized the Freudian negation I $\left\{ \frac{\text{DO NOT}}{\text{LIKE IT}} \right.$, corresponded to a less general variant of the model but one which was still empty, that is, extraliterary, or existing in the literary area not determined in any textual contents. Contrariwise, the fractions into which I translated the "symbolic negations" identified in the semantic system of the tragedy corresponded to entirely filled variants of the model, that is, determined in the textual contents. As for the symbolic fractions easily arrived at from the typology in the final chapter of the book, if one were to rewrite the typology thus: $\frac{\text{NOT ACCEPTED}}{\text{CONSCIOUS}}$,

17. Ibid., p. 252.

$$\frac{\text{NOT SUPPORTED}}{\text{ACCEPTED}}$$, and the like; their level of abstraction would be lower than that of the Freudian negation because it is circumscribed within the literary area, but higher than the "symbolic negations" of *Phèdre,* because it refers to undetermined textual areas or to textual areas determined only as an example. The *continuum* of these descending levels of generalization is broken in practice above all by the opposition between the empty, meaning textually indeterminate, variants, which serve the aims of theory, and the full, meaning textually determinate, variants, which serve the aims of analysis. In the latter case, the levels of approximation to the literally concrete may continue to be differentiated and to descend even after a first level of full variants is reached. The detailed analysis of a text requires abstractions at many levels.

Constants, Variants, and Misreadings

The concept to which I made the expression "addressee-function" correspond is certainly not in itself an original contribution of mine. Both because of its more or less recent, Russian or French formalistic origin, and because it is comprehensible only in opposition to the concept of "empirical-historical addressee", it is in danger of appearing inseparable from antihistorical implications. The internal coherence of the literary work should be contrasted with the confusion of its infinite links to the historical context in order to justify a lack of interest in the latter. Yet there is no need to ponder very long to realize that the concept is also concerned with the ideals of a correct reading, the right meaning, and the like, that derive precisely from the area of historicist-philological studies. Thus, it is concerned with their negative counterpart, the idea of a misreading, which has now been made unfashionable by a laborious diffidence toward the knowability of texts in which (to me, no philosopher) there seems to be projected, to a lesser extent, a not altogether innocent distrust of the knowability of the world.

For me to distinguish between an addressee-function and an empirical addressee merely means the following: to attempt to establish a determinate number of *constants* which the meaning of a work will maintain for every reader and every reading, and to distinguish them from the infinite series of *variants*, which involves the varying individuality of the reader, of the age in which he lives, of the moment in which the reading takes place, of whether the reading is individual or choral, integral or fragmentary, the first or the thousandth, and so on. The last alternative, whose consequences are hardly in doubt, is the clearest, didactically speaking. If, for example, I read for the first time a work in which an element of enigmatic ignorance, of *suspense*, is prolonged, or if instead I reread it as an empirical addressee, on the first occasion I take part psychologically in this ignorance, but not on successive ones. This, then, is a variant. Nevertheless, as one who has taken on the addressee-function, I shall be faced with a text that will always be written in the same way, that will be invariably contrived, played out on that suspense, and thus constant. (It should not be held up as an objection, even jokingly, that no one rereads a detective story once his curiosity to find out who is the murderer is satisfied: the "curiosity" to "find out" again which of the brothers Karamazov murdered his father must still continue to disturb the person who takes on the addressee-function again in Dostoevsky's novel, even if the question was solved long ago for him as an empirical addressee.)

An excellent example of constants of meaning, which I would venture to call blackmailing, since they give the reader no alternative but to understand constantly in *this* way or not to understand at all, are certain audacious metaphors *in absentia.* Anyone who reads "formidable of the earth yawn" in Góngora, and does not interpret it as a cavern, or "this very white diversion close to the ground" in Mallarmé, and does not interpret it as snow, or "this peaceful roof where doves walk" in Valéry, and does not interpret it as sea and white sails, anyone who substitutes his own variant at will for these constants (and I am not the first to observe this) is excluded from the meaning of the text, or has not understood it. Nevertheless, while the peremptory nature of more than a few constants of meaning, even among the problematic ones, has all scholars readily agreeing with each other, or at least, all those who do not defend a freely impressionistic reading, the number of constants recognizable by all is generally much more limited than one might expect. Sooner or later, all of them reveal a fear of "closing" the meaning of a text, and naturally, of impoverishing it by pinning it down to too many constants (if I had to explain the psychology of this attitude, I should not hesitate to speak of claustrophobia). Consequently, it happens that the scholar, according to his methodological tendencies, chooses to defend constants of the type that interests him, and willingly abandons the rest, not to the fear of arbitrariness, but rather to the reassuring unexpectedness of the variants of interpretation.

The scholar with some sort of historicist background will rightly take care that specific, secure relations with the context of an age are not misunderstood, whether concerning literary, ideological, or political history or concerning the general lines of the whole text or an allusion to be interpreted correctly in the small space it occupies. Instead, the text will contain a formal play of symmetries, repetitions, oppositions, which will seem significant to him, but not to the extent of authorizing him to establish seriously their signification. This is where an attempt at deciding upon any constant of meaning at the expense of all the possible variants might make him feel that he was stifling the text. On the other hand, the scholar with some sort of formalistic method will claim that the only things that can be identified with assurance are certain symmetries, repetitions, or oppositions, documented in the text, in the narration, the construction, or the style, on a global or microscopic scale. Where this ground, firm enough for him to tread, ends, he will say that the marshy and unsure ground of the interpretation of contents, including historical relationships, begins, and he will only be able to leap over it at his own risk, with all the freedom that deserves, moreover, the special talent or dilettantism...of other scholars. Indeed, both the former and the latter find a defensive means of escape or an offensive pretext in the intellectual division of labor. From the Freudian viewpoint I have adopted, however, there are two considerations of a general nature that may help the literary scholar to disentangle himself from the difficult situation in which the alternative of open or closed, of finite or infinite, meaning places him.

In the first place, both the decisive importance for the qualification of literary language accorded to the concept of figure (halfway between neorhetoric and the rhetoric of the unconscious) and the highly probable importance attributed to the presence of conflictive contents for the value and success of a work (pp. 174-

75) account for the resistance to recognizing constants of meaning in texts, or, in effect, for a fairly well diffused distaste for specifying, or seeing specified, one or more meanings *with the exclusion* of others. There can be no figure without polysemy, and the extensions of the concept of figure to which I referred project the semantic multivalence to all levels of the literary phenomenon. On the other hand, the adoption of conflictive contents in an implacable and doubtful compromise within a text can only lead to clashes of meaning; the most tendentious readings legitimize themselves when juxtaposed in the plural, since they can refer to opposite but coexistent tendentiousness. This is, in fact, the reason why anyone with doubts about the closed and precise meaning of literary texts is a defender of impressionistic freedom in reading. It also explains the great desire to abuse such skepticism: in the majority of cases, and with good reason, it has an air of "intelligence" compared to which I am well aware that the theorization I have attempted, to the detriment of the open and undefined meaning, risks seeming dogmatic, pedantic, or in the best of hypotheses, immature.

To choose to interest oneself only in the constants of meaning and, as compensation, in all kinds of constants, is a choice of study that I fear is both more naive and more difficult because it is condemned to appear overly humble if one adheres to minimal constants or overly ambitious if instead one goes so far as to injure that margin of ineffability, which many more scholars and readers care about than would actually like to admit. Nevertheless, it must be observed in the second place, that polysemy cannot mean infinite or indefinite but always finite and definite, meaning, however rich this may be, even to the point of ambiguity, or complex to the point of contradictoriness. The Freudian conception makes of the unconscious as a language a place of polysemy for the same reasons that it makes of it a seat of compromise; and the example of Freudian analyses of the manifestations of the unconscious, with their extreme abundance and range but their simultaneous tendency toward precision in the identification of meanings, offers probably the only premise possible for the elimination of that undoubtedly religious residue which is the tenacious and protean prestige of the ineffable.

I have based my use of the concept of addressee-function on these premises, as a summary, or rather organic whole, of the constants of meaning in the reading of a text. In this way, I attempted to attribute to the text itself an objective consistency, which is what remains (though I know well that according to many nothing remains and nothing ought to remain) once the infinite variants that must be debited to the complementary concept of empirical addressee have been subtracted. Among these we may distinguish: advantageous variants in reading, derived from the personal qualities or cultural knowledge of the individual empirical addressee, and pertinent enough to inure him to the comprehension of the work, even without going as far as imposing themselves as functionally indispensable for this purpose; variants in reading, which we may term harmless, such as most of the countless variants that supply the mental stuff of the associations of ideas, changeable from person to person, and from hour to hour; harmful variants in reading, or misreadings, which we may define only by referring to another definition, which, in turn, only acquires consistency according to each individual case, or which we may define as *variants incompatible with any constant* (while harmless variants, and, even more, advantageous variants, are compatible with all constants).

I should finally recall that the addressee-function, as the organization of the constants of meaning in a text, must be identical to an addresser-function (p. 185), though the selection of these constants, which always gives the same result, is obtained from two ever changing groups of variants, since every empirical addressee is different from the single empirical addresser. The variants which must be debited to the latter are intentions, hesitations, associations, and so on, of the author, that have disappeared without a trace, or have been documented by witnesses, declarations, variants in the philological sense, and so on, but which, in any case, have not succeeded in fixing themselves imperatively in the meaning of the text.

Definition of Literature and Literature as an Institution

In adopting for the definition of literature a criterion that was at least potentially objective and based hypothetically on its figurality, I set aside any criterion based not only on its value but also on its destination, convention, or institution, of the type: "literature is that which is produced to be just that or called just that or felt as that." At what point was I first impelled in that direction? When pondering the, so to speak, diluted or intermittent literariness of genres that might be termed "weak" with respect to the "strong" lyrical, narrative, or dramatic genres: those such as memoirs, diaries, the epistolary, or moralistic, as understood in French literature (my specialty), which has a particular wealth of masterpieces among these genres. All that is needed is for the literariness of a text belonging to one of these genres to be recognized and the text will become part of the institution even if the literariness is diluted and intermittent. This is confirmed by the practice of all histories of literature. Moreover, in the case of philosophical, historical, religious, political, or scientific writings, this practice follows a kind of interchangeability between their degree of importance as such and their degree of literariness: the same number of pages in a handbook will be dedicated to a work that is in itself more important but less literary than to one that is more literary but in itself less important.

If there is room in a history of German literature for *Capital,* it is because of the work's importance and not because Marx's writing is at times such as to cause him indirectly to create, in a context laden with summaries and surrounded by statistics, the terrible metaphor of the vampire behind the vision of modern machinery: "in the shape of capital, of dead labour, that dominates, and pumps dry, living labour-power."[1] Yet, once the figural possibilities of such a moment is recognized, we not longer have any valid theoretical motive for stopping short at forms of literariness whose density is equally irregular, merely because we receive them orally instead of in writing, and in moments that are absolutely outside the institution. One arrives inevitably at a definition in which, I am forced to admit, there is in practice more literature than nonliterature in the whole of human discourse.

It is not, however, this overflowing of the concept of literature from its

---

1. Karl Marx, *Capital,* trans. S. Moore and E. Aveling, ed. F. Engels (London, 1889; reprint ed., London: Allen & Unwin, 1946), p. 423.

traditional bounds that bothers me (at worst it could do so because of seeming fashionable, influenced by tendencies that are foreign to me, and anticonformist in a way that is already too facile). I believe that, in itself, this is an inevitable consequence, one of the extreme consequences, of establishing a relationship between the language of literature and that of the unconscious. The problem lies elsewhere. It is precisely from the decisive importance attributed to figurality that the temptation may arise to attribute an indispensable importance to particular macroscopic or synthetic figures which, when present, appear to circumscribe and organize all the others. On the other hand, these figures of figures occur almost solely in those texts whose literariness is strongest and which, consequently, are always a part of the institution. Thus, we can see ourselves being led back immanently from the criterion adopted for defining literature to the one set aside. I am thinking of the simple and crucial fact that a text has a beginning and an end, and it is inevitable that a succession of parts should come to be formed between them. Beginning, end, order of the parts: these are undoubtedly areas privileged to be the seat of every kind of figure of which literary language is capable. In texts whose literariness is strongest, I would say that these areas not only can but must, almost by hypothesis, be the seat of the figures.

It would be inconceivable for the first and last line of a sonnet by Mallarmé or the first and last scene of a tragedy by Racine not to be figurally overdetermined precisely because they are the first and the last. For many works just as markedly structured this emphasis on the textual confines will begin at the title, and in the entire space between one end and the other nothing will be figurally accidental about the order of the parts. It is clear, too, that the order of the parts, in a nonliterary or less densely literary text, will not be at all accidental either, but it will follow an entirely different logic. A historical work or memoirs will, for example, follow and articulate a chronological order. Yet what analytical instruments can one use, when faced with a masterpiece as eccentric with respect to the institution as Saint-Simon's *Mémoires,* to decide whether and in what way the order of the parts is also responsible for the literariness of an immense and chaotic text? It would be legitimate to suppose that here the immensity and the chaos would permeate the text in macroscopic and synthetic figures of various kinds; but considering the precise point at which an almost colorless account of war or a heraldic dissertation ends and a tale or portrait of overwhelming stylistic inventiveness begins, can I really say that something *begins* there, or should I rather speak of something that *begins again,* and, in that case, on the basis of which forms of intermittent continuity? What is the figural status of the "resumption" of a literariness that was interrupted or weakened during the discourse?

We can observe that the passage is quite direct from the problems posed by literarily "weak" genres to those posed by the "moment" of literariness that manifests itself in an ideological text or private letter, which is still a written text, or in an oral discourse, and perhaps even in a single sentence of that discourse. Such a moment, whether discourse or sentence, has as its context (not in the sense of historical context, here, but of preceding and subsequent language) a series of discourses or sentences uttered before and after by the speaker, and even by the addressee, which in effect extends infinitely on both sides. As a fragment of literature, it is framed by dispersion and stands out against shapelessness, as opposed to those texts in which the literary concentration above all strengthens the frame and gives form to the arrangement of each moment. One must thus admit that phenomena with such opposing aspects would not both seem able to be characterized by the name of literature unless all that distinguishes them within that common characteristic could also be defined with greater precision.

At the present time, I do not feel that any occasion arises from these considerations to reject the theoretical proposal based on figurality, which is not contradicted by any of them; but instead there arises a double task for the theory of figures. It would be useful to elaborate two distinct and complementary series of rhetorical concepts in order to define particular figures that are typical respectively of what I shall call closed literariness and open literariness, for want of better terms. On the one hand, figures belonging to titles, to beginnings, to ends, to beginnings and ends of a chapter, or paragraph, canto or verse, act or scene, to all the articulations of parts of a work that presuppose a closed and finished whole, except for the specific problems concerning the unfinished; on the other hand (and this would require a much newer and more difficult study), those figures that accompany a more or less durable opening or closing of a figural dimension in the language, in all situations in which this opening or closing does not coincide with a beginning or an end, which are absolute because they mark the limits of the discourse. We have perceived that the latter study would not only shed light on the transitory and unfortunately elusive literariness of oral discourse, but also on that which includes masterpieces of such importance that it is only in a relative and occasional sense that I have been allowed so far to call them "weak," and to a certain extent, on that of works belonging to strong genres. What actually occurs from this viewpoint, for example, in and around the digressions of Balzac, Tolstoy, and even Proust?

Appendix 4

Literary Identification
and Established Order

That literature has always maintained good relations with established orders and official ideologies would be as untenable a thesis as the opposite one, that it has always explained its effectiveness through some practical subversion. If we ask for witnesses on the role of literature from texts of all periods, in which literature either is the subject or speaks about itself by mirroring its own role, these witnesses *also* untiringly reflect the alienating identification mediated by literature; or, one might say instead, the identifying alienation, if this makes it clearer that a literary mediation is often represented as a means of finding a place in the culture and order of the world, and that the return of the repressed presses beneath or around the best values in which the repression takes pride. Nevertheless, there is no high-level testimony in which the recognition of the identification is not accompanied by conflict, contradictoriness, and compromise, even between alienations.

To begin with, few people have more intelligently penetrated the process than the great ideologists of repression, whose condemnation of art parried a threat to their order (but is there ever only one order?). This is true from Plato, among whose arguments of condemnation is this one: that emotional identification with another character or actor satisfies the inferior part of the soul, which rational repression would dominate if these were *our own* emotions;[1] to Saint Augustine, whose most famous lament is his regret at having cried over Dido, dead as a result of love, and not over himself, dead in God's eyes,[2] but who, elsewhere, actually sets up a double mirror effect, lamenting the lasciviousness contracted as a young man by reading a passage from Terence, in which the lasciviousness of a young man is in turn encouraged by the sight of a painting depicting that of Jupiter;[3] to that Pierre de Blois (ca. 1135-1204), mentioned by Auerbach, whose originality lies in his having deplored, as a rival to the sole identification with Christ, the identification with characters in a courtly epic who are not immoral at all, but actually exemplary;[4] to Pascal, whose sensibility in analyzing the moral

1. Plato, *The Republic*, 603d-606d.
2. Saint Augustine, *The Confessions*, 1: 13: 1-2.
3. Ibid., 1: 16: 1-2; Terence, *The Eunuch*, ll. 583-91.
4. Erich Auerbach, *Literary Language and its Public in Late Latin Antiquity and in the Middle Ages* (London: Routledge & Kegan Paul, 1965), pp. 303-6.

dangers of the theater has appeared to some to conceal a return of the repressed within the very act of condemnation;[5] to the extraordinary lines from Bossuet that I used and quoted in the first part of this book (p. 13); and finally, beyond Christianity, to Rousseau, who, in taking up all the Christian arguments against the theater, adds the impossibility of not boring one's audience by depicting virtue, except for conceiving a misanthrope whose virtue is not ridiculous, contrary to Molière's unpardonable character.[6]

More interesting still for our purposes are those texts which depict within their fiction the identifying alienation conveyed through literature. Even when they sometimes depict it as an access to a particular order, they tend more frequently still to dramatize a conflict between order and an individual, or between different orders. "While I was a boy, when I read in Homer and Hesiod about wars and quarrels, not only of the demigods but also of the gods themselves, and besides about their amours and assaults and abductions and lawsuits and banishing fathers and marrying sisters, I thought that all these things were right, and I felt an uncommon impulsion toward them. But when I came of age, I found that the laws contradicted the poets and forbade adultery and quarrelling and theft. So I was plunged into great uncertainty." The speaker is Menippus, in Lucian's homonymous dialogue;[7] and if he had only read Plato, instead of consulting too many philosophers and then descending into Hades, as he does to clear his doubts, he would have known immediately what to think of an education inaugurated with the gossip spread by those two poets concerning the Gods. Even in the sixteenth century, a talented pornographer like Brantôme had the cheek to show indignation at the pedagogical harm caused by the lascivious mythology of the Greeks and Romans, which helped preceptors become corruptors, and was no better than the fables of the French, the Italians, and the Spanish: "Je voudrais avoir autant de centaines d'écus comme il y a eu des filles, tant du monde que de religieuses, qui se sont jadis émues, pollues at dépucelées par la lecture des *Amadis de Gaule*" (I would like to own as many hundreds of crowns as all the young girls, as much of the world as all the nuns, who in the past have been moved, polluted and deflowered by reading *Amadís de Gaula*).[8] But the first example of a kiss and of a sin caused by reading a novel that I have been able to find occurs in the most famous lines in the whole of Italian literature, in the episode of Francesca da Rimini. I should be in a real predicament if I could not turn to an essay by Gianfranco Contini, in which he reconstructs with exemplary erudition all the reminiscences and rules that fit Francesca's passionate words, and thus the character herself, into the respect for a courtly, erotic, and literary code—into an order. This is not, however, to exclude the fact that "the affective complicity" of Dante, as character and narrator, enters into contradiction with "the condemnation of the demiurgic executioner," or that there is a "process of

5. Blaise Pascal, *Pensés,* 11.

6. Jean-Jacques Rousseau, "(Lettre) A M. D'Alembert sur son Article Genève dans le VII Volume de l'Encyclopédie et particulièrement sur le projet d'établir un théâtre de comédie en cette ville." See also my "Lettura freudiana del *Misanthrope*," *Micromégas*, 6-7 (1976): 19-55.

7. Heinemann, "Menippus, or the Descent into Hades," in *Lucian in Eight Volumes* (London: and Cambridge, Mass.: Harvard University Press, 1969), 78-79.

8. Pierre Brantôme, *Vies des dames galantes* (Paris: Garnier, n.d.), pp. 362-63.

participation and objectivity, of identity and differentiation"—conflict, in effect (and Contini wonders whether, in Dante, this is not "the usual dialectics of the other world").[9]

Indeed, it would seem that from the age of feudalism to that of Louis Philippe, which is not only "as long, within a society now politically and economically transformed, as the models created by feudalism survived as still capable of revealing a great force of attraction and conviction,"[10] but perhaps even beyond this, novels owe the social function of mirror and example of behavior to their chivalresque and courtly origin. Amadís de Gaula is Don Quixote's supreme model, but even in the homonymous novel, the hero's brother, Don Galaor, read chivalresque romances to the extent that "by this, almost as much as by the character with which he was born, was he moved to desire greatly to become a knight."[11] The emulative effect of the same novels was rather less edifying for Folengo's Baldus who "mox Orlandi nasare volumina coepit," began to make paper wrappings for cooking sausages out of the pages of the grammars which he was studying,[12] a fact which would still represent a conflict between two excessively bookish educations, even though the boy-hero was destined for a less rascally career. Nevertheless, the most tormented Don Quixote *avant lettre* would appear to be St. Ignatius of Loyola, who asked for chivalresque novels, to which he was *muy dado*, to while away the time during his convalescence, received lives of saints instead, and ended up by transferring to this stopgap reading matter the emulation which would seem to be an inevitable effect of his usual one, thus moving from the question "what would happen if I were to do this as St. Francis or St. Dominic did," to the decision: "St. Dominic or St. Francis did this, so I must too."[13] At this point, I shall not be prevented by the fear of a pun from stating that a saintly diverted literary identification mediates the foundation...of an order; and yet the Jesuit order was difficult to found, and was born bellicose, even though it was destined to become the antonomasia of conformity within a century.

The novelistic and theatrical imitation of the supreme imitator, Don Quixote, was protracted for a long time during the seventeenth century, but the sixteenth-century texts that I have just mentioned should give us some doubts as to whether the phenomenon was exhausted with the international fame of Cervantes. All three novels of the *genre comique* included in the volume *Romanciers du XVIIe siècle* in the "Bibliothèque de la Pléiade", devote some space to the reading of novels, serious ones, of course, which in Sorel's *Francion*, a later imitation of Cervantes,[14] are still only *chevaleries*, viewed nostalgically *de haut en bas* as readings

9. Gianfranco Contini, "Dante come personaggio-poeta della *Commedia*," in *Varianti e altra linguistica* (Turin: Einaudi, 1970), pp. 343-48.

10. Ivos Margoni, *"Fin'amors," "mezura" e "cortezia,"* (Milan and Varese: Istituto Editoriale Cisalpino, 1965), p. 108.

11. *Amadís de Gaula*, ed. Felicidad Buendía, in *Libros de caballerías españoles* (Madrid: Aguilar, 1960), p. 336.

12. Merlin Cocai, *Il Baldo* (Milan: Feltrinelli, 1958), 1: 90-91.

13. Saint Ignatius of Loyola, *Autobiografía*, in *Obras completas* (Madrid: La Editorial Católica, 1963), pp. 91-92.

14. Charles Sorel, *Histoire comique de Francion*, in *Romanciers du XVIIe siècle*, ed. Antoine Adam, Bibliothèque de la Pléiade (Paris: Gallimard, 1958), pp. 173-75.

of one's youth. Already in Scarron's *Roman comique, L'Astrée* appears as a much more respectable literary model, and there also appears a preceptor who begins by reading novels in secret while forbidding them to his students and ends up by declaring them as morally instructive as Plutarch.[15] The greatest ambivalence is reached in Furetière's *Roman bourgeois,* where in the five volumes of *L'Astrée,* to be kept hidden beneath the mattress, a very naive young bourgeoise seems to acquire the pretence of a rapid education while losing the innocence of her feelings, just as the donor of the volumes expected in his plan to seduce her.[16] In this case, there can be no doubt that the ambivalence is, at least partly, a conflict between the different moral and behavioral codes of two classes—the bourgeoisie and the aristocracy. Leaving aside its far greater literary richness and complexity, the same may be said about the first masterpiece by Molière, centered around a mania as protagonist and the only one of his masterpieces in which this mania is the result of alienating reading matter in the same manner as Don Quixote's—*Les Précieuses ridicules.*

With the arrival of the man of the new class, Rousseau, it seems that the need for models drawn from books increases as quickly as the prestige of the Holy Scriptures decreases. He dates his own uninterrupted self-awareness from his earliest reading and its effect. He traces to novels and to Plutarch respectively the bizarre-adventurous and the austere-unconquerable components of his character, and tells of how as a child, when narrating the story of Mucius Scaevola's action, he was about to translate it automatically into deeds over an open cooking flame.[17] When, as an adult, he wrote a book that was entirely a question of models, a pedagogical treatise, he set up as an inexhaustibly positive model the first narrative masterpiece to be produced by the new English class, *Robinson Crusoe,* where the subject is not love (though Rousseau was in fact writing his own love story), and where the literary genre is overturned by the substitution of bourgeois for aristocratic values, as well as by the change of hemisphere.[18] At the end of the century in Lewis's *The Monk,* the chivalresque romances of old are assigned the ridiculous task of mediating the unrequited love of an aging lady for a young man, and naturally the mediation only succeeds in provoking a misunderstanding.[19] In the meantime, however, early Romanticism had already appropriated the earlier model of Paolo and Francesca's literary tenderness, renewing it with completely different models: the only kiss between Werther and Lotte that is not followed by guilty enjoyment or theological condemnation but rather expiated in the imminent suicide, though gratified by the uncontested emotion of the addresser-addressee-function, takes place after the couple have been long and deeply moved in borrowing from the funereal voice of Ossian's songs: "The whole force of this passage fell on his heart."[20]

15. Paul Scarron, *Le Roman comique,* in *Romanciers du XVIIe siècle,* ed. Antoine Adam, Bibliothèque de la Pléiade (Paris: Gallimard, 1958), pp. 584-85.

16. Antoine Furetière, *Le Roman bourgeois,* in *Romanciers du XVIIe siècle,* ed. Antoine Adam, Bibliothèque de la Pléiade (Paris: Gallimard, 1958), pp. 1004-8.

17. Rousseau, *Les Confessions,* in *Œuvres complètes* (Paris: Gallimard, 1959), 1: 8-9.

18. Rousseau, *Emile,* in *Œuvres complètes* (Paris: Gallimard, 1959), 4: 454-56.

19. Matthew Gregory Lewis, *The Monk* (New York: Grove Press, 1959), p. 147.

20. Johann Wolfgang von Goethe, *Die Leiden des jungen Werther; Die Wahlverwandtschaften*

It is but a short step to the time in which Pushkin, after having shown us his heroine who "alone roams with a dangerous book" and naturally imagines that she is the heroine of a book by Richardson, Rousseau, or Mme de Staël, can pretend to regret the presumed heroes who were models of perfection, and openly joke about the scandal of the new literature influenced by Byron: "But nowadays all minds are in a mist, a moral brings upon us somnolence, vice is attractive in a novel, too, and there, at least, it triumphs."[21] Had not even the worthy Xavier de Maistre confessed the weakness, for which he often reproached himself, of the sympathy he felt for Milton's Satan, when reading about his deeds that were so fatal for mankind? "Je crois même que je l'aiderais volontiers, sans la honte qui me retient.... J'ai beau réfléchir qu'après tout c'est un diable..." (I believe that I would even help him willingly, if shame did not restrain me.... It is in vain that I consider that after all he is a devil...)[22] Maistre was writing during the French Revolution, and indeed the devil of old was about to become more innocuous to the new bourgeois order than were the values that Julien Sorel avidly derived from the *Mémorial de Sainte-Hélène* and Rousseau's *Confessions,* the potential holy scriptures of the new order, to its regressive phase which constituted the background order in *Le Rouge et le noir*—the Restoration. This review may be ended by another oversympathetic reader of novels, brought to life and led to suicide under the next regime—Madame Bovary, who has frequently been compared to Don Quixote. With the generation of her creator, Flaubert, with the symbolic divide of 1848, with the complete division of labor of the bourgeoisie, I believe that something was reversed and has remained so up to the present day. Literature no longer prefers to reflect the act of finding an identity through one's *reading,* but instead the act of searching for it through *writing;* no longer, therefore, in other privileged models of experience, but in the exercise of a privileged profession.

I have played the devil's advocate and devoted as much space as possible in this brief review to the always suspect complementarity between literary identification and established order. It should be superfluous to recall that at least after the symbolic divide of 1848, the established order has known instinctively how to repudiate that very art which it might have had some advantage in making an object of worship, of teaching, of spectacle; it knows perfectly well how to *divert its attention* from that art while in its presence. The historical forms of this inattention must have been thousands, but the two sharpest formulations of the phenomenon that I know both concern an artist considered supreme by many, judged ideologically as a reactionary by all, and, to my mind, notably misunderstood and misinterpreted—Wagner.

The audacity of this work, however, is of a kind that can be tolerated only when favored by a

---

(Basle: Birkhäuser, 1944), pp. 99-106; Eng. trans. as *The Sorrows of Young Werther,* trans. George Ticknor, ed. Frank G. Ryder (Chapel Hill: University of North Carolina Press, 1952), pp. 83-86.

21. Alexander Pushkin, *Eugene Onegin,* trans. Vladimir Nabokov (New York: Pantheon Books, 1964), pp. 99-106.

22. Xavier de Maistre, *Voyage autour de ma chambre* (Paris: Flammarion, n.d.), pp. 77-78.

complete misunderstanding, organized and maintained by a kind of social consensus, of blindness that is both avowed and unconscious.... Yet the harmful meaning of this message had to be denied to be acceptable, it had to be disguised at all costs, interpreted in a tolerable way, that is, in the name of the *good* sense.... Thus Wagner's *Tristan* may be quite safely taken up with impunity before moved audiences, so great is the general certainty that *no one will believe its message*.[23]

Moreover, in the one act play by Wedekind *Der Kammersänger,* the star, who is a Wagnerian tenor, claims:

We artists are a *luxury article* of the bourgeoisie, and to pay for this auctions are held everywhere. If you were right, how could a work like the *Valkyrie* be possible, when it concerns a subject whose exposure disgusts the audience to the depths of its soul? Yet when *I* sing the part of Siegmund, even the most scrupulous mothers bring along their thirteen- and fourteen-year-old daughters. And, when on stage, I am quite convinced that not one single human being in the audience takes heed of what we are performing up there any more. If they did, they would run away. That's how they behaved when the work was new. Now they have grown accustomed to *ignoring* it. They are about it as little as they care about the air between them and the stage."[24]

This is no doubt the height of alienation. The great bourgeois audiences did not even wait for the provocations of the avant-garde in order to begin to show habitual indifference to all that is problematic in art. Should anyone imagine that such a neutralization may not also come to oppose, sooner or later, works containing a much more progressive ideology than Wagner's, his error would be in failing to keep his distance from art, as I have done repeatedly in the guise of reservations about its relationship to praxis.

23. Denis de Rougemont, *L'Amour et l'occident,* Bibliothèque 10/18 (Paris: 1963), pp. 192-93.

24. Frank Wedekind, *Der Kammersänger* (Stuttgart: Reclam, 1959), p. 33.

Appendix 5

On the Intellectual
Division of Labor

Who would write an essay devoted entirely to the problems that are determined by the intellectual division of labor, which is in turn increasingly more determined by these problems? In order to master such material, one must succeed in temporarily freeing oneself from the effects of its reality, which generally tends to master us. This is an ambition that would have become more chimerical every twenty years over the past few centuries if someone had entertained it. And yet, that risk of being mastered instead of mastering, those diabolical effects that are weightier the subtler they are, that are armed with more reality the more they pass through illusions, do not always succeed in keeping it from the attention of those of us, scholars and students, who are directly concerned; and from time to time they reveal themselves, even if only in symptomatic form, as echoes, glimmers, in fits and starts. For example, the intolerance of the young toward didactic institutions, which became joined in 1968 with a crisis much broader than that of the educational system, *also* had its roots, though in an instinctive and confused but sometimes unambiguous way, in a diffidence toward the reifications introduced into knowledge by the division of labor. Among the many lessons learned from the crisis, the great amount of discussion about interdisciplinarity that has taken place since then, quickly becoming perverted from objection to convention, ought to count for less than the silent invitation to reflect upon the very act of division that *creates* the individual disciplines and their parts, and especially *on the fact that it does create them,* that it is this that creates them. Before looking beyond the boundaries and attempting to cross over or efface them, one should attempt to understand how they are drawn. Each and every one of their turns is a hieroglyph that should be interpreted historically, scientifically, and socially.

The antispecialistic impulses that have attempted or pretended to shake the university system since 1968 suggested to me a half-serious classification of the possible attitudes of scholars and teachers in the face of their problems concerning the division of labor. The "formalized" partition of this potential "semantic field" with the aid of two "binary oppositions" which, when combined, define four attitudes, might sound like a parody of the formalizations undertaken seriously in this book. I would therefore beg the reader to measure inversely all the importance that I attribute to the subject on the basis of the distance between the serious and the half-serious, of forced understatement. Let us note, first of all, that for some scholars the intellectual division of labor is an advantage, for others a disadvantage, and that for some it is necessary, and for others unnecessary. From the combination of these the following images of the scholar emerge, which are typical (to the point of being unreal) on the condition that the definitions are filled out a little:

(1) Those for whom it is a *necessary advantage*. This is a circle of academic-scientific hell, perceived as an Eden by those who inhabit it. Just as before Saussure's day it was thought that language was a nomenclature in which words corresponded to things, so these people believe that every area of study corresponds to an assured object of its own. The fact that the former is well delineated a priori is guaranteed by the latter's being equally well identified a priori. Inter-disciplinary impulses do not disturb their institutional faith, because the new relationships which must be established between the preexistent areas of study will have always existed between their respective objects, even if they are established belatedly. Nevertheless, they may die at a ripe old age without ever having been the least bit affected by the idea that really should disturb them: the idea that no field of study is ever specified and consolidated without carrying out a series of dissecting, if not mutilating, abstractions upon its objects. Their answer to anyone who might try to make them concerned about this dissection and mutilation would be similar to that of the pedant in Goethe's *Faust* to the protagonist, who is concerned about having murdered thousands of patients with his dubious medicine: "Why, therefore, yield to such depression?/A good man does his honest share/In exercising, with the strictest care,/The art bequeathed to his possession!"[1] Yet this confusion of the organization of knowledge is such that for some conscientious and precise works of undeniable usefulness we are indebted to the scholars of this first group, as all those who do not belong to it well know.

(2) Those for whom it is an *unnecessary advantage*. Here the first stage of innocence has been surmounted and these individuals realize more or less confusedly that *tout se tient* in the reality of this world. Consequently there are no guarantees that the areas in which one moves in order to study it are finite and neat like watertight compartments. However, human ability and prudence can always reach further than providence in ordering creation. If their studies are threatened by the inseparability of everything, with imprecision in their consistency, arbitrariness in their limits, and precariousness in their results, they will then solve the problem by dividing up the field safely and elegantly. Indeed it is in this that their capability will be judged. The act of the dissecting abstraction, which is automatic for the scholars of the first group, becomes meritorious for this one because it is optional, reassuring because it is defensive. Thus it is so much the worse for anyone who has not been clever enough to defend himself from the interference of problems other than those selected, should the operations effected not be impeccable on account of this interference. But in no case must the statement "this problem is neither pertinent to me nor within my competence," differ from "this problem does not exist." The scholars of the first group benefit

1. Johann Wolfgang von Goethe, *Faust* (Wiesbaden: Insel, 1959), p. 169; Eng. trans. Bayard Taylor (New York: Random House, 1912), p. 37.

blindly from the reification of fields due to institutions; these scholars go even further, for they collaborate with the reification and increase it. In their hands, specializations, attitudes, habits not only become converted one into another, but they are transformed into regulations and preclusions about what is or is not permissible or serious in the methods and objects of study. It is not easy to catch them out or make them contradict themselves; and their defense works equally well either with the aid of an ideology or with that of the utmost ideological indifference.

(3) Those for whom it is a *necessary disadvantage*. These are my positive heroes, as every reader must by now have expected. I admire them to the point that the mere aspiration to become one of them seems like the commission of a crime of immodesty. Not only are they aware that there is no progress in knowledge without a dissecting abstraction, but they do not restrict themselves to taking it into account to the extent needed to preserve their studies from risking imperfection. They are also aware that both a priori, and still more a posteriori, after an accumulation of human intellectual labor over thousands of years, there is no dissecting abstraction that does not sacrifice something of the real aspects or connections of an object, and perhaps even a great deal, in order to circumscribe a little operatively. They know that the indispensability of this price does not authorize them to close their eyes when paying it, because it goes onto the account of that progress in knowledge for which payment is indispensable. They, at least, know that one should not forget an opposite need: one must take care that the sacrifice should be reduced to a minimum, one must involve the greatest number of real aspects or connections in every operation, and not act as though all those set aside by the initial abstraction did not exist. In contrast with the cleanhanded scholars of the preceding groups, these are the scholars with dirty hands. They understand how harmful it is to remain entrenched in the single or few fields in which they are competent, as well as the improbability of their becoming competent enough in many other fields. Even more, they realize, like Rousseau: "l'impossibilité où l'on est d'un côté de détruire certaines hypothèses, si de l'autre on se trouve hors d'état de leur donner le degré de certitude des faits" ("the impossibility, on the one hand, of destroying certain hypotheses, though on the other, we cannot give them the certainty of known matters of fact").[2] They take risks, gamble, make mistakes, and know what they are doing. In their hands, the act of dissecting abstraction is uncertain and experimental, without illusion and responsible, but courageous; their errors are rarely useless, their position is the most uncomfortable and the most fertile.

(4) Those for whom it is an *unnecessary disadvantage*. Here is a final group of scholars whose irresponsibility rivals that of the first, though for exactly the opposite motives and with the opposite results. They assume that one need only be intelligent, restless and well-meaning in order to broaden the horizons (of discourse) at will, without meeting any obstacles along the way. Naturally, they overcome as many obstacles as they wish, but the horizons shift as each one

2. Jean-Jacques Rousseau, *Discours sur l'origine et les fondements de l'inégalité parmi les hommes,* in *Œuvres complètes* (Paris: Gallimard, 1959), 3: 162; Eng. trans. as "A Discourse on the Origin of Inequality," in *The Social Contract; Discourses* (London: Dent, and New York: Dutton, 1955), pp. 143-229.

proceeds, and each would have to stop in order to observe a more or less wide horizon attentively. Or, another fitting comparison might be this: they act like someone who tries to use a compass without centering it on any fixed point. Even when the dilettantism of their results induces one to claim, using an apt phrase from Raymond Williams, that their investigation "is not even specific enough to be wrong,"[3] the principal drawback to their attitude is not, despite all appearances, a question of means. It is not naive to hope that one may always compensate brilliantly and without diffuseness for a lack of competence in an informative, quantitative sense. It is rather a question of goals, if it is true that before reifying them, the intellectual division of labor historically outlined fields whose conditioning the dissecting abstraction cannot avoid, not even when it contaminates them, or overturns them. A talent that is strong enough to contaminate them advantageously is, of course, quite rare, not to mention a genius capable of overturning them and, with this act, to cause new fields to emerge of necessity. I do not believe that the aspiration to modify the boundaries between disciplines must be left to genius or strong talent, but it is indeed this fourth attitude that seemed condemned to being the object of a lengthy caricature in many of the interdisciplinary attempts that emerged from the rightful intolerance of 1968. It is an attitude that may easily appear sympathetic and even generous, almost always fragile, talkative, and moving, and always inconclusive.

3. Raymond Williams, *Culture and Society 1780-1950* (Harmondsworth: Penguin Books, 1971), p. 268.

The Johns Hopkins University Press

This book was composed in Alphatype Baskerville text and display type by David Lorton from a design by Susan Bishop. It was printed, on 50-lb. Publishers Eggshell Wove paper, and bound by The Maple Press Company.

DATE